CW01095547

MIRROR SYDNEY

MIRROR

We know you've been to
Sydney before but this
is an extra special trip
to see your brother.
♡ Trevor,
Beatrice & Alex

VANESSA BERRY

SYDNEY

AN ATLAS OF REFLECTIONS

First published in 2017
from the Writing & Society Research Centre
at Western Sydney University
by the Giramondo Publishing Company
PO Box 752
Artarmon NSW 1570 Australia
www.giramondopublishing.com

Designed by Harry Williamson
Typeset by Andrew Davies
in 11/15 pt Baskerville BT

Maps drawn by Vanessa Berry

Printed and bound by Everbest Printing Co Ltd
Distributed in Australia by NewSouth Books

National Library of Australia
Cataloguing-in-Publication data:

Berry, Vanessa
Title: Mirror Sydney: An Atlas of Reflections
ISBN: 9781925336252 (pbk)

9 8 7 6 5 4 3

FOR SIMON

We don't need to see anything out of the ordinary.
We already see so much.

ROBERT WALSER (1914)

CONTENTS

LIST OF MAPS

MIRROR SYDNEY

Once, looking through a clutter of bric-a-brac in an op shop, I found some old photo albums. They were empty of photographs but had soft-focus 1970s images on the covers: sunsets, beaches and golden fields. The one anomaly was a cover featuring an aerial photograph of Sydney Harbour. It showed the Bradfield Highway curving out from North Sydney and across the Harbour Bridge. Beyond the bridge was the city with its new high-rise skyline. Visible behind the 1960s office blocks of the AMP Building and Australia Square were cranes constructing the next city landmark, the stem and drum of Sydney Tower.

On the back cover of the album was the same image in reverse. The city was inverted, buildings in backwards order, with a second harbour bridge leading off in the opposite direction. I held the album open so I could see both Sydneys together, the city and its mirror image. They met in the middle of the spine, where a doubled-up Opera House opened like an origami flower. The highways branched off, one left, one right, beyond the cover's edges.

The doubled buildings and highways leading off into the unknown captured something of the way I feel about Sydney. In contrast to its most commonly celebrated description – a sunlit city of natural beauty, the harbour and beaches – the Sydney I know best is one of undercurrents and weird places, suburban mythologies and unusual details. These are the city's marginalia, the overlooked and the odd, the hidden and enigmatic places. They form an alternative city, a mirror or shadow Sydney that has the same shape as its better-known counterpart, but emphasises its ambiguities and anomalies.

Cities are made up of histories and memories as much as they are made up of their physical environments. As different as cities can be, all share the qualities of density and constant change. Traces of the eras they have passed through can be observed in their details and felt in the patchwork of atmospheres that shift from place to place. To write of a city's shadows and undercurrents is to use these details and atmospheres as thresholds, opening up the repository that is stored beyond them.

Sydney is a recent invention. The city was built on Aboriginal land, and the stories of the Sydney clans carry its first and abiding identities. These weave through in traces and embedded knowledge. In the centre of the harbour where the water is deepest is the island Me-mil, a name meaning 'eye'. From here the harbour can be seen in all directions. The British renamed it Goat Island and used it as a gunpowder store and for other functional purposes, but its identity as the harbour's eye has persisted. By thinking of the harbour as an animate, watching entity, another Sydney comes into being, one connected to this land's oldest stories.

There are many versions of Sydney. The architectural miscellany of the central city; the postcolonial city with the legacy of Indigenous dispossession; the party city of Mardi Gras and fireworks; the sprawling suburban network of traffic snarls and local enclaves. Sydney is all and more of these at once. Its landscapes hold the memories of everyone whose lives have taken place here, the imprints of past times and future dreams.

I grew up in the 1980s in the northern suburbs of Sydney, but like many of the city's residents I have roots elsewhere, threads leading out into the wider world. When I visited my grandparents in their small, square wooden house, they told me stories of their life in 1930s Shanghai, and then of wartime England, which I tried to imagine as the cicadas screeched outside and the lawn crisped in the summer heat. My grandmother told me of selling poppies on the street in Hong Kong on Armistice Day in the 1920s, my grandfather described his boyhood winters, skating on the ice of the River Calder in West Yorkshire. My mother recounted her shock on glimpsing Sydney for the first time, from the deck of a passenger ship in 1949, seeing the bare-looking, low-rise city she was told would be her new home. My father, born in the Sydney suburb of Croydon in the 1930s, gave me a link to a past Sydney of crowded trams heading to the races, unreliable old cars and inner-west dance halls. Once I learnt the right places to look I found that vestiges of this world still existed, but at first they seemed almost as remote as my maternal family's tales.

Sydney was the place I, too, would grow up to tell stories about. I have lived here my whole life, registering its changes along with my own. As a child I watched the suburbs slide past our car windows with an eye for particular talismans: the Wrigley's factory water reservoir at Asquith that looked like an enormous bubble of gum, the A-frame building on the highway at Gordon, the ABC TV transmission towers at Artarmon which I imagined to be Sydney's Eiffel Towers. These places were like resistors on a circuit board. My thoughts stuck to them. They had auras: each gave me a strong feeling that there was, embedded amid the everyday, an order of unpredictable things.

Back in my childhood the idea that a city could be enclosed in a book was an uncomplicated one. I had a fascination for the telephone and street directories, where I'd look up my surname in the A–K volume to find my address among pages of other Berrys. I took comfort in the fact that we had our place amid the index of the city's residents. I'd skim over the listings, read through the abbreviated suburbs and try to decode them. Crmrn, Bnyrg, Sn Sci, E Hls: stripped of vowels the names became a code. Or I'd open the pages of the Gregory's Street Directory at random and try to imagine the places on the pages I ended up at. If I opened to a page that showed the phrase 'limit of maps' on its edge I experienced a particular thrill, imagining this as a section of the framework that held the city together.

I felt surrounded in Sydney, inside an entity that extended far in every direction. If it seemed vast then, throughout my lifetime the suburbs have continued to stretch outwards. Now they only stop when they come up against national parks, the ocean or the mountains, or dwindle into the new developments and industrial parks of the south-west. The city's snaking roads and train lines cut through the sprawl.

Ever since the days of staring out the window of my parents' car I've felt compelled to know as much of Sydney as I can. As a teenager I caught trains to wherever the book and record stores were plentiful, grasping at the tail of the bohemian 1980s inner city. Like the suburban talismans I noticed as a child, these subcultural places undercut the surface of the city, requiring a different map and different knowledge.

These places were culturally and sometimes literally underground. It seemed fitting that I found Red Eye Records, with its red-painted walls and bulging bloodshot eye for a logo, in the cool, subterranean Tank Stream Arcade. The arcade was named for the stream that had, in 1788, determined the location of the British settlement, and now flows underneath the city through a series of pipes and drains. The entrance to the Tank Stream Arcade was at the north end of the city's central shopping plaza, Pitt Street Mall. Steps led down into it from the bright street and like the Tank Stream itself it seemed an undercurrent to the extroverted world above. Spending time in such places I often felt as if I was tunnelling beneath and around the city.

It's a feeling that has stayed with me, growing in strength and persistence. In 1999 I set myself the task of visiting all of the St Vincent de Paul op shops in Sydney, using the list in the phone book as a guide. It was part shopping trip, part expedition, and part public transport challenge. (I put off learning to drive until many years later; I liked staring out the passenger window too much.) Suburbs that hitherto had only been names in the street directory came to life, and by visiting them I entered into their everyday rhythms and patterns. My mental map of Sydney expanded in all directions. Before I set about my op-shop endeavour I'd had no imperative to visit suburbs like Galston, or Ermington, or Berala, or many of the seventy other locations on the list. As unfamiliar as many of these areas were to me, I knew that every place was for many people home. The details of the shops, streets, buildings and parklands I was passing by made up their everyday lives. I took in these places with the eyes of a visitor, alert to traces of past times that might transmit something of the area's history and identities. I did much the same in the op shops as I sorted through the miscellany of objects. Considering the polyester dresses and wedding-present dinner sets, I imagined I was sorting through the collective memories of generations of Sydney residents.

Ever since then, whenever I had some hours spare or if I was feeling restless, I'd go out into the suburbs. My destinations were places I'd never stopped at before, or ones I hadn't visited for years. As the yards of the houses that back onto the railway tracks slid by the train windows I felt my identity loosen. I saw myself from the outside, an anonymous traveller of unknown purpose. If I had ever been called upon to explain what I was doing I might have said I was surrendering to the details all around me. This was what it felt like: I was a screen that images of the city could move across.

No one ever did ask me to explain, of course, but as time went on I thought more about this habit of mine. After years of journeys I had a broad knowledge of Sydney's more obscure suburban details. Although most were small things, they didn't exist in isolation. Each of them had the potential to lead into understanding something deeper about the place, the suburb, the land, or the city as a whole.

To record these places and details I started a blog that I titled *Mirror Sydney*, inspired by the op-shop photo album and the shadow city I had spent so much of my life seeking out. The first post was a story I had written many years before about an abandoned and overgrown velodrome in Camperdown. It was a place of respite for me with its sense of ragged grandeur: the steep concrete surface of the velodrome track emerged from the tall grass like a forgotten amphitheatre. The velodrome is long gone now, the land turned into a park, but it encapsulated the qualities of the mirror city I was setting out to investigate. The velodrome had been tucked away in the back streets, seemingly forgotten and readily transformed by imagination.

Like all city residents I have my favourites among Sydney's myths and secrets. I know the faces that it shows to visitors and those it keeps for its inhabitants. I started the *Mirror Sydney* blog with a list of places in mind. These included specific sites like the velodrome, suburbs with contested or undercurrent identities, and parts of the city that carried with them some kind of enigma or resonance of past times. I set out to visit them one by one. Going into these places I paid attention to everything I passed by, staying ever vigilant to traces that hinted at the other identities, places and times that were folded into the present moment.

When I visited somewhere deliberately to write about it for the blog I let myself move into and across it, guided by instinct and the clues that I sensed all around me. It was a method led by intuition and a desire to move through time, all the while being anchored by the present and its details. My visits were often drifting ones that took me into unexpected places and perceptions. Drifting was one of the key tactics of the Situationists, a group of artists and activists in 1960s Paris. They would follow a chance pathway, a *dérive* ('drift') across Paris, guided by its atmospheres. This way of encountering the city mapped what they called its 'psychogeography'. The Situationists believed that by sensing and navigating the city in new ways they could produce revolutionary thought and action. Despite its definitions and lists of practices, in its most basic form psychogeography was to me a heightened version of everyday engagement with the identities and moods of places. It gave a name to the act of examining the urban environment and connecting to the latent forces within it.

My focus soon expanded beyond deliberate missions, and I found it equally important to pay attention to the incidental places I passed through in my everyday travels. This noticing became my life, moving through Sydney ever receptive to its details and atmospheres. This attention was in some ways not so different from my early scrutiny of suburban talismans, but now it was underscored by a sense of purpose.

This way of knowing Sydney involves a willing subversion of its identity, turning away from the monumental to the marginal. Many of the world's most prominent cities have been redefined in this way, their details and backgrounds brought to prominence by writers who identify with the underground and unrecognised.

The weird extrapolations of Venice in Italo Calvino's *Invisible Cities*, or the New York characters living in a city of the past described by *New Yorker* writer Joseph Mitchell, or the London of momentary scenes that Virginia Woolf encountered when she went out 'street haunting', all have at their core the same desire: to transform the city into something malleable that can be shaped and reshaped in thought and perception.

The blog posts that resulted from my missions and observations described moments within the ongoing life and history of the city, encounters with unusual, forgotten or overlooked places. If the blog was an album, I thought of each post like it was a photograph. I inspected and interpreted each snapshot, trying to put into words the connection between these everyday places and the experiences, histories and memories that underscore them. Collectively they formed an ever-expanding chronicle of Sydney's shadow identity.

Alongside the stories from the blog I drew maps of each of the places I encountered. Mapping is also a form of description, but maps show relationships and trajectories, revealing places as constellations rather than the linear pathways of the written word. The maps were put together more like star charts than topographical guides. The scrutiny I applied to their details as I drew them often made me wonder if anyone had ever lavished so much time on observing the form of the A&R Plastics transmission tower in Lidcombe, the sandstone elephant in Hallstrom Park in Willoughby, or the faded Superman cut-out in the window of Comic Kingdom on Liverpool Street in the city. But if there was one thing I'd learnt from doing the blog, it was that, even if their recorded histories were non-existent, I wasn't the only person who noticed such minor places and details. In the comments and conversations inspired by *Mirror Sydney* I found many others whose mental maps of the city were populated by these unassuming or unlikely places.

The maps show pathways and journeys through landscapes of time and space, capturing some of the systems of significance that underlie Sydney. No detail stands alone, but neither is it fixed in only one network or order. Maps can convert the city into a place of childhood memories or mystery structures, or elevate obscure suburban landmarks into dominant features, but always with the sense they could be rearranged to tell another story entirely.

It is easy enough to rearrange the drawings on a map, but to watch on as the city itself is rearranged is a much harder duty. When I started writing *Mirror Sydney* in 2012 I had a sense of what was coming for the city, but as changes escalated over the subsequent years they still came as a shock. I was right in suspecting that many of the anachronistic or neglected places I was documenting would not be around much longer. Cities are ever-changing entities, but in Sydney's drive towards reinvention there was this time something especially rapacious about the rate and scale of change. The city as I knew it was being overwritten as fast as I could chronicle it.

Construction cranes hover above the city skyline as if feeding from it, like ibis picking out its tastiest parts. The highways are choked with demolition trucks. One afternoon on Victoria Road I stepped back from the kerb as a truck turned out of a side street, painted black with no company name or logo to identify it, only the numberplate *HEARSE*. It rattled into peak hour traffic, black tarpaulins pulled taut over the rubble it was transporting away. I watched it until it was out of sight, struck by the now familiar feeling that the city as I knew it was being disassembled.

What started as a project to portray the significance of the city's details also became one of preservation. I wrote not only of places themselves but how they formed part of the city's memory, and how layers of time existed in them. As much as our past and future are woven into our lives in the present, so is the city's past and future entwined with our current moment. I thought of the deserted, ghostly photographs of old Paris streets taken by Eugene Atget in the early twentieth century. By staring into his photograph of a corset-shop window hung with cinch-waisted torsos I am there on the street in that moment; I can feel the city around me and can reassemble a feeling of it from what is captured in the image.

My favourite writing about Sydney gives me this same feeling. When I read Ruth Park's *Companion Guide to Sydney* I can reconstruct the 1970s city from its everyday details: the Mintie wrappers among

the trash at the entrance of the Great Synagogue, the sightseers
standing in the noise and dust to watch the tunnelling of the
underground railway station in Martin Place. Park was also writing at
a time of great change for the city, as it underwent, as she described
it, a 'maelstrom of destruction and construction'. By writing of
the city in this time of change she prevents it from slipping from
memory. Through her words I stand with the sightseers looking into
the chaos of the excavations, I watch the demolition of the Victorian-
era buildings, and I envisage the impending city of motorways and
high-rises, even with my knowledge of those plans that came to pass
and those that did not.

To write about places on the cusp of change is to feel keenly
the tide of time that underlies our experiences. What is present
and instantaneous swiftly finds itself stranded in the past. In the
moment of observation, what seems solid and vital can by the next
visit be gone or changed completely. This produces a paradox: places
with a tenuous presence are often highlighted by the fact they may
not be there for much longer, and come into an uneasy prominence.

As the places I had written about on the *Mirror Sydney* blog started
to disappear, and large-scale developments and redevelopments
reshaped the city and suburbs, I saw the shadow city that I had for
my whole life been drawn to also disappearing. The landmarks of
this more introspective Sydney, the places that I'd noticed out of car
windows, seen from trains, passed by on walks, are footnotes to the
city's history, unlikely to be investigated beyond a cursory notice,
and once gone, quickly forgotten. What I hope for is that the places
in *Mirror Sydney*, at the moments at which I encountered them, will
remain in collective memory, as a record of late twentieth- and early
twenty-first-century Sydney. This version of the city, an uneven
landscape of harmonious and discordant places, deserves this careful
scrutiny, for it is a complex city that folds many times and memories
within it. Recording the city in this way is to contemplate and care
for its histories, its inhabitants, its ecology and its future.

Among the recent changes are those of great social and political
significance, like the government sell-off of public housing at Miller's
Point and Waterloo, which has forced the relocation and dispersal of

entire communities. Other changes mark less dramatically the passing of time and the change of generations, as when old stores and milk bars close their doors after decades of operation. Such places come to be shaped around the life stories of the people who live and work there, and all the years that have accrued there. In former industrial zones new developments arise, their clusters of apartment blocks like micro-cities in themselves, but with all the spaces in and around them neatly prescribed, flattening the environment into tidy functionality. This physical change towards maximised density reflects the avaricious mood of the city. The real estate floodlight has come to illuminate every shadow, so no place is spared reduction to its economic value. The language of place becomes the language of ownership, and increasingly these owners are the wealthy and established.

The irony of owning property on stolen land underlies the anxious obsession with real estate, connecting back to the city's origins: British ships sailed into the harbour and took anchor at a cove with a freshwater stream trickling down from what was then a forest. This cove, known as Warrane by the Gadigal people, was renamed Sydney Cove after the British politician who had planned the antipodean penal colony; the stream was renamed the Tank Stream for the water storage tanks that were cut into its sandstone bedrock. The settlers cleared the land around the harbour, establishing farms where the crops failed to thrive, polluting the stream, and displacing the people who had lived in this place for many thousands of years. This dispossession and discord was the first step in creating the city that was to come.

Since the city's beginnings time and space have been carved up, made measurable and dispensable. But no matter how strongly these divisions are upheld, in our experiences moments and details are ever expansive. This is what I sensed as a child as I looked out at the water reservoirs and bushland gullies of the suburbs. Lacking other words to describe their atmospheres I thought it to be a kind of magic. But if it is indeed so, it isn't something otherworldly. It is very much of the world, this force that exists between us and the places that surround and shape us.

COMPASS POINTS

There's a question which follows you around if you live in Sydney. It's a familiar follow up to 'How are you?' and immediately reveals Sydney residents' obsession with location. I can sense when it's coming. There's a pause, then: 'So, where are you living these days?' The answer determines more than just physical location. It is a shorthand for allegiances, a shortcut to understanding who people are by where they live, whether it be by choice or by necessity. Then, once this has been asked and places attributed, the conversation is clear to continue.

Underlying the question lies another motivation less tied to status and stereotypes, one of genuine curiosity. The questioner hopes that the response might reveal a part of the city hitherto unknown. Sydney's sprawl is so extensive that places can seem to hide, or at least escape notice. Even for a person who has lived in Sydney a lifetime, there are places known only as names and vague presences somewhere on, or off, the map.

Sydney has a geography of hills and valleys, waterways and ridges. The suburbs reveal surprising vistas, where views of the city can suddenly appear from faraway hilltops, the drum of Sydney Tower like a pushpin denoting the centre. On the ground the road network is easy to feel lost in, a mess of freeways and roads major and minor that circulate traffic through the suburbs like an errant heart. The twists and turns inspire a feeling of anticipation, that over the next hill or around the next corner could be a scene never before encountered. All is revealed at the corner that gives the view of the ocean, or at the instant when everyone in the train carriage cannot help but look out the window as it crosses the Harbour Bridge. This unexpectedness exists in seemingly ordinary places too, even if it is at first not apparent. Every place has something more than it first seems to offer, once you stop to consider it.

Beyond the central city, Sydney quickly becomes a city of suburbs, each with its own sense of enclosure and identity. Those at the edge provide a dual perspective: you can look inwards, towards the city, or outwards and away from it – either feel absorbed by Sydney or perched on its margins. Wherever I am in the suburbs I think of Sydney as an enclosing system as much as a place. Walking down a residential backstreet or passing a construction site that heralds a new development, entering a dimly lit corner store or blinking against the harsh lighting of a night-time train carriage: these small moments make up the tiny components of a complicated machine.

With this sense of connection in mind the following are stories of the city's 'compass points', a suburb each from the north, south, east and west. Each has its own identity, distinct from as well as enclosed by the city. The compass formed by these places navigates through time as well as space. It points towards the layers of memories and histories that make up these places far from the centre: the ancient, recent and future versions that overlay them in the present.

Hornsby is Sydney's northernmost suburban centre, before ridges and valleys close in and narrow the land, pinching the suburbs to a stop. Like all junctions Hornsby is a place where influences mix, the sedate upper north shore, the miscellany of the western suburbs, and the potential of the city's edge and its promise of elsewhere.

Hornsby has two sides, the old and the new. The suburb is split in half by the train station, which divides both east from west and past from present. I'd first thought that 'the old side' and 'the new side' were my family's shorthand until I realised they were a common distinction used by locals. Both sides are centred around their shopping strips. On the new side is the Westfield shopping centre, on the old a Victorian-era streetscape of assorted small stores.

With this division between old and new, two versions of the suburb exist side by side, rather than the erasure of new replacing old. The tension between them is one of memory. The new side cannot forget its past and the old risks eclipse by the force of the new. This tension is not unique to Hornsby, although it is clearly defined here. It is a force that underlies cities, ebbing and flowing with time and circumstances.

The split identity has existed since the construction of the 'new side' shopping mall in the 1960s. As a child I was entranced by this multi-level shopping labyrinth. On weekends my grandfather would drive my sister and me here and give us spending money, one of the new $2 coins that had, in 1988, just replaced the paper banknote equivalent. The mall was a repository of knick-knacks and it lent everything on the new side a similarly consumable identity. As I grew older the novelty of Kmart trinkets faded, and I was drawn more to the old side, a place less easy to comprehend. It had an alluring sense of disorder about it, a combination of its motley cluster of businesses and the wilderness of the bushland and quarry behind the municipal park nearby.

Growing up in the suburbs is an exercise in making the most out of a limited landscape. I often pondered by what fate I was led to exist here, in Sydney, in the 1980s, rather than anywhere else at any other time. My life story was to be made up of these minor places, shopping centres and parks, train stations and neat houses which sat on blocks of land like cakes in boxes. It was a restricted landscape but one that was open to transformation, at least in my imagination.

I felt an affinity with the old side of Hornsby. There seemed more potential for interesting things here among the old, which fitted with my suspicion that there were secrets hiding just under the surface of everyday life. Even if I didn't exactly know what these secrets could be, I appreciated the old side's patina and unpredictable hodgepodge of styles and eras.

The core of the old side is a short stretch of highway which was once Hornsby's central shopping area. Under the stucco rendering and faux-Tudor facades were butcheries, grocers and draperies, and a funeral parlour with a morgue in the cellar underneath. Their present-day replacements are Korean and Indian groceries, real estate agencies and cafés, the kinds of small stores that reshuffle in use and ownership. Two solid brick buildings with serious facades have the unmistakable look of banks, but now one is a 24-hour gym, the other split between a real estate agency and a Korean church.

The old side's streetscape has been continually reshuffled over time but a more substantial change is coming. Plans to update the old side with high-rise development are progressing under the name Hornsby West: the 'old side' has always been a local's nickname, and never official. In the future the sides will switch, the old side becoming the new. Despite all the planning of its future, for now, day after day, the old side continues in much the same way: the secondhand bookstore sells paperbacks, Danny's Patisserie bakes poppyseed twists, films are shown on the Odeon Cinema's single screen.

If the old side of Hornsby holds the memories of past ways of life it also holds personal memories for generations of locals. My memories of the old side are teenage ones: on Coronation Street I bought hippie skirts and silver jewellery in the generically named 'Asian Market', and PiL and Siouxsie and the Banshees albums in Discovery Records. These were stepping stones to an imagined life elsewhere. I was walking around in Hornsby but thinking of London in 1977, of punks wearing garbage bags as dresses and stiffening their hair with egg whites.

Sydney is full of these small stories of connection and rebellion, of identities developing with the suburbs as their backdrop. Wherever they are, teenagers seek out places to make their own, whether it be a shopping centre or an abandoned house or a Red Rooster car park. Even the blandest of locations can have potential, as long as it provides enough scope to be reimagined.

There is still a record store on Coronation Street, Mix Up Music. From the entrance a Katy Perry song blasts out into the rainy street. The song's glossy production and motivational postcard lyrics clash with the shop's cluttered and musty interior. This is a mall music soundtrack to a place stocked with the mall's long-ago discards. My eyes stumble over the miscellaneous objects arranged together: a pair of satin high heels, a *feng shui* pack including CDs and a booklet, a home laminator, a set of wine goblets, ex-rental VHS tapes.

There is no one behind the counter and I think the shop empty until I notice a woman on a computer at the back of the store, scrolling through photos on Facebook. She stares at the screen, unaware of or unbothered by my presence. I look through a graveyard of 1990s pop albums, dust sticking to my fingers as I flip through the plastic cases. Behind the counter is a warning from the days when CDs could be hot property:

When dealing in secondhand goods, any official information you provide
will be reported to the police.

Every available surface is covered in notices and posters of
pop stars past, an '80s-era Bowie, the cryptic sign sticky-taped to
the end of a shelf containing plastic picnicware and computer-
game cartridges:

as the saying goes
everything has its price
anything in this shop
could be yours
if the price is right

What has no discernible price is the particular atmosphere of
the place, with its collection of obsolete formats and unusual
groupings of objects.

    In the café on the corner of Coronation Street and the
Pacific Highway I sit with a cup of tea, watching an elderly
couple at the table beside me read their individual copies of the
Daily Telegraph in tandem. They look up and start to discuss a
story and I quickly turn back to my own newspaper, the *Hornsby
Advocate*. The letters page includes the usual civic complaints
and congratulations and a photograph taken in local bushland
of lounge chairs and a coffee table set up among the trees.
The accompanying letter frets, 'Do parents know what their
kids get up to in the bush?'

    I leave the café and walk back along the highway, past the
oversized Sylvanian Family rabbit that guards the toyshop, then
across to the Odeon Cinema and on towards Forbes Footwear.
The interior with its ladders and shoeboxes stacked to the ceiling
is from a time of x-ray foot measuring machines and Brannock
devices. It now specialises in orthopaedic shoes, although it has
always been traditionalist. As a teenager I received a lecture on
Dr Martens boots here: they were not only bad for my feet but
erosive to society's morals.

Farewelling the old-world scene at Forbes I cross over to the new side of Hornsby. The connection between the old and new is a pedestrian bridge which spans the railway line. The concrete bridge is a well-worn path, its awning spotted with lichen and the railings sticky with grime from the removal of countless taped notices. It will remain there for only a few years more, its decrepitude inconsistent with the tidy civic square to which it is connected. Knowing its days are numbered, I make sure to stop and read the metal plaque commemorating the bridge's opening in 1980. It feels like reading the title page of a withdrawn library book, of animating long-neglected names. The plaque lists the councillors, the contractors and the engineers, all the key people who brought this grey walkway into being.

The new side of Hornsby is dominated by the shopping mall, made up of two linked complexes that enclose a central square. In the middle of the square is the water clock, one of Sydney's more eccentric public artworks. This unusual contraption is as misunderstood now as it was upon its construction in 1993. The clock's sculptor, local artist Victor Cusack, described it as a 'cacophony of movement and flying water'. His description is accurate. A tangle of metal bars, beams and cogs rise from the centre of a tiled pool, anchored by a bronze tree trunk hung with chimes and adorned with sculptures of birds, bats and lizards. The movement of water through the fountain animates it into a thrashing, sloshing monster, equal parts steampunk fantasy, garden ornament and folly.

At the 'Rock Around the Clock' festival, an event organised in 1993 to celebrate the already controversial structure, officials praised its iconic presence and likened it to landmark European civic sculptures. It was said to be the world's second-largest pendulum clock after Big Ben but local conservatives were having none of it: 'Many pensioner ratepayers would rather eat than tell the time,' wrote a reader of the *Advocate,* one of the many protesting the cost of the clock. 'Maybe the council could recover some of the funds spent on this monument to monstrosity by hiring it for any future version of *The Addams Family,*' another reader suggested.

Others predicted that it would become a receptacle for rubbish, or the target of detergent-wielding saboteurs. They were not wrong: when the clock repeatedly stopped working during its first few months the culprit was found to be chicken bones flung into the water by littering passers-by. Local residents may not have liked the water clock but it did inspire spirited and sometimes extravagant responses. One contributor to the *Advocate* letters page wrote a free verse poem about the structure, linking it to the social and economic mood of the 1990s recession. The poem evokes how the clock 'weeps by the bucket' and is 'timed to clank and persuade by robotic arcade'.

After more than two decades of dividing opinion the clock's agglomeration of cogs, pipes, and bronze wildlife continues to slosh and see-saw. Due to inconsistent maintenance over the years the clock face has ceased to tell the time but the fountain is as vigorous as ever. I watch long perspex troughs at the centre fill until they overflow, spilling out a stream of water as the contraption emits hoots like a steam train.

Nearby two teenage girls are busking at the shopping centre entrance. Both sing and one plays an acoustic guitar covered in a collage of postage stamps lacquered under a coat of shiny varnish. During a lull in their performance I go over to ask if she decorated her guitar herself. She replies yes, polite but distant, and I drop a dollar into her guitar case. My dollar triggers Florence and the Machine's 'Dog Days Are Over', a song especially calibrated to evoke a sense of wild emotional freedom even in the most commonplace of circumstances. Their voices echo around the rainy square, punctuated by hoots from the clock.

Back in the early days of the water clock, my own teenage musical adventures found expression on the new side of Hornsby in the form of all-ages punk shows. I wasn't the kind of teenager who found solace in the donut shops and surf stores of the shopping centre, but neither did I expect to find it at the Police Citizens Youth Club. Despite the unlikely connection between police and punks, this plain brick building, under a defunct neon sign of dancing feet for the 'Stomp Café', was the venue for monthly gigs by local punk bands. At these shows I stepped into a messy, subversive world, where teenagers in the kinds of boots disparaged by Forbes Footwear slammed into each other to the raucous sounds of the club's most frequent performers, a punk band named Savage Cabbage. Across the street was the AMF bowling alley, where before the bands started I would sit on the fire escape under the lanes, listening to the crash of the balls and pins above. In my memory these are secret night places, settings for adventures. But I stand now before the bowling club and see a windowless grey slab. The PCYC is a worn brick building shrouded in scaffolding.

I avoid the maze of the Westfield and cross back over the train line to the old side. As I do I try to imagine how it might look in the future with high-rise towers. My mental image is derailed by thoughts of the *Advocate* front-page headline which described how, based on the plans, 'Paris Rises in the West'. I imagine the earth opening and an Arc de Triomphe rising up, the Aquatic Centre spilling over to become a river, spanned by a Pont-Neuf with lovers and tourists strolling under lantern streetlights.

Instead I have come to a demolition site where the CWA tearoom once stood. A flat-roofed building from the late 1950s, it sat modestly at the edge of the park, screened from the street by a row of lavender bushes. Its demure, reliable form suited its function as a place of tea and respite. Looking at the rubble where the building used to be I imagine this must be the start of the old side's big change. The demolition of the CWA was a preliminary tea-and-scones sacrifice to appease the force of the new.

The park is deserted on this chilly day. The fountain has its water jets switched off and the water in the tiled pool is greenish and dirty. A plaque on the side commemorates the fountain's construction in 1970 to mark the 200th anniversary of Captain Cook's discovery of the east coast of Australia. Another plaque revises the claims of the original:

Hornsby Shire Council acknowledges that when Captain James Cook claimed possession of the east coast, the land which is now Hornsby Shire had already been occupied by the Darug and Guringai People for many thousands of years.

The significance of the slab of rock at the centre of the fountain is left up to interpretation. Perhaps it came from the nearby quarry, which is now disused and overgrown. Sydney suburbs are pockmarked with old quarries, which have modified the shape of the land whether they have been filled in or remain as sudden cliffs interrupting the flow of the streets. Of these, the most renowned were the three sandstone quarry sites that operated in Pyrmont in the 1850s, known by stonemasons as Paradise, Purgatory and Hellhole, each named for the quality of its stone. Yellowblock sandstone from Paradise gave many of Sydney's grandest nineteenth-century buildings a golden blush, among them the Sydney Town Hall and St Mary's Cathedral. But rather than sandstone, the Hornsby quarry was mined for blue metal, gravel made of volcanic rock which is a raw material for concrete.

The road to the quarry is fenced off and an abandoned rock-crushing plant decays behind the gates. The factory buildings are rusty and graffitied, the rooms ragged and smashed up, the tagged names ghostly on the walls. Beyond the factory is the winding path that leads down into the quarry pit. At the centre is a lake surrounded by steep cliffs of dark, volcanic rock. It's a tranquil place but a little spooky, the rock faces scarred and scraped, with trees growing out of them at unusual angles. There are houses only a few hundred metres away but the quarry seems far from the suburban streets, a wilderness within the artificial shape of the gouged cliffs.

I follow the worn asphalt down the spiral to the lake's edge. The surface is a gemstone green, and deep waters lie beneath it. The blue metal that was mined here was rock formed after a volcanic eruption 200 million years ago. With the quarrying came the excavation of this ancient memory of the earth. After the quarry closed, water filled the pit to form the lake, a different kind of water clock to the one in the centre of the civic square. The water's green surface dissolves time. Here time feels still or absent.

In the balance of old and new the quarry landscape is neither. It's a place reclaimed by trees and vines, birds and insects, dormant to human activity except for the occasional curious visitor. By the lake's edge even the hum of traffic seems to have disappeared. It's a weird mixture, the exhaustion of the landscape inside the disused mining pit, but the flourishing of non-human life on its surface.

Although the quarry feels disconnected from the surrounding urban scene of the old side of Hornsby, I know that in years to come it will be filled in and converted into a park. The spot where I'm sitting will be buried underneath tonnes of rubble from the construction of the NorthConnex motorway. On the grassy slopes of the future park people will have picnics, walk their dogs, go jogging, sit and daydream. But for now this is a sidestep place, quiet and latent.

A wild ride of hairpin turns, through bushland populated by roosters.

OLD SIDE

The Highway north.

GORGE

OP SHOP

The Jersey St op shop zone, Vinnies & The Wombat Wardrobe.

Once I bought a large collection of pinned butterflies from Vinnies.

QUARRY

Peaceful & eerie, an emerald green lake, post-industrial wilderness.

MiX UP MUSiC COLLECTIBLE CDs

Repository of obsolete formats.

◉ CORONATION ST. ◉

The Hornsby version. Classic old side collection of miscellaneous businesses.

CWA

Tea and scones headquarters (now demolished).

FACE

Ivy-clad restaurant, go in & look out the eyes.

Pacific Highway

Since 1914, once one of many Odeons, now the only one left.

ODEON

Footwear and shopfitting time-travel.

FORBES

NEW SIDE

HPCYC

Police Citizens Youth Club

Unlikely mid-90s punk venue. See the Hard-Ons by night, learn badminton by day.

WRIGLEYS

The Wrigleys Factory water tower, like a big gum bubble.

The factory has produced gum since 1958, & recently expanded to take over production of Eclipse Mints.

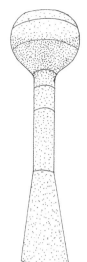

ＷESTFIELD

The world of the mall.

THE BRIDGE

Between old & new.
The intermediary zone.

WATER CLOCK

Florence Street Mall's sloshing centrepiece, dividing opinion since 1993.

More
ＷESTFIELD

Mall, continued.

HORNSBY
OLD & NEW

Structures, shops & wild places.

Flipping through a box of old postcards at an antique shop, I stopped on one that featured a black-and-white illustration of 'South Reef at Sydney Heads'. The card depicted a night scene, the full moon shining across the sea and rocks. 'Hope you are taking advantage of fine weather. H.A.B.' was written underneath in neat fountain-pen script. I turned the card over. Postmarked 1906, its addressee was 'Miss Bury' of Leichhardt. I picked up the next card in the box, from the same pictorial series and with an image titled 'Breakers on Rocks at Coogee'. Also from H.A.B. to Miss Bury, it carried the inscription: 'If fine, why not take a run out to this place?'

When they arrived at Miss Bury's house in Mackenzie Street, these postcards must have brought with them the ocean and the full moon, a clear night and the sound of the waves. More than 100 years later, their messages are obscure. I am tempted to think of them as romantic suggestions, but they are not necessarily so; whatever innuendoes they contain remain a mystery.

To take advantage of fine weather and visit the sea, Miss Bury would have had to make a long journey. First she would catch the tram along Parramatta Road into the city. Sydney in 1906 was a metropolis under constant expansion. It was a new century, Australia had been declared a federation only a few years earlier, and on her journey Miss Bury would have travelled past the latest addition to the city: the new Central Station, built on land that, in the nineteenth century, had been the Devonshire Street Cemetery.

The lofty ceilings of the station's grand concourse provided a cathedral-like atmosphere, inspiring wonder at the ever-advancing technologies of travel. From here the tram turned to travel up George Street, past rows of commercial premises with awnings that stretched out to cover the pavements, their side walls painted with advertisements for shopping emporiums, tailors and patent remedies. The street was the city's main thoroughfare and was busy with trams, horses and carts, boys on bicycles and people dashing between the traffic. At Martin Place Miss Bury would have stepped out to join the throng, before boarding the Watsons Bay tram that ran all the way to South Head.

The journey to South Head, then as now, is to the eastern edge of Sydney, where the land meets the ocean. The entrance to Sydney Harbour is between two headlands. The larger and more remote of the two is North Head. The isolation of this headland from the centre of Sydney made it the chosen location for the city's quarantine station, which operated for almost 150 years and was many immigrants' first experience of Sydney. By contrast South Head, the innermost headland, has a stronger connection to the city. It is a thin finger of land at the very tip of the promontory that is now the city's eastern suburbs, with both a sense of urban order and the wildness of land's end.

The tramlines followed the inner edge of the headland. It was a sightseeing journey with views of grand houses and the harbour, past Barracluff's ostrich farm at Diamond Bay and ending at the ocean cliffs. At Watsons Bay there were day-trip attractions and amusements: tea rooms for refreshments and an octagonal wooden building housing a camera obscura. Inside this dark room, as if by magic, a view of the Heads and the ocean hovered over the walls.

People travelled here then, as they do now, for a sense of distance from the city. Here they could turn their backs on Sydney and look out across the ocean. South Head was a place many associated with their arrival into Sydney by boat. Until passenger flights became commonplace in the 1950s the Heads were the physical as well as the symbolic entrance to Sydney. The high cliffs, jagged and striated with waves crashing against the rocks down below, created a sublime

panorama of nature's power. In the nineteenth century this view was
a common postcard subject, often including people standing at the
cliff's edge looking out to sea. In these images the women in white
dresses and men in suits appear small against the rocks, like a Caspar
David Friedrich painting of tiny figures against a vast natural vista.

Though South Head is known for its beautiful and dramatic
outlook, it is also a tragic place. Since the first recorded case in 1863
the high cliffs of The Gap have been the location for thousands of
suicide attempts. Many people have lost their lives here, countless
others have contemplated the cliff edge and fought with the urge
to cross it. Some people's attempts have been intercepted by locals
like the 'Angel of the Gap', Don Ritchie, who for forty years lived in
the house across from Gap Park and saved the lives of hundreds of
people by talking them away from the edge.

It is a sunny November day. The streets look fresh with the pale
green of spring leaves and the mauve of jacaranda trees in bloom.
Though it is more than a century after H.A.B.'s messages, taking
advantage of fine weather remains a good suggestion. Ever since
buying the cards I'd kept them on my desk, scrutinising them for
long enough that I felt H.A.B.'s directive applied to me too: Berry
and Bury are close enough as names. The day had arrived for me
to take up H.A.B's suggestion to 'take a run' out to South Head.
I set out in my car where the tramtracks once used to lead east,
following the hills and bends through Double Bay and Rose Bay
until I reach Watsons Bay, the end of the road.

The path that leads to the place on the postcard, the rocks
known as South Reef at the tip of South Head, begins at Camp Cove,
a small, sheltered beach on the inner side of the headland. Near the
beach is a lengthy timeline information panel. The first section of
the panel is 'Triassic Period–1788' and in six paragraphs it covers
some 220 million years, beginning with 'Hawkesbury sandstone
forms from accumulated layers of sediment'. I ponder this geological
prehistory as people stroll past me on the way to the beach with
towels draped over their shoulders. Cars prowl along Cliff Street in
search of parking spots. The wooden cottage on the corner, its white

paint peeling, has a garden planted with mother-in-law's tongue under a gnarled frangipani tree.

The next point on the timeline is six thousand years ago. The Birrabirragal people lived here then, fishing in the waters of the bay now named Camp Cove. The Aboriginal name for the inner side of South Head is Barraory and the inscriptions carved into rocks around the headland showed the people, kangaroos, fish and whales that inhabited the headland and the ocean surrounding it. Then comes the first fixed date on the timeline: 21 January 1788. After this day, time and the land are increasingly divided up. The headland was used by whalers and the military, a marine biology station was constructed, as were lighthouses and lodgings. Then came the tourist age. It started with a swimming hole, tearooms and trams, and continues now with their equivalents: the beach, a kiosk selling ice creams and crisps, and buses squeezing along the tight streets.

A path begins at the eastern end of the beach and traces the edge of the headland. On either side are tangles of lantana and morning glory with cuttings through them leading to the cliffs. On the harbour side of the headland the cliffs are not so high or dramatic as those facing the ocean, but they are dangerous nonetheless. Signs show a cartoon figure slipping off a crumbling edge, but these often go unheeded as people are compelled by the lure of an uninterrupted view. The rocks at the edge here feel secluded, hidden from the path by the thicket.

South Head was once inaccessible to anyone but the military, and beside the path there is a glossy black cannon mounted in a concrete well, pointing in the direction of the harbour and the city beyond. From here the city looks small, an outline of vertical shapes against the sky. The then Prime Minister Tony Abbott's voice comes blustering through my thoughts, a soundbite from the radio news I'd been listening to in the car. Describing Sydney in a speech to the British Prime Minister, Abbott had said: 'As we look around this glorious city…it's hard to think that back in 1788 it was nothing but bush'.

From here the city has a tenuous presence. The harbour and the

zigzag shoreline of the bays and headlands are the glorious thing.
I stand here where sandstone boulders rise up like whales from
the grass, my eyes tracing the shapes made by the land against the
water and feeling the temptation to erase the city and its structures
altogether, imagining it three hundred years ago, or three thousand.
As tempting as this thought is, to imagine the reversal of time is not
so simple. My existence here is a consequence of the colonial history
that has named and changed this place, transforming the land and
its meanings as it did so.

South Head was the site of some of the first contact between
the British and the Aboriginal clans of the harbour. Later it became
a camp for many displaced Aboriginal people including Cora
Gooseberry, an elder who was well known in the colony as Queen
of Sydney and Botany. In the 1840s she described to the artist
George French Angas her father's reaction to the arrival of the
British ships in 1788. He had thought them terrifying sea monsters,
and fled far inland from the coast to hide.

For the early British arrivals the headland was a place where
people would stare hopefully out to sea, looking for boats that might
bring food or news from the rest of the world. They were looking
out for invading forces too, and over time the vegetation was cleared
and the headland became a bald landscape, pockmarked with gun
emplacements, circular concrete wells sunk into the sandstone.
Now these concrete blocks have more of the look of stone, their
appearance softened by decades of weather and wear.

The track continues past Lady Bay, the nudist beach below.
Men are stretched out on the rocks above the beach, sunbaking
and chatting and smoking. A group of walkers makes jokes about
averting their eyes as they peer curiously downwards. On the
other side of the path is the naval base HMAS *Watson*. Through
the tall wire fence I can see another group of men sitting, smoking,
although these ones are in uniform. They have their backs to the
harbour and face the cluster of utilitarian buildings that make up
the base.

The path emerges from the shrubs at the lighthouse-keeper's
cottage. It is behind the Hornby Lighthouse, built after the wreck

of the *Dunbar* passenger ship in 1857. One hundred and twenty two people perished in the *Dunbar* disaster, most of them wealthy Sydney residents returning home after a trip to London. The lone survivor was deckhand James Johnson. He survived the wreck by clinging to a rock ledge for almost two days, while the bodies and wreckage from the ship washed up on the rocks below. The waves bobbed with debris, the bonnets and shoes, hams and petticoats, barrels of figs and bags of mail that the Dunbar had been carrying. Eventually Johnson was spotted. He was rescued by an Icelandic apprentice watchmaker who was lowered down from the cliffs above by a rope, while a crowd watched on.

After recovery from his ordeal James Johnson became the first lighthouse-keeper at South Head. He lived here in the cottage for many years, at the edge of the ocean that had almost claimed his life. The lighthouse, painted in red and white stripes for visibility, looks cheerful, like a candy-cane. Its doors have long been sealed up as the light operates automatically, but I climb up its external stairs and look out to sea from the top of them, thinking of Johnson looking out over the very same view. From here too I can see the scene on H.A.B.'s postcard, the rocks of the reef with the waves crashing against them and North Head in the distance. In between the Heads a few sailboats are out catching the wind, their white sails tiny against the ocean.

I return to the track and cut through one of the trampled paths among the brambles and lantana. It's just wide enough to avoid scratching my legs and I step through it carefully. At the end is a flat rock above the reef and I sit here watching the men fishing on the rock platform down below. Near me a metal ring sunk into a section of concrete has a cluster of engraved padlocks attached to it. I carefully lean forward to read the initials and messages inscribed into the locks: 'Steph, you have made me the happiest man on earth. Will you marry me?'

Whoever H.A.B. was to Miss Bury, he or she did not end up her lifelong companion. Miss Bury married an A.N.W. in 1917. But I like to think that on a fine day Miss Bury and H.A.B. might have caught the tram to Watsons Bay. Like the figures in a postcard they would have stood at The Gap and looked out towards the horizon, feeling the sea air on their faces.

For a long time the South Reef view on the postcard, below the tip of the headland, was an inaccessible military area. The pits of the concrete gun encasements are now an obstacle course of interconnecting tunnels. Most end in bricked-up walls or gaps too narrow to pass through, although there is a network of passageways and bunkers which connect up with the naval base. The entrances are closed off, but I find one door with a view into a gloomy series of rooms. Scratched into their walls are sets of initials inscribed by previous visitors. Alert for coincidence I look for an H.A.B., but none of the engravings match.

The track loops around and I return to Camp Cove, snaking my way over the sand between groups of people sunbaking until I find a place in the shade at the other end of the beach. Women wearing bikinis eat strawberries, read mystery novels, bask in the sun. The scene I have entered is very different to the restrained one Miss Bury would have encountered in 1906, when women were only permitted to 'bathe' in loose-fitting dresses with sleeves and skirts.

The propriety of beach activities was a topic of great debate in the 1900s. In 1903 a law that had prohibited 'daylight bathing' at Sydney beaches since 1833 was repealed. With its repeal came arguments over appropriate swimwear. A suggested mandatory skirt for men's costumes led to the 1907 bathing costume protests, for which men wearing women's underwear, curtains and tablecloths marched on Bondi Beach, crying a vigorous 'No' to the question, 'Will we wear skirts?' Men didn't want to wear a skirt to swim but neither did women. The baggy dress and pantaloons that were acceptable nineteenth-century women's bathing attire made it impossible to do anything but wade, as these outfits quickly became waterlogged. Frustrated by this, professional swimmer Annette Kellerman designed the first one-piece women's swimsuit and, following her controversial lead, by 1910 women began to wear close-fitting costumes known as 'Kellermans' that more closely resemble swimwear as we know it.

After swimming I take up a spot on the sand. Around me groups of people lie out on towels, sunbaking. Others sit reading or stroll along the shoreline. I watch a man and a woman at the water's edge. They have the look of a retired couple on holidays, wearing matching bucket hats and sunglasses with side panels. The woman has a stick and is tracing it across the sand, writing something. The man tries to snap a photo of what she has written but she's too close to the tide line and a wave dissolves the letters. I managed a glimpse of it, though, before the water washed it away. She had inscribed their initials, the letters side by side in the wet sand.

The Graphic Series. G 20.   South Reef, Sydney Heads.   Copyright.

Hope you are taking advantage of fine weather. *sgd*

Fine

Martin Place

POST *Graphic* CARD.

Miss Bury
"Rathmines"
Leichhardt

Postal nexus in the
city centre, "a semi-
conscious organism of
the public life".

Daily Telegraph
1886

Leichhardt

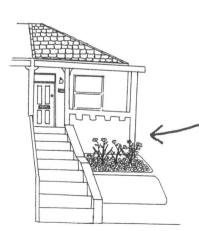

A little house
with Miss Bury
in residence.

Weather

Postcard journeys
across the city.

At Sydney's eastern edge,
the cliffs and the ocean
and a camera obscura.

South Head

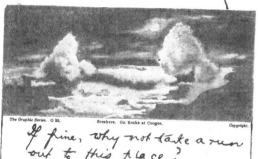

The Graphic Series. G 22.   Breakers. On Rocks at Coogee.   Copyright.

*If fine, why not take a run
out to this place?*

The Coogee Aquarium
with baths and pleasure
gardens, a dome decorated
with gold and silver stars
and with the 'largest
living alligator' on
display.

Coogee

Kurnell is most often seen from above through the windows of planes as they come in to land over Botany Bay. Passengers look down over the white polka dots of the petrol and oil tanks at the Caltex plant, then rows of houses and a thin strip of sandy beach, and then the expanse of the bay. For most visitors to Sydney this is all they will see of Kurnell. The plane descends towards the runway and the views of a moment before are forgotten in the anticipation of touchdown.

The name Kurnell comes from Cunnel, the Gweagal name for the headland at the end of the long, curved peninsula of land at the southern end of what is now called Botany Bay. The suburb of Kurnell is small and remote with only one road in and out of it, Captain Cook Drive. The road passes coastal bushland and industrial sites, a wastewater treatment plant, a sand mine, the nature reserve, and Caltex. Since the 1950s the Caltex oil refinery has been Kurnell's most dominant feature, especially at night when its glow can be seen from across the bay. When it was in full operation flares of flame emerged from the chimneys like giant Bunsen burners and the buildings were illuminated with what looked to be strings of giant fairy lights.

In our early twenties, my friends and I would sometimes take a midnight drive to Kurnell. We did it for a scare, pretending to see ghosts in the dark at the side of the road as we awaited the lights of the refinery. It was an adventure that only worked by night. Come daytime the disguise lifted and the truth was a grimy, industrial scene. The refinery's tanks, pipes and chimneys were a man-made yet inhuman landscape, a reminder of the toxic industries that, in Sydney, are usually tucked out of sight. Although in 2014 the refinery's operations were downgraded to fuel import and storage, it has the same dominant presence on the peninsula as before.

It is day when I visit Kurnell this time, rounding the curves of Captain Cook Drive and waiting to see the chimneys and tanks of Caltex. It's always a surprise to be so close to a substantial industrial plant. Although there are industrial areas in the Sydney suburbs, most of the large-scale enterprises – power stations, mines – are beyond the city's edges. Like an ambassador between the two worlds there is a small petrol station in front of the refinery. Here two old brown Holden Commodores are being filled up direct from the source. Alongside the petrol station is a playground, a tennis court, and a weathered wooden sign welcoming visitors to Kurnell, 'the birthplace of modern Australia'.

The modern Australia of Kurnell is a grid of residential streets. After the kilometres of bushland and factory gates it is a surprise to be in a suburb again. It is a mixture of 1950s cottages and the behemoth two-storey homes with porticos and double garages that are slowly replacing them. Many of the houses facing the bayside beach are newly built in this style. They have wide patios designed for hours of leisure and watching the planes fly in and out of the airport across the bay. Beside them, the older cottages look small and neat as dollhouses.

There is a row of these little houses remaining at the end of Prince Charles Parade, the road which follows the inner edge of the headland. Collections of trucks, horse floats and rusting machines are gathered in their long yards. In one driveway is a trestle table with a jumble of household objects arranged on top. A cardboard sign nailed to the side announces the 'Golden Coin Sale' in neat script. Among the jars and plates and vases for sale is a riding hat, which I try on and find to fit me. I offer the man at the stall $2. As I hand him the money I ask what it is like living in Kurnell.

'I love it!' he says.

'Do you feel like it's a part of Sydney?'

He pauses. 'Not really,' he says, as if this is one of the things he loves about it. 'It's a village, surrounded by a city.' He points behind his house and tells me he keeps a rooster, horses, everything he could want back there.

A riding hat seems an apt souvenir for a Sydney suburb with more than the usual population of horses in its backyards. But horses are not the most unusual pets to be found here. On the nightly television news I once watched a report about a home in suburban Sydney where a 2.5-metre saltwater crocodile was being kept in a backyard pool. The pool had been enclosed by a cage, but as it is illegal to keep crocodiles as pets the zoo had come to claim the beast, citing fears that it might get loose and escape into Sydney's waterways. Although the crocodile's owner wasn't home to comment at time of the raid, someone from National Parks must have spoken to the nearby residents, who reported that the neighbours had grown quite attached to it. As I watched the footage of the backyard pool the location appeared on the bottom of the screen: Kurnell. I wasn't surprised. If one did want to keep a crocodile covertly, Kurnell seemed far enough removed from the city to allow one to get away with it.

This part of Kurnell is a regular pattern of houses, lawns, fences, garden ornaments and letterboxes. Australian flags fly outside fibro cottages and beachfront mini-mansions. Looking closely I find weirder details. From the patchy grass of a vacant lot an abandoned Space Hopper toy leers with a buck-toothed expression. A garage door wears the outline of angry spray-painted warnings, now faded and indecipherable. Parked in a driveway is a van advertising a white dove release service, for weddings, funerals, birthdays and special occasions. A nonsense word is painted on a boarded-up window – *noughtuiew* – and I stand there trying to decode it in case it's an anagram. While irregular details exist in every suburb, in Kurnell the incongruous things, the white doves and nonsense words, appear to be quirks arisen from isolation.

Prince Charles Parade faces onto Silver Beach and the calm waters of Botany Bay beyond it. The long strip of sand is interrupted by a succession of rocky breakwaters on which people perch to fish. Interrupting the beach is the Caltex wharf and pipes which stretch a kilometre out into the bay. Underneath the wharf barnacles grow thickly on the pylons, and the light is dappled as it comes through the gaps between the pipes. A CCTV camera watches all who pass by. While standing underneath the wharf I hear the long, droning sound of a factory siren. Details of the refinery are a constant presence: the chimneys and tanks visible behind the houses, the strips of vacant land over which the pipelines run, the red and green star of the Caltex logo.

The other prominent presence in Kurnell is Captain Cook. On weekdays convoys of buses transport school children to the site of Cook's landing place in 1770. The colonial significance of this spot was marked in 1870 by another colonial appropriation, an obelisk. It has a funereal look to it, surrounded by a low sandstone fence like a family plot in a graveyard. Set into the path leading to the obelisk are the words *Warra warra wai* – 'go away' – documented as the first words spoken by the Gweagal people to Cook and his crew. These words are proud, and lonely to imagine. I hear them in my head over the zip of jet skis from the bay and they activate the past in a way the obelisk could never do.

In 1970 a reenactment of Cook's landing was staged here with the Queen in attendance, watching from under a marquee on the beach. As Cook's party approached the shore in a rowboat the event was upstaged by a group of Sydney University students who roared through in a speedboat, claiming the land for the allegedly 'mad' monarch King George III. While this was occurring there was another gathering on the opposite side of the bay at La Perouse. Here Aboriginal people threw wreaths into the bay in a mourning ceremony to acknowledge the dispossession of their land. Around them people stood with signs on which were written names of the Sydney clans, among them Cammeraygal and Gweagal, Wangal and Gadigal, names connected with the Sydney landscape for many thousands of years.

The Dharawal people were the language group of the south side of the bay, which they called Kamay. The British first named it Stingray Bay – the bay is shaped like a stingray, and stingrays were once plentiful in its waters – and finally renamed it Botany

Bay. It was originally intended as the site for the penal settlement that would become Sydney. However, in 1788, Arthur Phillip chose the deeper and larger Port Jackson to the north. Botany Bay is the city's alternative harbour, a parallel city of utility, dominated by the functional structures of the airport and the shipping container port. I watch planes taking off from the runways and a freighter stacked with red Hamburg Süd shipping containers moving slowly towards the ocean. Beyond the cranes of the container terminal is the Sydney city skyline, muted by a bluish haze. I try to imagine what kind of Sydney would exist if the settlement had been built in Botany Bay instead. The bay has none of the drama of Sydney Harbour, being wide and almost circular and surrounded by flat land. The Botany Bay Sydney would have been a calmer place, perhaps.

It is difficult to imagine Kurnell expanded into a city. It is Sunday and the park at the tip of the peninsula is crowded with picnics. A trio of teenagers plays boules on the grass as kookaburras watch from a branch of the banksia tree above them. Around a table decorated with Happy Birthday bunting a family drinks Coronas and converses in Russian. On the far side of the park a group of divers remove their tanks and peel off their wetsuits. People photograph the monuments and plaques, of which there are many, marking Aboriginal and Cook-related sites, or stop to rest among the eucalypt trees. The bushland of the nature reserve seems like it might be the original coastal vegetation but the area was cleared long ago and these trees are recent replantings. The environment has had to withstand much modification, from the clearing of its ironbark forest to provide timber for housing, to nineteenth-century gentlemen's shooting parties converging on Kurnell to hunt koalas.

On the eastern side of the peninsula are sand dunes, a shifting terrain that has been eroded by mining but is still a conspicuous landscape. The dunes have been put to many different uses, from families visiting for a day of sand sledding to the filming of scenes for films such as *Mad Max Beyond Thunderdome*. For *Mad Max* the dunes became a desert with a Boeing 747 brought in and half-buried in the sand as if crashed there.

The dunes also have a more sinister history. The discovery of

human bones during the construction of the desalination plant in
2007 was a reminder of long-held rumours that the sand dunes
are a place for criminals to dispose of bodies. It was soon suggested
that these could be the remains of Juanita Nielsen, the activist
whose 1975 disappearance and presumed murder is one of the
city's best-known mysteries. But DNA tests on the bones ruled this
out and their identity remains unknown. The dunes are the site of
another notorious unsolved crime, a case known as the Wanda Beach
Murders. In January 1965 the bodies of teenage friends Marianne
Schmidt and Christine Sharrock were discovered in the sand
behind Wanda Beach on the southern side of the headland. Despite
exhaustive investigations and the reopening of the case the crime
remains unsolved.

The isolation of the ocean side of the peninsula makes it an eerie
place of shifting sands and lonely structures. At Potter Point a series
of slender ventilation pipes rise up from the rocks like sentinels.
Surfers know this place as Voodoo, a stretch of ocean with powerful
waves. In the 1980s the nearby dunes were a dumping ground for
old cars, their windows smashed, spray-painted with graffiti. Despite
being a lonely place this area has absorbed a lot of human activity,
especially from industry, as decades of sandmining have depleted the
once abundant dunes. Many of the dunes have been hollowed out to
become pools clogged with building debris.

Compared to the peaceful waters of Botany Bay on the other
side of the peninsula the view of the open sea from the cliffs is
wild and boundless. For decades this was the outlook of the people
who lived in cliff houses built against the rock face. Prior to the
construction of the oil refinery in the 1950s there was no road
leading into Kurnell. The peninsula's isolated position made it an
appealing retreat in the early twentieth century and, as in other
coastal areas around Sydney, a shack community was established
here during the Depression. While the shacks were often hastily
built from available scraps, the cliff houses were more elaborate feats
of construction. Around the contours of the rock face rooms and
passageways were assembled. These structures clung to the rocks
like the outcrops of a peculiar castle.

Despite their precarious location and the irregular assortment of building materials used to create them the houses had a cosy atmosphere. Photographs of Bert Adamson's home show neat rooms with carpets and potted plants, a calendar on the wall, a single bed with a carved wooden headboard. The white painted walls and pale blue ceilings reflected the colours of the sea below. Outside, a ladder led down to a rock platform for fishing. Adamson began to construct his cliff house in the 1920s, continually extending and improving it. These improvements stalled as he grew older and he had to deal with the increasing vandalism that finally saw the destruction of his home by fire in 1974. There is no trace of the built structures today, though the cliffs still hold the shape of Bert Adamson's rooms.

There's a long walking track that follows the headland around to Cronulla but I choose the easy way out of Kurnell and travel back along Captain Cook Drive. I reverse my journey through the suburban streets, passing the petrol station and the tennis courts, the tanks and chimneys of Caltex, the gates to the nature reserve and the wastewater treatment plant. The road goes on to join up with the network that links the peninsula to the Princes Highway and the rest of the city.

Just before the road branches out, at the neck of the peninsula, is Greenhills Beach, a new housing estate. Once an area of dunes, and then mined for its sand, a section of this land has been released for housing. Behind the perimeter of the new estate rises a steep sandhill, crisscrossed by pathways. Below it are new streets lined by lots marked out by SOLD signs posted into the sandy soil. The one structure built so far is the frame for a house, a square timber skeleton. It looks lonely rising up from the sand, as if it could equally be the first to be built or the last to remain.

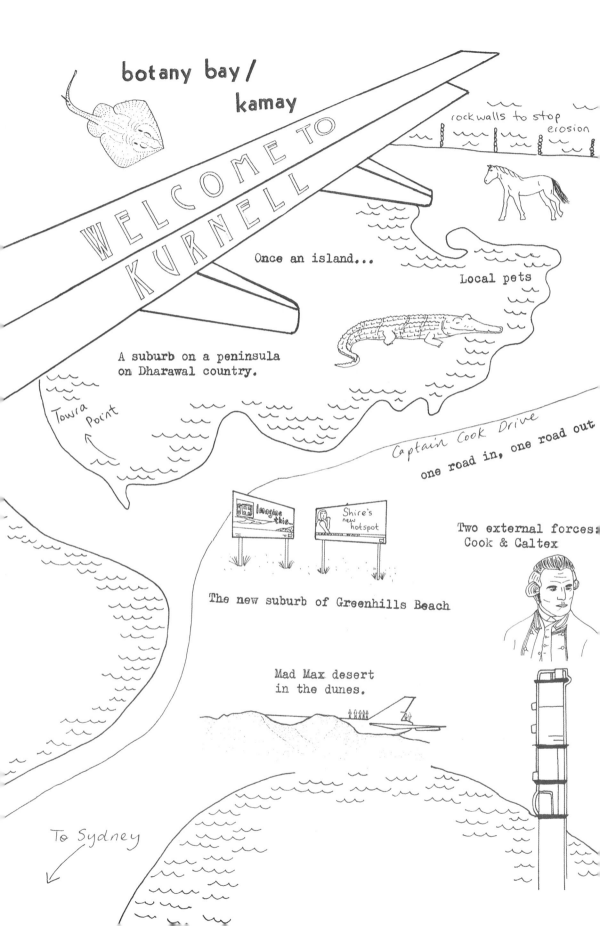

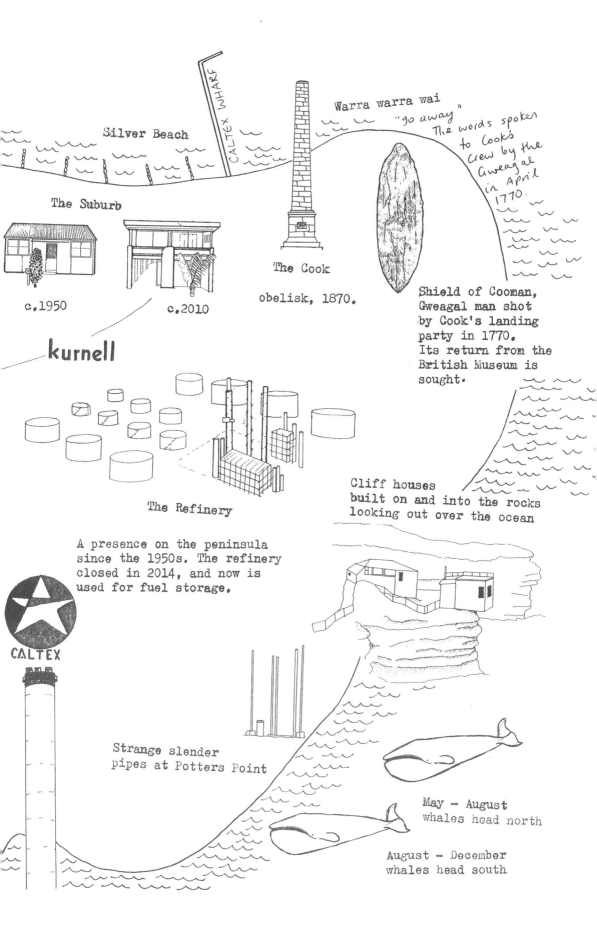

Silver Beach

CALTEX WHARF

Warra warra wai

"go away"

The words spoken to Cook's crew by the Gweagal in April 1770.

The Suburb

c.1950

c.2010

kurnell

The Cook

obelisk, 1870.

Shield of Cooman, Gweagal man shot by Cook's landing party in 1770. Its return from the British Museum is sought.

The Refinery

Cliff houses built on and into the rocks looking out over the ocean

A presence on the peninsula since the 1950s. The refinery closed in 2014, and now is used for fuel storage.

CALTEX

Strange slender pipes at Potters Point

May — August whales head north

August — December whales head south

Penrith is at the western extremity
of Greater Sydney, that wide halo of ever-spreading suburbia
that forms the city's sprawl. Here, on the hottest of summer days,
Sydney's harbour and ocean feel like a faraway world. Penrith is
a city in itself, a low-rise city with long, straight streets. It has the
Nepean River for a harbour and as an Opera House either the
Joan Sutherland Performing Arts Centre with its productions of
Shakespeare, or Panthers World of Entertainment with its Neil
Diamond show. If Parramatta is the business centre of the western
suburbs Penrith is its far-flung domestic centre, a landscape of family
homes, cars and shopping centres.

The journey from Sydney to Penrith passes through the many
rings of suburbia, a gradual expansion from the tight inner-west
streets to the broad plains of the outer suburbs. Along the motorway
is a string of western Sydney landmarks: the Blacktown drive-in
cinema, the cartoonish waterslides of the Wet'n'Wild water park,
and the huge white sheds of the Arnotts factory. The train ride has
its own series of landmarks: the painted mural of fields, bulldozers
and Superman at Seven Hills; the kangaroos in Featherdale Wildlife
Park; and the ever-expanding Rooty Hill RSL. The RSL once had
a sign over the entrance proclaiming it the 'Vegas of the West' until
in 2003 advertising laws banned it: 'Vegas' was too evocative of
gambling to be a permitted slogan.

A visit to the centre of Penrith involves a choice between the
Westfield mall or High Street. Westfield is a hermetically sealed

grey hulk with an ambience shared by mega malls the world over: air conditioning, chain stores, noisy food courts, bland background music. Life gets lived here as much as everywhere else, but such places are a wipe-clean surface, designed for nothing to stick.

The businesses that don't fit into Westfield, being too small or too niche in their appeal, their profits not great enough to meet the shopping centre rent, populate High Street. This is the part of town with the op shops, party supply and hobby stores, the new-age shops, bargain stores and independent retailers. Arcades lead off High Street like secret passageways. Penrith has seventeen shopping arcades, not the Victorian-era galleries that might come to mind upon hearing the word, but their 1960s and 1970s equivalents, with small shops on either side of passages paved in brown tiles.

In the 1920s German philosopher Walter Benjamin began what has become one of the world's most influential creative works about cities, the *Passagenwerk*, or 'Arcades Project'. The Parisian arcades that were the subject of Benjamin's research had been constructed in the nineteenth century but, by the 1920s, were well in decline. He found the arcades anachronistic, full of mysterious signs, strange objects, antiquated trades and vacant stores with secretive atmospheres. When Benjamin investigated the Parisian arcades and their traces he found, by looking deeply into their details, that he could reconstruct the Paris of the nineteenth century. The arcades contained the essence of the city as a whole through their preservation of objects, technologies and preoccupations. Benjamin's suicide in 1940, after attempting unsuccessfully to flee from Nazi-occupied France, meant he never completed the 'Arcades Project'. The manuscript was hidden in the Bibliothèque Nationale in Paris until after the war, and the collection of aphorisms and fragments finally published only in 1982, in a volume of nine hundred pages. A vast, unfinished collection, it examined how the Paris arcades were 'a past become space', and brought to attention how cities, and particular places within them, can act as repositories of memory and history, ideas and atmospheres.

The Parisian arcades of Benjamin's day have a far greater romance than their namesakes in the outer suburbs of Sydney. But despite the differences in time and scale, Penrith's arcades share something of the links to past atmospheres that Benjamin found so worthy of investigation. Layers of times past are preserved within them. In the 1920s, High Street was lined with tearooms, barbers, bakeries and estate agencies. By the 1950s there was a movie theatre, Greek milk bars and electrical stores where people would gather to watch the televisions through the windows. In the 1970s the arcades opened, tucking even more stores away in their shadowy interiors.

I start my arcades project at Memory Mall, the arcade at the corner of Woodriff Street. Its curious name is advertised in blue neon lights, in a flowing script as though written by hand. Inside I expect to find stores selling mementos to fit with the arcade's name, but the memories sold here are momentary ones, in the form of sandwiches and haircuts. Despite the unexpected poetry of the name 'Memory Mall', the title comes from its proximity to the war memorial Memory Park across the street with its monuments, wilting floral wreaths and plaques listing the names of fallen soldiers.

Although arcades were for Walter Benjamin time capsules, malls aren't generally regarded as places of memory. Memories do inhabit malls though, often childhood and teenage ones. My arcade memories from the 1980s have a sense of extended domesticity. There was something about such arcades that was almost like houses in their mixture of public and private, interior and exterior. Yet they were exciting in a way that houses usually weren't, with endless promises of new things to contemplate, and perhaps to buy. Rather than the objects within them, my memories of the arcades are of their atmospheres, the tiled floors and potted palms, their cavernous acoustics, the static faces of window display mannequins. Sometimes I imagined being locked in one at night and having it as my domain, how I'd read through the newsagent's magazines and eat chocolate bars before curling up to sleep in a bedding store.

Memory Mall is lively with a constant traffic of people buying sandwiches and shortcutting through to High Street. Other arcades are ghostly, such as the nearby Nepean Walkway, which keeps its roller shutters part-way down and has an entrance flanked by a tobacconist and a funeral parlour. The majority of the shops inside are for lease apart from Lorraine's. A sign hand-lettered in blue marker on a sheet of A4 paper describes Lorraine's merchandise as 'hand made baby's wear and pretty dolls'. The store is shut so I gaze through the window at a display of hand-knitted baby jumpers, devotional items, tapestries and 1970s beauty guides. These are arranged on a series of long tables. As I peer in, the beady eyes of a trio of nun dolls wearing knitted black habits stare back at me from amid the jumble.

Each arcade has two faces, the face it turns to High Street and the face it turns to the car parks and laneways behind. They're often used as shortcuts between these places and in the more dimly lit arcades the people entering at the other end look like advancing shadows. Even in the ghostliest of arcades there's the sense of sidestepping the obvious route, and while some are empty of tenants, they're not quite uninhabited. At the far end of the Nepean Walkway is an empty hair salon, Maxim's, the window decorated by a decal of a twice-lifesize gentleman in a tuxedo with a carnation in his buttonhole. He smiles and tips his top hat to people passing by, despite the For Lease sign on his shoulder.

Turning back along High Street I come to Penrith's fantasy supplies arcade, The Cottage Lane. On the awning are signs for past businesses – Floraison Design, Power of Beauty, Devine Creations – none of which can be found inside. Instead there is the Prima Ballerina ballet shop and Behind the Mask Fancy Dress store, with a window display of masks and a leering green Incredible Hulk as its mascot. This is the arcade of masks and costumes, where people leave with new identities as astronauts, flamenco dancers or superheros. The Cottage Lane also has another commonly encountered arcades business, a New Age store, this one listing the prices for psychic services in glittery adhesive letters under the invitation to 'come in and say hi'.

The next arcade, the NK Centre, is a solid brick building with arched windows on its upper storey, darkly tinted so there is no clue as to what goes on inside. Also mysterious are the initials NK, although their likely namesake is Nicholas Kepreotis, a man who owned a milk bar and a fruit and vegetable store here prior to the construction of the arcade. This arcade is liveliest at the car-park end, where a cake-decorating store is in a hobby-store face-off with a wool shop, both stores busy with shoppers and crowded with merchandise.

Inside the Wool Inn, a queue of people wait at the counter for advice from women wearing hand-knits. The shelves are stacked with plump balls of wool and knitting patterns, in as much abundance as the cake tins and figurines in One Stop Cake Decorations opposite. Here I look through drawers of plastic decorations, tiny kewpie dolls and roses, soccer balls and wedding bells. There's a rack of every imaginable shape of cookie cutter, cake tins in the contours of ladybugs and monsters, and shelves of figurines: bowlers, ice-skating couples, football players. At the counter a woman inspects a tray of sugar-paste roses while her two little girls watch with rapt attention. One Stop Cake Decorations contains the potential of celebrations yet to come, birthdays, successes and surprises, as the Wool Inn holds the potential of future jumpers. The neatly stacked balls of wool will become thick winter cardigans, or novice knitters' first scarves.

Across from the tinted upper-storey windows of the NK Centre, behind the advertising placards for Nepean Pizzas and Charcoals, is a faded sign with three words. *Pelmets. Blinds. Advice.* This is a relic from a long-gone store, from the days when people knew that a pelmet was a piece of fabric that goes along the top of the window to hide the curtain rail. I imagine the pelmets store as precursor to the arcades' abundance of psychic services. Penrith citizens would come to the pelmet store with their troubles and questions, about their lives as well as their curtains. Who better to offer advice than experts in concealment?

In this section of the street, the entrance to each arcade is painted a different shade of blue: Elizabeth Arcade a pale hydrangea colour, the Broadwalk Arcade turquoise, the Calokerinos Arcade a bright blue, the same colour as the sky. It has an angular roof like the tailfin of a Cadillac but underneath all the shutters are down and the businesses relocated. It's sealed up tight with not even a gap to peek through.

At the centre of Elizabeth Arcade is a bookstore with a sale table out the front. I browse through these cheapest of books, a library of past preoccupations and entertainments. Well-worn airport novels, Mills and Boon romances, canary owners' manuals and various versions of *The Blue Day Book*. Propped up among *How to Raise and Train a Bulldog* and *Chicken Soup for the Woman's Soul* is the familiar cover of *Dinkum Dunnies*, a book so readily available in secondhand stores that every household must have owned one in the 1970s, along with their sets of the *Encyclopedia Britannica*.

One of the mainstays of Penrith's arcades are the hairdressers, and most arcades include at least one barber or salon: Rod's Hair Shoppe or Jon's Salon, Male Look Hairdressing or Man About Town Gents Hair Stylist, Cherie Hair Fashions or Pamela Hair Boutique. Of all types of suburban businesses, hair salons are linked most consistently with the identity of the owner, and their decoration varies accordingly. At the Central City Arcade the sign for Rod's Hair Shoppe is a drainage downpipe ingeniously painted to look like a barber's pole. Inside Rod's a couple of scruffy-haired boys fidget on the vinyl chairs as they wait for their turn. A few doors along there is a more patient scene in Afro Varieties Salon, where a woman is having her hair plaited into many tiny braids.

On the top level of the Parker Arcade is the Active Career College, the place where apprentices learn to cut hair, dreaming of the day their names will be painted on the awnings of future salons. Many of the arcades have businesses upstairs, small colleges or solicitors' offices, the kind of companies that don't need street exposure and can hide away upstairs. The stairwells leading to these upper levels, with their exposed bricks and worn steps, lead me to imagine offices with wood panelled walls, clunky telephones and secretaries wiping dust from the leaves of indoor plants.

On the corner of Station Street is the Penrith Centre, decorated by pebblecrete rendering and shingle tile awnings. Inside I walk over the speckled linoleum on the floor, past parlour palms in pots beside rigid metal tables and chair sets painted burgundy. Although the arcades have many stylistic similarities – strip lighting, brown tiles – each has a particularity, a colour and a mood, to differentiate it from the others. The adjacent Skiptons Arcade shares the pebblecrete of the Penrith Arcade but has a central atrium with stairs leading to an upper terrace. Up here is a real estate coaching business and a guitar school. Its logo is an acoustic guitar resting against an open book of sheet music, a contrast to the guitar school in the City Centre Arcade, advertised by a cartoon of a purple-haired, shirtless punk playing a Flying V with a raven on his shoulder.

The final arcade is Riverlands, at the western end of High Street. Riverlands has the now familiar arcade combination of hobby stores, hair salons and niche businesses: the Quilt Shop, Hair Fanatics, The Shoe Shed. The list of businesses on the sign in the Riverlands car park includes Bish's One Stop Bowls Shop, but Bish's has been replaced by Derby Skates. The window is now decorated with an image of fierce roller-derby women posing in an alleyway in short skirts, ripped tights, and chunky black rollerskates.

Across from Riverlands the grey wall of Westfield stretches out behind a screen of eucalypts. I've reached the end of the arcades and having worked my way through the pasts contained in their tiled and pebbled interiors I look back down along High Street. The buildings are a patchwork of different facades with landmarks standing out: the pebblecrete Penrith Centre, the bright blue fin of the Calokerinos Arcade roof, an old sign for Reuben F. Scarf Hand Tailored Suits, the serifed letters of *SUITS* golden in the afternoon sun. People walking down High Street disappear into the arcades, to have their hair cut or to buy cake-decorating supplies, or just to walk back to their cars, past the pretty dolls in Lorraine's and the temptation of a psychic reading, and the For Lease signs that make them remember what used to be there, or imagine what might be in the future.

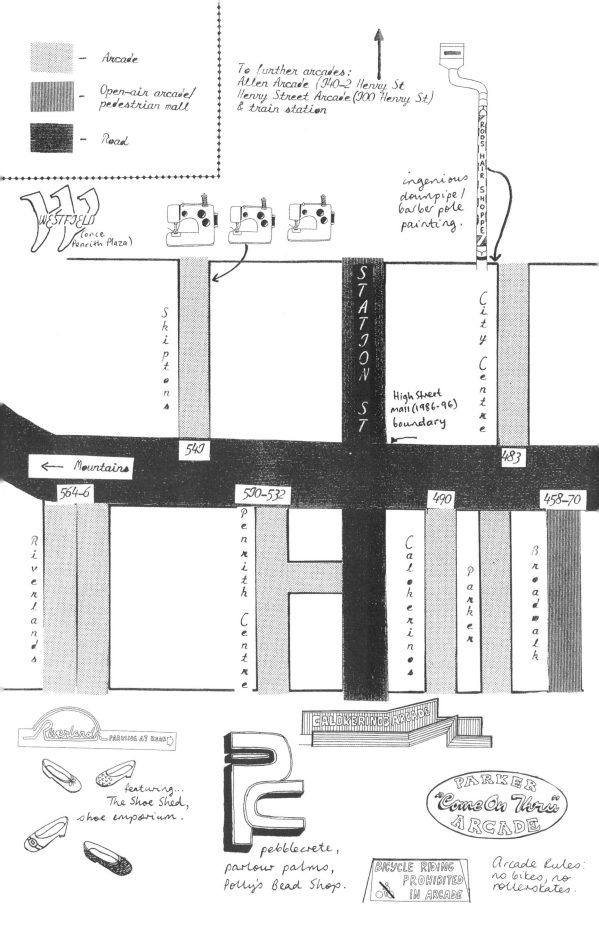

Legend:
- Arcade
- Open-air arcade/pedestrian mall
- Road

To further arcades:
Allen Arcade (140-2 Henry St)
Henry Street Arcade (900 Henry St)
& train station

ingenious downpipe/barber pole painting.

ROD'S HAIR SHOPPE

WESTFIELD (once Penrith Plaza)

Skiptons

STATION ST

City Centre

High Street mall (1986-96) boundary

541

← Mountains

483

564-6

590-532

490

458-70

Penrith Centre

Calokerinos

Parker

Broadwalk

Riverlands

CALOKERINOS ARCADE

Riverlands — PARKING AT REAR

featuring... The Shoe Shed, shoe emporium.

PC pebblecrete, parlour palms, Polly's Bead Shop.

BICYCLE RIDING PROHIBITED IN ARCADE

Arcade Rules: no bikes, no rollerskates.

PARKER "Come On Thru" ARCADE

RUINS AND
RECENT PASTS

The recent past still lingers around the present like a shadow, lurking in the shapes of buildings and shop signs, echoing in rumours. Past places and times have a ghostly life, not quite present, not quite absent, sometimes persisting for many more years than one might have expected. Sometimes in the moments before their disappearance such places have a final moment of distinction, suddenly noticed before they are gone. Others just slip away.

Cities are cyclical, founded on change and shaped by a complex network of forces. Go beyond the surface of any place, even the most weed-choked vacant lot or the blandest structure, and there are events and meanings that animate it. Often these reside in small things, minor details of no immediate significance or importance that are nevertheless present.

Nowhere is the recent past more noticeable than in a suburban ruin. An abandoned movie theatre or string of old houses set for demolition, a long-empty shop or a burnt-out shopping centre. To call them ruins perhaps confers a misleading grandeur upon them, for often they are eyesores, without the picturesque ambience of older ruins from a less immediate past. Their emptiness stretches out towards those who pass them by. Some quicken their pace, others stop to contemplate them, others go to the hole in the fence and step inside to investigate.

I'm somewhere in between the contemplators and the investigators as I regard these ruined places. Often these ruins are a target for urban explorers, who seek out abandoned and dilapidated places to infiltrate them. Although I will slip through the fence if there are no obvious impediments, my interest is not in infiltration, nor the sense of challenge and personal achievement that motivates many urban explorers. To me ruins are disruptive places, symbolic of the passing of time and changing values. In their neglected state they are not tidy memorials, linked to one meaning alone. They are unrestrained places where memory and imagination can twist and turn.

Ruins become symbolic places as well as material ones, embodying particular fears and dreams. The decaying environs of Parramatta Road, a strip of highway which runs west from the centre of Sydney for which the most commonly repeated metaphor is a varicose vein, acts upon the city's conscience. The demands made of it exceed its capabilities and the traffic-choked road has a poisonous effect on its surroundings, which exist in various states of either decay or fortification.

The highway itself intensifies while its surroundings wither. It wears its history sporadically: the creeks it travels over hint at a former landscape, the old warehouses its industrial past, the decaying rows of shops a quieter era of men's fashion boutiques and milk bars. The demolitions along the road for the WestConnex motorway are part of this historical process too. The swathes of cleared land, now occupied by earthworks and machinery, indicate that something has been removed, but what exactly used to be there can be hard to remember even a few weeks afterwards. Here the recent past exists as a sense of absence, as something that can readily disappear physically and then soon after from memory.

Other recent pasts escape ruin or disappearance and continue to exist as anachronisms. They are journeys into the particular dreams of the era in which they were constructed. The retro-futurism of the Domain Express Footway is one such place, as was the Sydney Monorail before its deconstruction. Both anticipated an imagined future city of smooth and efficient transit, but their futures never quite came to be. Now the walkway is a surreal, subterranean thoroughfare, and almost all signs of the monorail were swiftly erased from the city's streets after it was scrapped in 2013.

Of all the levels of time perceptible in the city these recent pasts are the most impermanent, readily subject to erasure. Their traces can exist one day only to vanish the next. But when something halts this process and they linger on for years or for decades, they become objects of contemplation.

Alongside Auburn station, at the perfect height to be seen from the windows of the trains as they go by, is one such trace. On the top of a shop building is an old neon sign, a string of words that form a promise. The shops below it are a restaurant and a barber now, but in the mid-twentieth century this was a pawnbroker and the words *FOR YOU A LOAN* glowed on the rooftop every night. The lights have long since ceased to shine, but the words remain visible and illuminated in my thoughts.

PARRAMATTA ROAD

At the start of the Patrick White short story 'Five-Twenty', the elderly couple Royal and Ella Natwick watch peak hour traffic on Parramatta Road from their front veranda. The cars and trucks, 'big steel insects', move slowly past. The Natwicks often sit out there during the afternoon rush hour. As the cars stream constantly by Royal says: 'I reckon we're a shingle short to'uv ended up on the Parramatta Road.'

Parramatta Road is a place to move through rather than end up in, to view with frustration through a car window as the traffic crawls. It's Sydney's oldest thoroughfare, a six-lane highway running twenty kilometres east to west from the city to Parramatta. It was established as a road by 1794, although like many of Sydney's major roads it incorporated Aboriginal tracks. Now travellers along it have a view of run-down shopping strips and warehouses, and sometimes a glimpse into first-floor apartments where the contemporary equivalents of the Natwicks live. For many years I was one of them, living with a view onto Parramatta Road. Through the veil of black diesel dust that coated my bedroom window I could see into the Stanmore McDonald's car park. This was a 24-hour stage, host to drama, romance, action and the occasional moment of science fiction when the 3 a.m. ambience of seagulls, thumping car stereos and burger wrappers swirling in the wind seemed all too weird. Even when I wasn't watching it the sound of the road was omnipresent. It crept into my dreams, a constant backdrop to my thoughts.

Parramatta Road is a resistant place. The thick traffic makes walking along it an almost unbearable combination of noise and exhaust fumes. Any business that tries to operate here is either a remnant from past days, like the archetypally anachronistic Olympia Milk Bar, or fills some kind of niche that people have to seek out: wedding dresses, guitars, kitchen equipment. The road has its own culture, a combination of decay and utility, that exists mostly separate from the suburbs it travels through. Turn off Parramatta Road at any point and there are distinct neighbourhoods: the Italian population of Haberfield; Burwood and Strathfield's Chinese and Korean communities; or the Turkish and Lebanese culture of Auburn. It's a relief to escape from Parramatta Road into these suburbs, where there are people on the streets and a spirit of place not subdued by the overwhelming traffic.

Parramatta Road's culture is cars and factories, warehouses and outlet stores. Feeding the traffic cycle, long stretches are dedicated to car dealerships. They line the road from Sydney City Subaru at Petersham, where a four-wheel drive is displayed atop a lump of concrete painted to resemble a boulder, to RA Motors in Granville, which has for decades been guarded by the patron saint of Sydney's used cars, a shop mannequin in fancy dress named Fiona. Between these landmarks almost every kind of car you could think of is for sale: secondhand Cube Cars imported from Japan; gleaming new Jaguars arranged in the glass edifice of their showroom; rows of ex-government white vans at Capital Light Commercials. Capital was once known as The Jalopy Shoppe, a name which stood out vividly since it was painted across the side wall along with a huge, grasshopper-green cartoon Model T Ford. It appeared like a ghost of cars past, from the days when Parramatta Road traffic was made up of these slow, puttering vehicles with running boards and canopies. It is gone now though, buried beneath a coat of severe black paint.

For as long as it has existed Parramatta Road has been a problem for Sydney. Take any moment from its history and there are descriptions of it as dangerous, poorly maintained, congested, dreary, or a combination of all of these miserable traits. In 1855, visiting English economist and urban chronicler Stanley Jevons decided that of 'a more disagreeable road it is impossible to conceive'. This is an impression that still applies today for the motorists who sit with engines idling, stuck in relentless traffic. The only consolation is the miscellany of roadside scenes that motorists can meditate upon while stationary. The Korean barbecue restaurant, decorated with a maypole of coloured lights. A pair of drooping, piano-playing mannequins on a carport awning advertising piano lessons. The billboard in the Dental Evolutions car park, picturing a diagram of a replacement tooth with a screw attached to the base tunneling into a gum. On a particularly bad day of traffic, a trip to the dentist may seem like a less torturous experience.

Yet Parramatta Road has its fans, lovers of urban decay, anachronisms and modern ruins. It's a place that doesn't hide its ravages, and its ugliness is a kind of honesty. The traffic and drive-thru restaurants, car dealers and discount warehouses are as much part of the city as its most lauded sights. They're an alternative series of postcards: the ruins of the Brescia furniture warehouse, burnt out in 2006 to leave a blackened concrete shell; the car yards with their rows of palm trees attempting to evoke a Los Angeles boulevard.

The road officially starts at Sydney University, stately with its sandstone quadrangle and perfect lawns, separated from the traffic below by a long retaining wall. Then there is the inner-west cluster of bedding, guitar and bridal stores. At the top of Taverner's Hill is a tall orange building, once a brewery but now a self-storage facility, its bulk visible from far away and from the planes which fly above it on their way to the airport. As the road continues west its landmarks accrue, like the huge teddy bears which stare out from the windows of the Urban Flower florist, or the AR Plastic compound at Lidcombe, made up of breezeblocks and shipping containers, and with a transmission tower on the roof like a jerry-built spire. Or the Costco warehouse at Auburn, where shoppers drive away in cars loaded with cartons of tinned tomatoes and pallets of toilet paper. At Granville there's an incongruous moment when, twice hourly, boom gates come down at a level crossing. The traffic stops to wait for the Clyde-to-Carlingford train to pass as the alarm clangs like a cowbell. After this moment of pause there is a run of discount furniture stores and more car yards before the road eventually dissolves in an intersection on the outskirts of Parramatta.

This is a familiar kind of ragtag and piecemeal suburban Sydney landscape, unevenly developed. Among it sites of utility, commerce or neglect can become places of significance for those who care to look into their details. The Arnott's bird is eternally mid-nibble on a Sao cracker on the railway overpass at Strathfield, a last remaining symbol from the days when the road had many biscuit factories. At Homebush the derelict Midnight Star Theatre is as solid and tragic as a ruined wedding cake. Once a cinema, then an ice rink and a theatre restaurant, the Midnight Star was squatted briefly in 2002 and became an anarchist social centre before lapsing into a barricaded ruin. Apartment complexes have been built up to every side of the Midnight Star, and I expect it to be gone each time I approach it. Then the road curves and it comes into view, boarded up, the facade marked with water stains and peeling paint. It operates on the slow time of material degradation, rather than the racing clock of the new developments surrounding it.

Here and there along the road are rows of old commercial buildings, shops with residences above them built a century or more ago. Their awnings are decorated with For Sale and For Lease signs, some praising the 'high exposure' of the position or, looking further ahead, 'groundbreaking development site'. Less than a lifetime ago this was a busy shopping destination. The signs for these businesses can still be seen here and there. In Leichhardt a once-grand facade displays a gallery of extinct beers, the painted logos for Tooths Lager and Reschs Draught. On the side of this building a sign advertising KB 'Cold Gold' Lager was cunningly placed so that motorists driving home would see the red KB initials on the yellow background like a duplicate of the setting sun. Then it was obscured by the bright, cartoon letters of a graffiti writer's tag. The journey into the sunset is an archetypal Sydney commuter experience for those on the westerly drive home. The most awkward moment comes when the sun descends so low in the sky that it is no longer blocked by the car's sunshade, leaving no choice but to squint into the piercing, yolky light until it dips below the horizon.

Parramatta Road has gone through a number of cycles of regeneration and neglect. One cycle hinged upon the construction of the railway to Parramatta in the 1850s, which meant that the highway was no longer the preferred choice for land travel. Trains were much faster than the slow coach ride up Parramatta Road and its condition gradually declined. Photographs from the early twentieth century show the road surface rough and crumbling, and the newspapers were full of complaining letters. In 1900 the *Sunday Times* described it as 'a track through a morass…in summer travellers are exposed to the dangers of suffocation and blindness from the clouds of dust which permeate the atmosphere'. The road was disgraceful, deplorable, awful, a death trap, an 'example of what a road should not be'. In response to the outcry, the road was upgraded and resurfaced and re-opened in 1921 with a grand parade of cars and lorries. At the celebration in 'gaily beflagged' Parramatta Park afterwards, speeches praised the resurfaced highway and the passing of the days when the ruts were filled by rabbit skins and rubble.

Parramatta Road is reaching the end of another cycle and the start of a new one. The concerns in 1921, as cars became established as a mode of transport, were the road's surface and condition. Now the volume of the traffic and the decline of the areas surrounding it are the problem. Behind the plans and debates is another motivation: to fix it for good this time around. The scheme that aims to do this for Parramatta Road is called WestConnex, a government masterplan with which the traffic-choked road will become a leafy boulevard lined by residential towers. The traffic will be diverted underground, transforming Parramatta Road into a desirable place to live for tens of thousands of people. In the artist's impressions the car yards have disappeared and the pavements are busy with people, their shapes slightly translucent and ghostly in the computer rendering as they stroll along with prams and dogs and sit at pavement cafés.

These potential scenes are coming ever closer towards realisation

as the WestConnex scheme progresses. The weird features of
Parramatta Road, its remnant places and unlikely landmarks,
either have already gone or face erasure. No one could argue with
descriptions of its congestion and deterioration, nor the desire to
make it more inviting. But until its haphazardness is swept away it will
reward the curious with its details. It's a museum of twentieth-century
offcuts and twenty-first-century hopes, a snarled jumble of traffic and
strange attributes, disorderly, deteriorating and compelling.

Ligne Noire

Ligne Noire, perfumerie and gift shop, hasn't opened its doors for
a long time. Zigzags of graffiti come and go across the facade as the
pile of mail on the doorstep grows wrinkled and dusty. The windows
reflect the Parramatta Road traffic as it lurches endlessly past.
The antidote to this constant motion is to peer in through the glass.
Inside has the frozen look of a museum diorama. 'Perfumerie.
c. 1996, Parramatta Road, Sydney.'

Ligne Noire is on the ground floor of a two-storey corner
building on Parramatta Road in Annandale that has, over its time,
had such identities as a butcher's shop, a jeweller, a milliner's
workshop and a loan office. In the days before shopping malls, and
before the traffic escalated to unbearable proportions, Parramatta
Road was where people came to buy clothes, have their hair cut,
get rolls of film processed, buy toasters and lamb chops. Most of
these businesses are long gone and few traces of them remain.
But Ligne Noire is under a spell, frozen in time.

On a shelf near the door are displays of stagnating bath salts and
perfumed lotions. The green bottles with fat round stoppers are
arranged according to their various scents, rose, vanille, magnolia
and citron. On the lower shelves are gift baskets with bottles of bath
products mummified inside plastic wrappers. Cakes of soap wear
beads of sweat from the heat of many summers. Another cabinet
is filled with signature Ligne Noire products, the name embossed
in silver on the labels for anti-wrinkle night cream, dermatological
soap bars and *lait demaquillant fluide pour le visage*. There are bottles
of perfume, the kind now most often found in chemist shops:

Old Spice, Drakkar Noir, Royal Navy, medicinal-looking eaux de cologne. Beyond the perfumes are racks of outmoded clothes, tartan blazers and boldly patterned dresses bolstered with shoulder pads. Sunhats, handbags and Glomesh purses are all displayed as if one day the owner might wake from a twenty-year sleep and open up shop again.

My eyes skip over the details of the cluttered interior. The Snap Printing calendar on the wall behind the counter shows the year 1996. In the glass cases under the counter are arrangements of costume jewellery, faux pearls and chunky gold earrings. Beside this is an imitation plant festooned with ribbon rosettes in the place of leaves. Around the store dusty fabric lilies stand in tall vases. In a corner a koala toy wearing a straw hat stares out mournfully.

As I stand at the windows of Ligne Noir, in a reverie about a black-and-white gingham Miss Shop bodysuit, someone walks past behind me and I jump. To stare through the window at the objects inside is to enter into a different world, and it is easy to forget the real one outside. The person who surprised me slows down, curious about what I am looking at, before continuing on to the kebab shop a few doors away. It is not, as I had for a moment thought, the owner, come to claim their shop. Whoever they are I am free to imagine. This is the reward of such enigmatic places. They can be read as a crime scene photograph or a movie set, the setting for a fiction or a museum display. Like its hampers of bath salts and talcum powder, Ligne Noire waits, sealed up, a forgotten gift.

Bears

The giant teddy bears stare out from the florist store on the corner of Burwood and Parramatta Roads, marking a boundary of sorts. For those travelling east they are a sign that the city is approaching. For those going west the bears signal the transition from the inner west to the suburbs beyond. They are the road's sentinels, along with the costumed mannequins and the inflatable mascots that come and go outside the car yards and factory outlets. The beady eyes of the bears watch the tens of thousands of cars and trucks that pass by each day. They are similarly observed, the subject of countless conversations in the cars stopped at the intersection as people wonder: what would you do with a bear that big?

On Valentine's Day the window is in disarray. Bears have fallen over and onto their sides and there are gaps in the display that have yet to be refilled. The showroom is busy as people pull at the bears' ears to check the price tags. The biggest, a colossal beast over six feet tall, costs just short of $2000. A man reads the tag and I ask him if he's thinking of buying it. 'It's too expensive!' he says. 'I should just get her a diamond ring.' I agree that the ring is safer. A bear that big would need a room of its own.

It is the busiest day of the year here at the florist. Staff rush back and forth with armfuls of roses, inflate balloons from cylinders of helium, and conduct conversations with people in the market for giant plush bears. Most of the people considering them are men confused at the variety of sizes, styles and fur textures available. Despite the rush the bears outnumber the people in the room and the effect is claustrophobic. Anywhere you look the small shiny eyes of a bear meet your gaze. Outside, staff load deliveries of floral arrangements into a van parked on the footpath. Soon they roll the doors shut, and it accelerates off the kerb to join the Parramatta Road traffic, leaving behind a confetti of rose petals on the pavement.

Karp

The junction with the M4 motorway, at the midpoint of Parramatta Road in Strathfield, is a moment of hope for motorists heading west. Here their slow, stop-start journey gives over to the relief of the motorway, unless it too has become clogged up with traffic. At the lights before the turnoff there is one last wait to endure, a final moment of frustration. Drivers sit in their idling cars, staring across at the decaying row of shops on the opposite side of the street.

Most of the shops are empty, the businesses closed down or relocated, the buildings rapidly deteriorating. A layer of soot covers every surface. Tags mark the walls and windows like scraps of lost conversations: *Arvo*, *Grime*, *This*. On other walls there are so many layers of bill posters that the corners have formed a thick, curling rind.

At one end of the row of shops the sign for Karp Chemist has fallen askew and pigeons roost on the beams of the awning. The letters of the sign had once been hand-cut in an elaborate typeface but now are grimy and broken. Like a fading memory it has slowly reduced from D. Karp Chemist, to Karp Chemist, to Karp Che. For many years the 'he' of chemist has hung down as if held by a thread. Above it the red and gold Kodak banner is faded and peeling. Photo processing, once such an important service, is now a memory preserved on fading signs, the last public reminders of an analogue technology that was so much a part of everyday life.

The cars and trucks grind past, having just exited the motorway and joined Parramatta Road. I feel fragile standing on the pavement, self-conscious. The few traces and flourishes left here do little to counteract an overall sense of entropy. I'm torn between observation and imagination. I want to transform this almost-ruin, to pick up the details and bring them to some kind of life where they are reconstructed or redeemed. Yet my imagination is always pulled back by the reality of the place itself. Its power lies in its continued ragged existence against the odds.

Amid the decay the Da Franco Restaurant is open for lunch, its folding sign perched by the roadside. Inside there are pictures of Venice hanging on the wall, an upright piano in the corner, potted palms and chalkboards in the shape of scrolls with the specials written on them. In here you can try to forget the surrounding disaster of boarded-up facades and car exhaust, although the sound of the surging traffic is omnipresent.

Beside the restaurant is a passageway which leads to the suburban streets behind. The passage was once lined with shops but now the windows are painted over and it's a minor thoroughfare, used as a Parramatta Road escape hatch by people going to and from the bus stop. Along its length the walls are painted green, which gives it a cool ambience, like stepping into an urban cave. Turning away from Parramatta Road always brings with it a feeling of respite. The deeper into the rows of red brick houses I walk, the more protected I feel.

RA Motors

It's State of Origin night and the traffic is worse than usual. It crawls in both directions, slow enough that it would be easy to overtake the cars on foot. But this is Parramatta Road, and there are no pedestrians. There is a gathering of people, though, at the road's western end. Cars honk their horns as they drive past, the bleats rising above the cacophony of motors and the trains rushing along the overpass towards Granville station.

There are four figures on the pavement outside RA Motors. One is a man in a kilt playing the bagpipes, his ginger moustache curled into points. Beside him two girls in cut-off denim shorts and singlets wave blue and white chequered flags. On wide sheets of paper taped to the side of a truck is painted: *HONK 4 THE BLUES*. Blue balloons have been tied to the side mirrors of the cheap Mazdas and Toyotas for sale in the lot. Amongst all this is Fiona, the inanimate mascot of RA Motors, overseeing everything.

Fiona, a shop mannequin whose costumes and wigs change with the seasons, has watched the traffic go by on Parramatta Road since 1983. She has been knocked down by cars swerving off the road, and kidnapped and then returned piece by piece – yet each time she has returned to her position of roadside prominence. Tonight she has long black hair under a white sunhat and is wearing a grey mini-dress and stiletto boots. The fluorescent lights of the car yard illuminate her and her companions as if they're on a stage.

The bagpipes' nasal drone continues as a party clusters in the driveway of the car yard. On a trestle table are the remnants of an earlier barbecue, plates of sausages and bread rolls, plastic bottles of tomato sauce. The group sips at their beers and watches two guys coming from the Vauxhall Inn across the street. They weave through the stationary traffic. One has his phone out and is ready to snap a photo of his mate in between the flag-waving girls and Fiona. The honks from passing cars intensify. As we watch them posing the car-yard manager smiles and says, 'It's a bit of fun. No one does things like this anymore.'

We talk about traffic for a while. He tells me that to beat Parramatta Road you have to be strategic and travel very early in the morning, before the rush. Sydney's roads are a mess and even a minor accident can cause havoc. After a pause, he says he has a good idea. To remove broken-down cars that are holding things up there could be a helicopter with a strong magnet hanging from its undercarriage that would lift the troublesome vehicle out of the way. I can't quite tell if he's joking.

A silver Rolls Royce drives slowly by, gleaming like a cloud, an apparition among the regular traffic. We watch it glide past as we stand under the billboard proclaiming 'Sydney's Cheapest Cars'. I get talking to Moses, who has a tailoring and upholstery workshop in the shed behind the car yard. He tells me about his plans to make Fiona an outfit. 'It's winter,' he says, 'I'll make her some ugg boots, maybe a jacket.' We look out to where the famous mannequin stands at the roadside, beside the girls waving flags, imagining her in her cold-weather ensemble.

Then the nasal drawl of the bagpipes stops. It's getting towards kick-off time and the party is over. The girls put down the flags and head back towards their bags and jackets. I watch as Fiona is carried in from the roadside to spend the night in the office, her duties as the goddess of used cars over until tomorrow morning's peak hour.

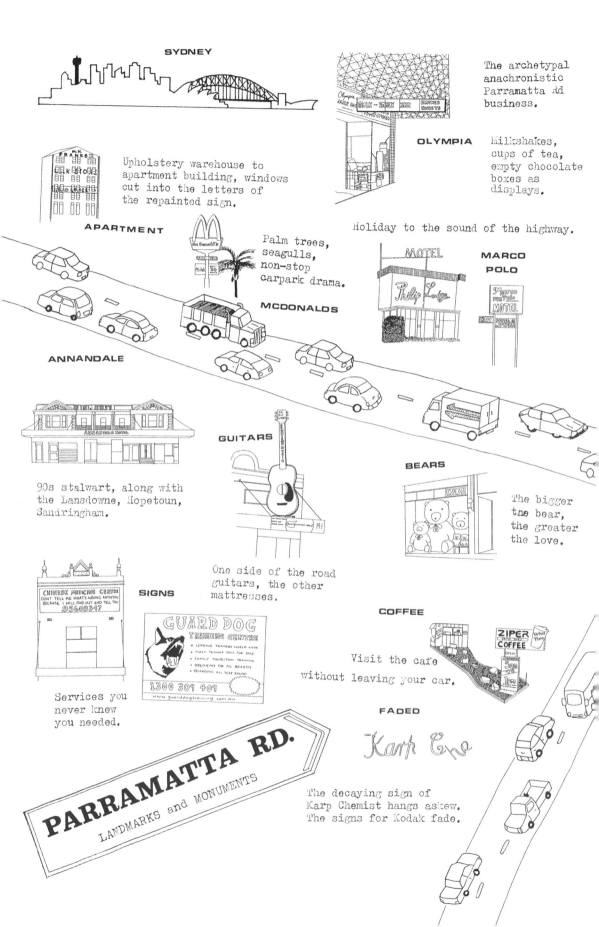

SYDNEY

The archetypal anachronistic Parramatta Rd business.

OLYMPIA

Milkshakes, cups of tea, empty chocolate boxes as displays.

Upholstery warehouse to apartment building, windows cut into the letters of the repainted sign.

APARTMENT

Holiday to the sound of the highway.

Palm trees, seagulls, non-stop carpark drama.

MCDONALDS

MARCO POLO

ANNANDALE

90s stalwart, along with the Lansdowne, Hopetoun, Sandringham.

GUITARS

BEARS

The bigger the bear, the greater the love.

One side of the road guitars, the other mattresses.

SIGNS

CHINESE MEDICINE CENTRE
DON'T TELL ME WHAT'S WRONG WITH YOU BECAUSE I WILL FIND OUT AND TELL YOU
95609347

GUARD DOG TRAINING CENTRE
• LEADING TRAINERS WORLD WIDE
• FULLY TRAINED DOGS FOR SALE
• FAMILY PROTECTION TRAINING
• OBEDIENCE FOR ALL BREEDS
• BOARDING ALL YEAR ROUND
1300 309 409
www.guarddogtraining.com.au

Services you never knew you needed.

COFFEE

ZIPER COFFEE

Visit the café without leaving your car.

FADED

Karp Cho

PARRAMATTA RD.
LANDMARKS and MONUMENTS

The decaying sign of Karp Chemist hangs askew. The signs for Kodak fade.

RUIN

Burnt out in 2006.
Left as a
monument for 10
more years.

PIANOS

Mannequin duet.

PERSPEX

Shipping containers,
breeze blocks,
public weighbridge,
transmission tower.

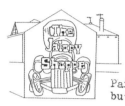

JALOPY

Painted over,
but not forgotten.

SPHINX

Keeper of secrets
outside Euro Iron
Pty Ltd.

BISCUITS

Arnotts in Homebush, Peek Frean
in Ashfield, Westons in Camperdown.

CONCRETE

The concrete for
building the city.

The Vauxhall,
the first (or
last) pub
of many.

MIDNIGHT STAR

Once theatre restaurant,
once anarchist social centre,
now grand ruin.

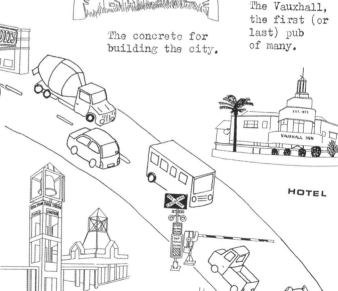

HOTEL

COSTCO

Consumer chaos upon its
opening in 2011. Buy in bulk.

HOMEWARES

Office furniture,
lounge suites,
pine, leather,
carpets, lighting,
showrooms, megamalls.

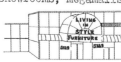

Car
dealer-
ship
goddess.

FIONA

PARRAMATTA

MAGIC KINGDOM

At the corner, where Hollywood Drive turns a sharp right, is a wild, overgrown lot enclosed by the remains of a breezeblock fence. Across the bricks, carefully spray-painted in neat black letters, are the words:

HAUNTED FUNPARK DEMONS GHOSTS

This is the entrance to the ruins of the Magic Kingdom amusement park in Lansvale in Sydney's south west. Lansvale is in Darug country, occupying a hook of land that curls around the Georges River on the north side. This area is a low-lying river flat where water and land seek to merge despite attempts by the built environment to keep them separate. The Magic Kingdom closed a decade ago, with the park owners selling what rides they could, leaving the giant slide, a giant concrete shoe, a few buildings, and the ghosts.

The fence, with its unofficial warning, does little but mark the boundary. In many places there are gaps where the bricks have crumbled, revealing a mess of broken furniture and fallen real-estate signs with optimistic descriptions – *walk to the Georges River, elevated site with good access, vendor wants it sold*. These hopeful sentiments peel and fade as the land beyond becomes a wilderness.

The Magic Kingdom is a Sydney ruin with origins in the amusement-park boom of the 1970s and 1980s. This era was not the first wave of such places. Their precedents can be found in the Victorian period and its fascination with leisure activities. In the 1880s visitors had flocked to the Bondi Aquarium, later renamed Wonderland, at Tamarama, where a rollercoaster ran along the beach and there was a clifftop miniature railway and elephant rides. On the other side of the harbour, Manly was also well supplied with amusements. 1903 was the year of the Water Chute, a combination rollercoaster and waterslide contraption with carriages that slid down a steep incline into a pool below. In 1931 the Manly Fun Pier opened, with its carnival rides and slogans: 'Built for fun in '31' and '7 miles from Sydney, a thousand miles from care'.

In the first half of the twentieth century the Sydney seaside was home to fun palaces and piers but by the 1970s and 1980s the focus had shifted to amusement parks on the city's outskirts, in step with the ever-expanding suburbs. In the west, at the African Lion Safari, tigers, bears and lions roamed the grounds freely as visitors drove their cars through the park. To the north Paradise Gardens was home to a collection of life-size fibreglass dinosaurs. The south was guarded by the dancing Andalusian horses of El Caballo Blanco. Television advertisements for all these places promised adventure, fun and magic, wrapped up in catchy jingles. The advertisement for the African Lion Safari from the early 1980s culminated in the strange refrain, 'it's scary but nobody cares', sung by a chorus of children, further emphasising the park as a place where everyday rules didn't apply.

Watching them now, the advertisements are amusingly low-tech, but to children in the 1980s they were captivating. The idea of these magical, extraordinary places embedded somewhere not very far away was tantalising to me as I sat on the scratchy carpet of the living room, waiting for the breath of the pedestal fan to turn in my direction and provide some relief from the hot summer-holiday afternoon.

Most parks had a theme – replica dinosaurs, lions and tigers, colonial re-enactments, Andalusian horses, circuses with Cossack riders, koalas – but the Magic Kingdom had no exotic drawcards. Of all the amusement parks it was the most suburban, more like a surreal backyard than an otherworldly wonderland, its main attractions a giant slide and an oversized concrete shoe.

Lansvale might be a small suburb but it was once home to two amusement parks, the Magic Kingdom and Dizzyland, an establishment known for its cheap carnival rides and the hillbilly nights at its Hollywood Country Music Club. Dizzyland had salvaged some of the Luna Park rides after the ghost train fire of 1979, and in its sheds stored herds of old carnival horses. There is no sign of Dizzyland today, just a golf course with figures in white trousers strolling the putting greens. The well-manicured lawns of the Liverpool Golf Club extend alongside the Magic Kingdom wilderness like a more successful, professional sibling who has shaken off youthful folly.

Stepping through a hole in the fence and into the Magic Kingdom I feel a sense of trespass, half thrill, half fear. The grass has grown high and thick and the gum trees trail curtains of balloon vine, baubled with pale green seed capsules. Palm trees and cacti mix in with the weeds, and burrs cling to my clothes as I stamp through the long grass.

The road that circles the park is still visible although grass encroaches on it from either side. I follow the faint arrows on the road's surface until I reach a path that leads towards the rusty scaffolding of the slide. The slide sticks out from the weeds and tall grass like the rippled yellow tongue of a giant. Close up the scaffolding that supports it is a lacework of crossbeams, an intricate cat's cradle. High up in the scaffolding two white cockatoos look down at me silently, with none of those birds' usual boisterousness.

Abandoned places bring about dystopian fantasies, the sensation of picking over the fragments of something long vanished. The weirdness of abandoned theme parks makes them particularly enticing. Empty houses are still domestic even when they are in ruins. Abandoned industrial sites, while often dramatic in their scale, still contain traces of their past usefulness. Amusement parks were dreamlike from their conception, and in their abandonment they provide a different kind of fun. To encounter the rusting rides, bright paint faded, is like climbing inside childhood memories or inside a dream.

Others think less of memories and more of thrills. At the foot of the slide is a pile of plastic bread delivery trays, used in place of mats to ride down the slide by those who come to visit the park after dark. The Kingdom has never ceased to be a playground for some. Their names are spray-painted on the edges of the slide, *Jared 4 Mel*, *Ash*, *DEBT*. For local teenagers the slide is a challenge, and to climb to the top of it at night and look out across the darkness below is to become the Magic Kingdom's royalty.

Across a field of matted grass is a derelict house, its windows dirty and smashed. It watches me with its broken eyes in the ominous way of all destroyed houses. Its sinister appearance is somewhat tempered by my knowledge of an unusual happening that occurred there. In 2007 a young man faked his own kidnapping in the house to avoid telling his parents he had skipped work to spend time with his girlfriend. He called police emergency saying he was tied up inside, and there they found him, bound and gagged by his own hand. Later, in the hospital, he confessed to having staged it all.

The grass twitches with unseen creatures and the sound of racing motorbikes buzzes like massive insects in the distance. I read the warning that is posted beside a small, weed-choked waterslide:

The proprietor accepts no liability whatsoever for any injury to any person or for any injury to any property (Howsoever caused.)

The legalese of the sign contrasts with the pale blue fibreglass pool it guards, which looks too shallow to cause injury to anyone.

In the years since its closure the park's demise has been furnished with rumours, the most common of them the story of a child dying in a fall from the giant slide. All amusement parks attract these sacrificial myths, but the Magic Kingdom claimed no lives. It closed due to some of the same factors that shut down other Sydney amusement parks: dwindling visitor numbers and the rise of insurance costs. Sydney's sole theme park disaster occurred at Luna Park in 1979. In this tragic incident seven died after a fire broke out in the ghost train. Despite suspicions of arson the cause of the fire was never determined. Adding to the mythology of theme-park dangers were some less catastrophic incidents. The escapes of a grizzly bear and then a lioness from the African Lion Safari in Warragamba in separate incidents in the 1990s could have been more of a disaster had the escapees not been tracked down and shot. But the Magic Kingdom had only simple rides, and their most exotic animal was a goat that had the distinction of eating everything it was given.

The paths through the grass dwindle into mud, which bleeds black water with every step I take. It soon becomes impossible to go further. I turn back to the slide and climb through underneath it to get to the stage on the other side. The stage is rotted through in places and the Pepsi advertisements painted on the backboard have faded. A cartoon Ginger Meggs, holes poked in place of his eyes, points towards a sign for the Magic Kingdom painted in gothic script. I climb up onto the stage. Kids receiving prizes, and teenagers working their first jobs, acting as Batman and Robin in the superhero show, must once have done the same thing. The wood feels spongy underfoot and I follow the beams as I cross it, looking out over my audience of weeds.

On the stage I feel the same confused sense of scale I encounter whenever I return to a childhood place and find it much smaller than my memory's version of it. The Magic Kingdom, however, is not part of my childhood memories, apart from a vague recollection of the song, 'Magic', that played in its TV advertisement, the one hit of a 1970s band called Pilot. I can only imagine the Magic Kingdom in its prime, in images like those of faded and blurry old photographs. All I know of it is contained in this ruin and the myths that circulate about it, which are mostly to do with the ghosts that inhabit the place after dark, and the bad luck that will stick to you if you dare to enter it.

Of all of the Magic Kingdom lore, my favourite is the rumour that it is impossible to get up close enough to kick the big boot which, along with the slide, is the park's most prominent feature. Its peeling red and yellow painted form rises from the undergrowth

like the discarded footwear of a giant. I push my way through
the grass in its direction, my feet crushing a new path among the
weeds. My presence in the park feels like a disturbance of a place
long settled into decay. Beside the scrawls of graffiti, the bread-tray
toboggans and the occasional beer bottle or Fanta can, there are
few signs of other visitors. If the park feels spooky, it's mostly due
to its emptiness.

The boot is on an island in the middle of the lake at the centre
of the Kingdom, once traversed by rented paddle boats and
rowboats. Now the closer I move towards it the marshier the ground
becomes, until it is impossibly swampy. The lake has leaked into
the surrounding earth so under the grass there is the same glistening
layer of black mud that stopped me before. I can only observe
the shoe from a distance, derelict and inaccessible, unkickable.
On the side of it are the painted figures of the Old Woman Who
Lived in the Shoe and her many children, and a cat dreaming the
first verse of the nursery rhyme in a thought bubble, like escapees
from a picture book.

Once this area was a swamp, and this is the true spirit of the
park, gathering force in wet weather and softening the ground
into black mud. The sturdy boot is a fitting symbol for the futility
of attempts to control the sodden land. On nearby Knight Street
the houses are built up on high foundations to combat the
flooding. Numerous times the river has broken its banks and
floodwaters have swelled, rising to drown the houses' lower levels.
Newspaper articles documenting past floods record the residents'
despair, although some seem perversely proud of it. 'Lansvale
is like Texas,' said Mr Stan Leszewicz, whose house was cleaved
in two by a tree in a storm in 1990, the story documented by the
Sydney Morning Herald. 'We have bigger floods, bigger mosquitoes,
bigger everything.'

While Knight Street is at the edge of suburban order, the Magic
Kingdom returns to the wild. Saplings grow through the holes in
the rotting stage. A grey heron roosts on Mother Hubbard's shoe.
Ducklings swim in a puddle atop buckled bitumen. The swamp and
its creatures are the inhabitants of the Kingdom now.

As I turn back from the shoe I see a flash of movement behind some trees ahead of me and feel a stab of fear. A ghost? I head towards one of the gaps in the fence and back to the car. Two more cars are parked in the side road now. One is a four-wheel drive with a decal covering the back window, picturing a serene portrait of the spiritual leader and vegan guru Supreme Master Ching Hai alongside an exhortation to 'Be Veg Go Green'. A group of people stand near the most recent real-estate sign – *Great Zoning, Great Block* – deep in discussion.

The shape behind the trees resolves into a person who looks neither like a ghost nor a denizen of the Kingdom – just a man in jeans and a T-shirt out for a walk. When he passes me I ask him if he lives nearby and he says that yes, he moved back to the area recently. I point to the *DEMONS, GHOSTS* warning on the fence, but he shakes his head as if it's nonsense. 'The park closed because it kept flooding,' he says. 'And there was a story about a child falling from the slide, and dying,' he adds, as if he feels he has to say it but doesn't really believe it. I look towards the real-estate sign and suggest that maybe the site would become a residential development, as it almost certainly would if it were in the inner suburbs of Sydney. He laughs and says it isn't likely. We turn our attention to the rolls of pigeon-grey clouds in the north-west, and I wonder aloud if it is going to rain.

'It's raining somewhere,' he says. But the downpour has yet to reach Lansvale. The sun glints off the lake inside the Magic Kingdom and illuminates the red covers of the old electricity boxes that stand at intervals in the nearest corner of the park. The 'Be Veg Go Green' car starts up and slowly drives away. I say goodbye to the man, who continues his walk up Hollywood Drive. For now it's quiet, apart from the birds. Occasionally a light plane flies over, on its way out from Bankstown Airport.

I take a final gaze around the Magic Kingdom, past the slide, the boot, the ruined house and the overgrown grounds. The place looks familiar to me now and, despite the warning on the fence, it seems more placid than haunted. Back on Hollywood Drive I pass slowly through the streets of Lansvale. An elderly man tends his lawn, watched by an immaculately painted concrete kangaroo.

A mint green fibro house is fenced like a compound, its garden decorated with frogs and gnomes. Every yard has at least one such concrete mascot, smaller domestic versions of the boot at the heart of the once Magic Kingdom.

As I travel home I think about suburban wastelands. They are places disruptive to order, sites of failure but also of potential, places to dream in. Places like the Magic Kingdom, with their surreal amusement park leftovers, only bring these dreams closer to the surface. Their neglected buildings and overgrown grounds became somewhere to slip away from the present day into the past or the future, or at least into a different version of the present.

A few months after my visit to the Magic Kingdom I travelled to another former amusement park, this one in Catherine Field on the city's southern outskirts. It was once an El Caballo Blanco, one of a number of these equestrian parks that operated around Australia in the 1980s, all of which featured Andalusian dancing stallion shows, with riders in red velvet suits and glittering dresses with layers of ruffled skirts. Passing by construction sites for new housing developments I don't hold many hopes of it remaining. Then I catch sight of the gates. They are still in place at the entrance but without the statues of white horses that once decorated each side, rearing up on their hind legs. These tempting souvenirs must have by now been relocated to an urban explorer's trophy room.

There is a green sedan parked under a tree on one side of the gates and a man in a security guard uniform in it, seat reclined all the way back. I go over to reassure him that I am just going to take some photos, nothing nefarious. He immediately sits up brightly, happy to have someone to talk to. He explains that his job is to stop trucks as they try to shortcut through to the surrounding developments, as they are destroying the surface of newly laid roads. 'But most of the time I sit here reading mystery novels on my e-reader,' he says, taking a swig from the two-litre bottle of Black & Gold brand mineral water on the seat beside him.

'The horses on the gates are gone,' I say.

'Yes, there's only a hoof left now,' he replies, pointing to where there is indeed one shiny black hoof attached to a pillar.

From the gates I can see over to what was once the centre of El Caballo Blanco, buildings with Moorish arches and painted tiles, their courtyards overtaken by weeds. After the park closed the buildings became a storage area for a rug business, a use that would normally signal impending demolition. This time the place was gutted by a fire and then left abandoned. The ruins are broken and overgrown, walls sprayed with graffiti, the parking lot scribbled over with tyre marks. Like the Magic Kingdom it is the plants and birds that have run of the place now.

As amusement parks had their heyday, now so have their ruins. The era of theme park wastelands is coming to an end. The El Caballo Blanco site has made way for a residential estate with a golf course designed by Greg Norman. The Magic Kingdom, despite the swamp and its stale presence on the real estate market, was finally sold. The pale blue breezeblock fence has fallen to rubble, taking with it the warning of its haunted interior. The demons and ghosts have fled Lansvale, but they will reappear in another guise in another ruin.

SYDNEY THEME PARKS
of the past, present and future.

AUSTRALIANA VILLAGE

A collection of 19th century buildings assembled into a pioneer village. Inspired an obsession with writing in chalk on slates with my sister & I in the 80s. 1960s-present

PARADISE GARDENS

Once a pre-historic world and enchanted forest — now a golf course. 1970s-1986

KOALA PARK

Visited by celebrities such as Johnny Depp and Liberace.

1930-present

MOUNT DRUITT WATER WORKS

1980s

The subject of inevitable razor blade rumours. Manly Water Works still operates.

FEATHERDALE WILDLIFE PARK

1972-present

Once home of Fatso, the wombat from A Country Practice.

Often a target of thieves, most recently stolen: an emu.

BULLENS ANIMAL WORLD

Circus themed animal park owned by Stafford Bullen, who owned the nearby African Lion Safari. 1969-1985.

AUSTRALIAS WONDERLAND
1985 - 2004

Australia's largest theme park — the Bush Beast was the country's largest wooden rollercoaster.

WET & WILD

Weird construction work beside the M4: Wet & Wild opened summer 2013.

AFRICAN LION SAFARI
1968-1991.

"It's scary but nobody cares" Lions, tigers & bears roamed free, to be watched from "the safety of your own car"

EL CABALLO BLANCO
1979-2000s

The gates remain, but of the horses, only one hoof is left.

OLD SYDNEY TOWN

1975-2003

Pistol duels, floggings, pit-sawing, the Magistrate's Court - Sydney as it was in the 1800s, recreated on the Central Coast.

AUSTRALIAN REPTILE PARK

1959-present

Eric Worrell's wildlife park had Australia's first big thing constructed: a diplodocus, still visible from the F3 today.

HORNSBY MODEL RAILWAY

Ride tiny trains every second Sunday of the month. See also the Bankstown Steam Locomotive Society.

WARATAH PARK

1966-2006

Home of Skippy. After the series was filmed in the 60s, the park became a tourist attraction.

MANLY FUN PIER

Enter the shark aquarium through the shark's mouth.
1931 - 1989

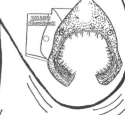

LUNA PARK

After the ghost train tragedy of 1979, the park closed and the face fell into disrepair.
1935-present

PARRAMATTA SLOT CAR TRACK

From the 1960s there were many slot car tracks around the suburbs...there are still some to be found today, although the Parramatta one is gone.

SEGA WORLD

"Australia's Interactive Disneyland" only lasted 4 years.
1997-2000

KINGS CROSS WAX WORKS

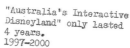

"World Famous People of Past and Present in Authentic and Lavish Scenes"

1960s-1980s

MAGIC KINGDOM

1970s-2000s

The Magic Kingdom is abandoned and said to be haunted. Urban explorers make journeys to the giant shoe at its centre.

LA PEROUSE SNAKE MAN

The tradition of La Perouse snake men goes back to 1897, making this perhaps Sydney's longest running (slithering) attraction.
Last show 2010.

INSET

JAMBEROO RECREATION PARK

"Where you control the action"
Constructed in 1980 for the Australian Grass Ski Titles.
1980-present

The north-eastern boundary of Hyde Park is bordered by some of Sydney's most celebrated buildings. There's the solemn Hyde Park Barracks on the corner of Macquarie Street, and across from it the spires and buttresses of the gothic St Mary's Cathedral. Even the roundabout on the road between these two buildings is ceremonial, decorated by a domed nineteenth-century water fountain with ornate pillars and gargoyles.

I'm about to leave this grandeur behind and go underground. At the edge of the park is a stairway leading down below street level. A sign spans the stairwell, announcing the entrance to the 'Express Walkway'. At first the walkway seems bland, the kind of white-walled passage that might be a service corridor in a hospital or an office complex. But as I travel along a noise arises, a mechanical hum accompanied by long, high shrieks. The further I go into the tunnel the more intense it becomes. I expect to round the corner and discover an immense cavern of machinery, the secret heart of the city where complicated contraptions churn.

Instead, the white walls end at a protruding fibreglass ledge painted grey to resemble a rocky outcrop. Beyond it is a three-dimensional mural of Sydney Harbour, the water with a bushland backdrop and smudgy white clouds in the sky above, painted by a careful hand. Thus begins a pictorial history. Painted above the rock ledge is a group of Aboriginal people. The man at the edge of the rock points to the tall ship which, like the rock, protrudes from the wall's surface. The ship tows behind it a three-dimensional

Sydney Harbour Bridge. Incarcerated behind the bridge is the sorrowful face of an Aboriginal elder, whose hands clasp its rungs like prison bars. The bridge morphs into the white sails of the Opera House, then a stretch of harbour bushland continues beyond it. A relief panel cut out of the wall shows the foreshore crowded with high-rises, a window into the built-up city of the future. In twenty paces I have travelled from colonial invasion to the present day.

The source of the grating noise has now come into view. Rather than the city's secret mechanical heart I am standing on the edge of two adjacent paths of smoothly moving black rubber tread. This is the Domain Express Footway, a moving walkway that links the city with the multi-level parking station built underneath the parkland of the Domain. At the time of its construction in 1959 it was said to be, at just over two hundred metres, the longest moving footway in the world. Although very much a technological curiosity, it was a functional construction. It eliminated the steep walk up the hill from Woolloomooloo to the city by following a gentler incline underneath the Domain.

Above ground, the same walk takes in the parklands between the Art Gallery of New South Wales and the Cathedral. To the east the view stretches over the rooftops of Woolloomooloo towards Kings Cross. Underground, the only view is this string of bizarre murals painted along the walls of the tunnel. Fluorescent strip lights on the roof provide an artificial sky, and the cacophony that accompanies its operation is an entire sonic landscape of mechanical groans. It's a claustrophobic, immersive environment, one dislocated from the above-ground world.

I step onto the footway and am conveyed along. I feel like a rock in a stream as people with armfuls of documents power past me on their way to or from important meetings. Footway travellers are a mixture of business people, shoppers, families and tourists. Some walk along the footway, combining velocities to travel as quickly as possible. Others take it slowly, and stand still for the duration of the five-minute journey, watching the murals go by.

The first mural scene is a painting of two children leaning over bright green hills. Beside them a girl holds up a spiky yellow orb, a substitute for the sun, which feels far away in this underground gloom. The mural was painted by both professional artists and local children and the styles vary accordingly, some neatly accurate, others naive figures painted in loose brushstrokes. More Opera Houses appear, one salmon pink against a blue bridge, another indigo in a night cityscape with wheels of stars above it. As I watch the pictures slide by, the footway continues to hum and shriek. When I inch to the side to let people pass, the edge of it shudders underfoot.

While it seems an unlikely city attraction, the footway has been remarkably enduring in its mixture of utility and novelty. Constructed along with the Domain parking station in the late 1950s, it was officially opened in 1961. Following his speech and the cutting of a ribbon, the first to ride the footway was Lord Mayor Harry Jensen with his thirteen-month-old son. Afterwards, the Lord Mayor and guests of honour gathered for a celebratory lunch of lobster mornay and salad-filled pineapple shells, as eager and curious members of the public tried out the footway. Thousands of people were to follow in the coming week as parents brought their children in from the suburbs to experience the future.

The dark side of the footway was quick to manifest, and excitement soon gave way to doubts and fears. There were incidents: a child's finger crushed, a man's trousers ripped and the two five-pound notes in his pocket shredded. Remarks about the footway's 'taste for pedestrians' appeared in newspaper commentary, as well as articles detailing its newest victims. A man had his trousers torn from his body when they became caught in a gap at the end of the footway; an attendant had to drive him home to put on another pair. A woman lost a galosh. A Pekingese puppy's hind leg was caught in the gap. This string of incidents led to instructional signs at each end: STEP OFF FOOTWAY – DO NOT SLIDE.

Moving walkways were a fairly new civic phenomenon in 1961, although the technology had debuted in the late nineteenth century at a World's Fair in Chicago. A film exists from the 1900 Paris Exposition Universelle of people on the *trottoir roulant*, or moving walkway. They awkwardly stumble on and off, some tentative, some joyful, some hamming it up for the equally novel motion picture camera. Having never encountered a moving footway before, they are clumsy, their bodies adjusting to the unfamiliar motion. The women in hats and gloves and the men in suits pictured in the Sydney newspaper reports of the 1960s were similarly inexperienced with moving walkways and the accidents can be at least partly attributed to the public's adjustment to unfamiliar technology. The small gap at the end of the footway was a trap for the unaware.

The footway, and the parking station it connected to the city, were constructed at a time when Sydney's city streets were undergoing great change. The modernist city of cars and office blocks was taking shape as Victorian-era buildings were demolished. By 1960, most of the city's trams had run their final journeys and tram tracks dug up and sealed over. Everyone had an opinion on how to deal with the growing demands of automobile traffic. Various alternative transport plans were proposed: in the 1940s industrial designer Charles Beauvais made sketches of an 'Aerobus' station at Wynyard. Outside the station a donut-shaped craft with a propeller whirring at the top and the destination – Mosman – on the front soars up into the sky. Beauvais put a lot of thought into Sydney's infrastructure, in 1945 proposing an elevated railway dubbed the SOS, short for 'Silent Overhead Service', to replace trams and ease traffic congestion. A model of the Beauvais-designed City of the Future was then exhibited at the Sydney Royal Easter Show in 1947. Visitors watched from a viewing area above the model as miniature plastic cars moved along freeways made from rubber conveyor belts. The network of roads skirted the monumental high-rise buildings of the future city.

Proposals to deal with the traffic were usually smaller in scope than the visions outlined by Beauvais. One was for the demolition of the unpopular Queen Victoria Building and its replacement with a city square and an underground car park. Headlines such as 'Only a Bomb Will Shift It' and 'Tear Down This City Horror', accompanied by the familiar image of what is now Sydney's retail showpiece are surprising, even shocking to the contemporary eye. But Sydney's planners were thinking unsentimentally of the future. The Victorian architecture now celebrated as historically significant was considered by many to be irrelevant, a relic of a less sophisticated age.

The footway is an unusual pocket of space and time. Since its opening day it has existed as the trace of a future city of maximum efficiency that would never come to be. Yet its continued presence has been for the convenience of motorists who leave their cars in the parking station. It might seem in some ways anachronistic, but it is also practical, and this has ensured its survival.

In the science fiction novella *The Roads Must Roll*, by Robert Heinlein, moving footways are the main mode of transportation in a dystopian future America. Their smooth running is vital to the country's economic and social order, and when one of the main footways is sabotaged the Chief Engineer must go 'down inside' the workings of the footways to try and restore control. 'Down inside' is a noisy environment of roaring rotors and the whine of rollers in constant movement.

While Sydney's footway is hardly sinister in the manner of Heinlein's story, it has a similar sonic presence, the churn and whine of machinery. The footway also suggests a feeling of being 'down inside'. Travelling along it you are inside the workings of the city, moving covertly underground, undetected by those above. If the Domain footway were to break down, the city above wouldn't stop functioning. It would, however, lose a reminder of one of its alternative identities, as a mechanical city of efficiency and retro-futuristic novelty.

The Sydney of 1960s urban planning was one of maximised efficiency: expressways, underground car parks and high-rise towers. In the 1970s a plan for an extensive underground network of moving footways and walkways was considered. The cars would have the run of the streets while pedestrians travelled expediently underground. While this network was never realised, parts of the underground walkway system were indeed constructed. They tentacle out from the city's train stations, a sometimes confusing sequence of thoroughfares which bypass the congestion of the streets above. Navigating them is a covert pleasure, of knowing the best path through the labyrinth.

Most of Sydney's underground walkways are shopping arcades, which camouflages to some extent their subterranean location. Riding the Domain Express Footway, however, the only distractions are the mural scenes. Towards the middle of the journey mobile phone reception falters, so there is no link with the outside world as you pass by an ocean of lopsided sharks and turtles. The ocean swells into a frothy wave before it breaks over a long strip of yellow sand. On the sand are dotted rainbow umbrellas and towels, with tiny sunbathers lying beside their beach bags and thongs. Max Dupain's 'Sunbaker', here with a pink sunburn tinge rather than the silver sheen of the original photograph, appears like Gulliver beside the Lilliputians of the beach scene.

The footway was refurbished in the 1990s. A worn-out mechanism meant the footway no longer moved and it was for a time uncertain whether it could be replaced. The original manufacturer of the components was no longer in business, but eventually two huge, steel-reinforced rubber bands were fabricated in Holland by a company that made conveyor systems for mines. These were shipped to Australia and installed as the footway's surface. The 'Tunnel Vision' mural, painted by a team led by artist Tim Guider, was added to decorate the walls of the tunnel. Then the walkway was set rolling once again.

Three quarters of the way along the footway's course, the mural paintings portray a suburban scene with tiny people loading cars and heading back to their houses with shopping bags. Then there is a forest of sorts, trees and leaves on a green background. In places I can see the ghost images of graffiti where it has been scrubbed away. Here and there are markings and messages added to the mural: 'Gustav K was here'; a black pen moustache on the face of the sunbathing woman in a bikini; 'Drown' written in small, angry letters above the head of one of the swimmers.

I register these details as the footway carries me onwards, as I notice each of the people travelling past me on the other side, on their way toward the city. Most look away when I meet their eyes. It is not a place where I can imagine striking up a conversation, although the footway was at least once rebranded the 'traveldator' for a speed dating event. Couples conversed for the five-minute journey, before making the acquaintance of another prospective partner on the return trip.

There is an incline and now the car park is in sight. The final mural panel at the end of the footway shows an inner-city back lane. From the window of a terrace house a boy looks down onto a girl in a pink dress who stands inside a cone of light that comes either from a streetlight or from extra-terrestrial forces. I carry this weird Beatie Bow scene in my thoughts as I step off and out into the car park, propelled by the inertia of my journey.

Spaces designed for vehicles are rarely easy to negotiate by walking, and it is difficult to work out how to exit the parking station. I pass row after row of grey and white cars, a monochromatic scene, as if I am inside a black-and-white film. Eventually I find my way out through one of the caged archways of obscure architectural purpose that run along the length of the parking station and emerge, blinking, into the sunlight. I feel like the mural girl in her cone of light in this sudden brightness, returned to the world above ground.

MURALS
& GHOST SIGNS

In and around Sydney City.

King George V
Mural
Cumberland St.
1983
The Rocks
by Peter Day

ROZELLE

Was hidden behind trees & fading, but still intact, the woman peering down from her window at one edge still visible from Darling St, until painted over in 2017.

CYSS Mural 1980
Darling St. Rozelle
by Michiel Dolk

Over 150 metres long - one of the longest murals in the southern hemisphere.

trompe l'oeil viaducts above the basketball court

Redfern Railway
Bridge Mural
by Carol Ruff
1983

ANNANDALE

48,000 YEARS IS A LONG LONG TIME........
48,000 YEARS STILL ON MY MIND........

The Crescent Mural 1980
Public Art Squad/ Rodney Monk

on the long wall under the light rail line, recently repainted.

The bay, the trucks, the planes

REDFERN

Think Globally
Act Locally 1984

James St. Redfern
Public Art Squad

Dinosaurs and terrace houses with people peering down from the balcony

Painted illegally, but now heritage protected.

I Have a Dream Mural 1991
King St.
by Juilee Pryor & Andrew Aiken

Idiot Box Mural 1993
Erskineville Rd
by Andrew Aiken
Now painted over a uniform shade of mustard yellow.

NEWTOWN

Three Proud People 2000
Pine St. Newtown
by Donald Urquhart

THREE PROUD PEOPLE MEXICO

King St.
Ghost Sign Photo processing ghost signs, like tea & soft drinks, are classic above-the-awning sights.

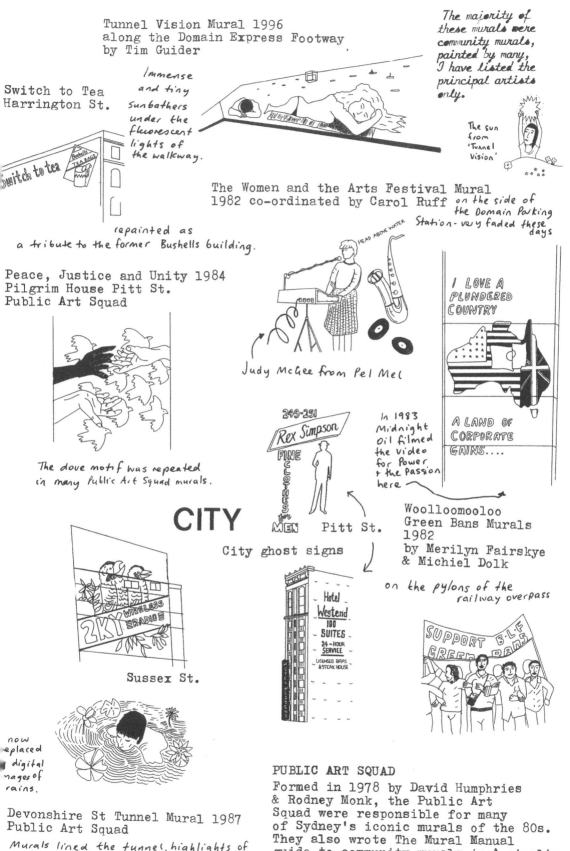

Tunnel Vision Mural 1996
along the Domain Express Footway
by Tim Guider

Switch to Tea
Harrington St.

Immense and tiny sunbathers under the fluorescent lights of the walkway.

The majority of these murals were community murals, painted by many, I have listed the principal artists only.

The sun from 'Tunnel Vision'

repainted as a tribute to the former Bushells building.

Switch to tea

The Women and the Arts Festival Mural 1982 co-ordinated by Carol Ruff on the side of the Domain Parking Station - very faded these days

Peace, Justice and Unity 1984
Pilgrim House Pitt St.
Public Art Squad

HEAD ABOVE WATER

Judy McGee from Pel Mel

I LOVE A PLUNDERED COUNTRY

A LAND OF CORPORATE GAINS....

The dove motif was repeated in many Public Art Squad murals.

CITY

249-251
Rex Simpson
FINE CLOTHES for MEN   Pitt St.

City ghost signs

In 1983 Midnight Oil filmed the video for Power + the Passion here

Woolloomooloo Green Bans Murals 1982
by Merilyn Fairskye & Michiel Dolk

on the pylons of the railway overpass

2KY WIRELESS RADIO

Sussex St.

Hotel Westend
100 SUITES
24-HOUR SERVICE
LICENSED BARS & STEAK HOUSE

SUPPORT B.L.F GREEN BANS

now replaced digital nages of rains.

Devonshire St Tunnel Mural 1987
Public Art Squad

Murals lined the tunnel, highlights of an otherwise tedious journey.

PUBLIC ART SQUAD
Formed in 1978 by David Humphries & Rodney Monk, the Public Art Squad were responsible for many of Sydney's iconic murals of the 80s. They also wrote The Mural Manual guide to community murals in Australia.

The final weeks of the Sydney Monorail were met with a surge in public interest. With its demolition imminent, it was finally acceptable to enjoy this often-maligned feature of Sydney and people made pilgrimages to the city for a final ride. While some now realised they would miss the monorail, many celebrated. Over its history it was consistently unpopular, condemned as a kitsch interruption to the streetscape. In the years before it was built the Sydney Citizens Against Proposed Monorail group held protest marches attended by thousands. They called it the 'monster-rail', an offence to the city, ugly and unnecessary. On the monorail's first day of operation, in July 1988, protesters gathered outside the Queen Victoria Building waving green cardboard spanners and placards. Nearby, the monorail glided along its metal track, full of curious travellers clutching their First Day Cover commemorative envelopes, postmarked in the shape of the monorail carriages.

The year 1988 was marked by the duelling energies of protest and celebration. As a child in primary school, caught up in the fervour of Australia's '200th birthday', I accepted the Bicentenary as a joyous event. Every schoolchild in Australia was given a souvenir coin in a cardboard folder patterned with streamers, including a page for autographs that my friends scribbled fledgling signatures on. Adults told me to keep it, as the coin would be worth something one day.

Later I realised that, despite all the hype, the truth of the day was that it marked the Aboriginals' dispossession of their land by the British colonists. While the harbour hosted flotillas, fireworks, and the return of the First Fleet, more than 40,000 people marched through the city protesting Invasion Day. At Mrs Macquarie's Chair a tent embassy was set up, and during the 'Parade of Sail' the point was dense with Aboriginal flags. As the ships went by, two protesters stood in the shallows with a banner:

WHITE AUSTRALIA HAS A BLACK HISTORY

Those who congregated there and marched through the city were marking a day of mourning.

1988 was also a year of reinvention, of Sydney as a world city of multinational investment, office towers and high-rise developments. The city had modernised during the 1950s and 1960s but now was looking further ahead into a post-industrial future. Of all the 1988 projects the reconstruction of Darling Harbour was the most ambitious. The harbour, known as Gomora by the Gadigal and Wangal people, is a long inlet between two ridges, leading onto an open flat valley. The British changed the harbour both in name and in shape. Parts of the foreshore were reclaimed, and factories, goods yards and wharves were constructed. The harbour became a cluttered, industrial scene, with the chimneys of the Pyrmont power station rising above a cluster of warehouses. In 1988 this was replaced by a convention centre, shopping malls, restaurants and parklands. Advertisements in newspapers of the time announced 'Welcome back, Darling Harbour', with the declaration that it had been returned to the people of Sydney. It was now a landscape of equal parts leisure and business. The monorail was part of this plan, connecting to Darling Harbour via a loop around the southern section of the central city, in an 'ultra slim' and 'pollution free' and 'whisper quiet' way.

In 1988 a child's first ride on the monorail was perhaps akin to the children of 1959's first ride on the Domain Express Footway: it was a taste of the future we would grow to inherit. During my first journey I imagined that by the time I was an adult the rest of the city would have caught up with the monorail. What this would look like overall I was not sure, but its details included features of a cartoon future such as jetpacks and hovercraft. At the time, for all the new elements of the city, grime and decay were equally present. The monorail trip quickly became a journey into the past, a reminder of late-1980s optimism for the city's renovation. By the time of the 1990s recession the monorail provided a good look into the excavated holes of stalled building developments, with their weeds and pools of stagnant water. A 1991 newspaper article referred to it as the 'ghost train', with a view onto the 'gaping chasms' of the Chinatown Triangle, Park Plaza and World Square.

From the perspective of the streets below the monorail was forever unexpected. Despite the heavy pylons which supported the track at street level, the train's appearances were usually a surprise, accompanied by a soft whine as it whirred by overhead. At this moment some would curse the monorail for any or all of the usual reasons: ugly, useless, only used by tourists, expensive, ridiculous. Those more sympathetic enjoyed the sight of it gliding along its track, a reminder to look up and discover the city above street level.

The monorail gave its passengers a new way to experience the city. Here was a subversive way to travel, hovering between the world of the street and that of the buildings. Its route traced a loose circle around the city, travelling anticlockwise. No doubt this was for technical reasons, but as the years passed and the monorail became retro-futuristic rather than just futuristic, it seemed ever more fitting that the monorail moved in the direction of a clock's hand rewinding.

In 1988, like many Sydney children of the time, I had my first monorail ride. In 2013 I had my last. In its final week of operation the monorail attracted interest at a level almost equal to its opening twenty-five years before. Places on the final trip were allocated via ballot, a range of 'Farewell Monorail' merchandise was produced for sale, and the carriages filled with people going around one last time. I joined them for a final lap of my own, to record some final observations of Sydney's most divisive mode of transport.

I board the monorail at World Square, a station that in 1988 ran alongside a construction site covering an entire city block.

Up until a few years earlier the Anthony Hordern Palace Emporium had stood here. It was a vast department store that was, upon its opening in 1905, Sydney's largest building. Advertisements of the time list its impressive statistics, almost fifteen acres of floor space, twenty-one hydraulic lifts and approximately three thousand employees. It was an expansive wedding cake of a structure with a grand entranceway. Inlaid into the floor of the entrance was a terrazzo slab a metre across which pictured Hordern's emblem, an oak tree. The Emporium had a reputation for selling 'everything from a hairpin to a harrow', from sewing needles to anchors, corsets to farming machinery. After the demolition of Hordern's, the site remained a hole in the ground for almost twenty years until the World Tower was built in its place. It continues to be a site of excess; World Tower is the city's tallest residential building. When it opened in 2004 people stared up at it, trying to imagine what life would be like on the seventy-fifth floor.

Selecting the least crowded carriage, I join a family visiting from Japan and a young woman who holds a map of Sydney in one hand and a half-full packet of chocolate biscuits in the other. Despite Sydney residents' objections to the monorail, it has always been popular with tourists. We all peer out the windows as the monorail turns to travel up Pitt Street. Slowly it passes a sign advertising the long-defunct Bristol & Co. Real Estate, showing a picture of the kind of square, red-roofed cottage that once epitomised a suburban dream home. On the other side of the street is the neon sign for Diethnes Greek restaurant, which has served roast lamb and moussaka in Athenian surroundings for sixty-three years.

The city that exists just above street level is revealed through the monorail windows with its unexpected views. A series of images pass by like a flipbook. An office with people busy at their desks, plants and figurines lined up on the windowsill, a kitchen with big tins of instant coffee and Milo. An empty meeting room with a bowl full of mints in the centre of the table. Two guys in suits playing ping-pong in a Pitt Street office building. A woman reading a thick paperback as she pedals on an exercise bike. A class having a lesson. The boarded-up windows of Druids House, obscuring the magical rites going on inside. Once I see it, it's gone: the monorail glides by with only just enough time to register each scene before the next one appears.

Despite its visual intrusiveness on the streets, the monorail has always offered passengers a contemplative perspective on the city. It is similar to riding the train through the suburbs, thinking of the homes and lives and people busy out there, too many individual stories to comprehend. The monorail view inspires this kind of feeling, but also one of trespass, of seeing into the usually unobserved city workings that occur above the street.

At the next station there's a row of people standing with phones at the ready, waiting to take photos. A girl with an iPad in a pink rhinestone case stands at the beginning of the platform with it held up towards the arriving train. Once the train goes past she lowers the device, shrugs and turns away. A few solo travellers board, people who like me are riding the monorail in farewell. An elderly man wearing shorts despite the cold weather takes a seat and looks pensively around the carriage as it takes off again. The track turns up Market Street, past the decorated exterior of the State Theatre with lions and men in armour, like guardians of the city's last grand picture palace.

The monorail travels downhill, away from the central city, so that we can suddenly turn to look back at it. On this overcast day it is a wall of grey office buildings, with Sydney Tower like an olive on a toothpick rising above them all. Ahead of us is the conglomeration of Darling Harbour: floating restaurants, the Maritime Museum with its attendant warship and lighthouse, and the Harbourside shopping centre. Harbourside, made up of a central galleria and long market halls, is a 1988 version of Joseph Paxton's Crystal Palace, the iron-and-glass building that showcased the 1851 Great Exhibition in London. This is not the first Sydney version of the Crystal Palace. In 1879 Sydney had its own exhibition building, the Garden Palace in the Botanic Garden, an immense glass, iron and wood structure which stood for only three years. When it burnt down in 1882, many records and objects were lost, most significant among them a large collection of Aboriginal artefacts and artworks. The building then slipped from public memory, only to re-emerge in recent years.

As new developments remodel the city, there has been a surge of interest in the city's lost structures and in the memories lost with their passing.

Darling Harbour is a place that is destined to be reshaped yet again. There's something bittersweet about its failed promise of a civic wonderland. Even a few years after it opened it was obvious that it hadn't captured the public imagination as had been expected. Many tourists preferred a trip to The Rocks and the immediate sense of history provoked by the old terraces and narrow streets that trace the sandstone rise of the headland. By contrast Darling Harbour seemed to have little connection to the land on which it stood. The rows of palm trees along the promenade gave it the atmosphere of a holiday resort, and it was hard to know what to do there apart from wander. Its most consistently popular feature was the spiral fountain where kids splashed along the channels of water, down to the smooth, round stone at the centre. There was a sense of accomplishment at reaching the bottom of the fountain, of having finally reached a point of purpose in Darling Harbour's constructed landscape.

At Darling Harbour station the mood of the carriage changes as new passengers board. People are eager to talk about the monorail's last days. A man with a bushy white beard shocks a young male tourist holding a pungent Subway sandwich with the news that this is the last week. Soon the entire carriage is involved. 'You'll never get to do this again,' another man says to his son, who had been in a kind of Thomas the Tank Engine trance about the joys of monorail travel. His face falls, but he is appeased with the promise of a souvenir coin.

We pass a backstage scene of loading docks and tour-bus parking zones, and then the monorail maintenance sheds. A couple of trains rest, one covered over in a white shroud, the other stripped of its advertising, already decommissioned. The conversation in the carriage turns to its fate. People like the idea of the monorail being transplanted elsewhere, to Tasmania, to the University of New South Wales, to Asia. This hopeful discussion is wishful thinking. Despite plans for its revival, the monorail's eventual destiny is for the carriages to be dispersed among historical collections and individuals, and corporations with ideas for their reuse. The Sydney office of Google bought two for conversion into meeting rooms.

Back on the monorail, I am travelling through a condemned landscape. The convention centre, which would be demolished soon after the monorail was decommissioned, has a tired, barren look. Further along the track passes the Entertainment Centre, another soon-to-be casualty of the impending redevelopment of Darling Harbour. As a child I had imagined the curved external walls of the Entertainment Centre to be the sides of a colossal UFO, about to lift off into space. Colloquially it was known as the 'Ent Cent', a lopping off of extraneous syllables that seemed too familiar a term for me to ever feel comfortable with. It was a place for mega-concerts and ice spectaculars, Rock Eisteddfods and repeated visits by Elton John, who holds the record for the musician with the most performances staged there.

The monorail crosses the square outside the Entertainment Centre, past peppercorn trees and advertising banners for an upcoming Fleetwood Mac tour. We glimpse up the laneways into Chinatown and into a succession of restaurant and hotel windows. The monorail glides through Chinatown station without stopping. Although the platform is brightly lit, there is no one in the ticket booth and the barriers are closed. It's the monorail version of a *Geisterbahnhof*, the closed stations in the divided Berlin that bridged the east–west divide but that trains nevertheless travelled through.

Most of my traveling companions are peering out the other side of the carriage rather than at the shuttered station. I turn to join them in looking towards the thicket of trees and the curling roof of a pagoda that rise up behind a high wall. This is another Bicentennial project, the Chinese Garden of Friendship. The gardens were designed in Guangzhou, Sydney's sister city in China, as a symbol of affinity between the two countries. In the early years of the monorail, souvenir postcards were produced with a photograph of the track passing by the gardens. The trees are newly planted and the outline of the pagoda rises from above the wall. Behind it are the masts of the convention centre, forming a triple layer of 1988 reinvention. Of all of these it is only the gardens that have endured, the wishing pond filled with coins many times over and the trees grown tall.

The monorail turns up Liverpool Street. There are more glimpses into offices, a group of people having a conversation in a stairwell, then the faded cutouts of superheroes in the windows of Comic Kingdom. Superman and Batman look across into the dusty windows of Kent House opposite. Kent House is an unusual building, a tall Federation-era warehouse with a facade decorated by ornamental brickwork with a pattern like playing-card diamonds. With its long, skinny drainpipes and attic windows I'd always thought it a relative of a New York tenement. In 1962 the Spanish Club, which for decades was the centre of the Spanish community in Sydney, was established in Kent House with bars and a restaurant, dancing nights and language classes. Towards the end of its days in the late 2000s the club, following the Sydney tradition of club premises becoming underground music venues, hosted gigs organised by the Sydney record label Dual Plover. These featured the kinds of obscure, experimental performers particular to the label: Justice Yeldham smearing his face against a sheet of glass and producing knife-edge bursts of distorted noise; or the tap-dancing Singing Sadie, performing what sounded like jolly 1920s show tunes until you were able to decode the ribald lyrics.

I've looped around the city and am now back to where I started. I stand on the platform at World Square watching the monorail leave the station. It turns the corner of Pitt Street and disappears from view. A few weeks later the dismantling begins. There is no conversion of the track to a miniature version of New York's High Line, as one optimistic plan proposed; it is sawn into pieces and sent to a St Peters scrap yard. Later, the carriages are advertised for sale on Gumtree for $3000 apiece.

For a brief time, sections of track remained in place, edges blackened where they had been cut. Then, one night in September 2013, in the early hours of the morning, the final piece above George Street was taken down. A small crowd looked on, a mixture of monorail aficionados and drinkers from the nearby pubs. They watched the rain of sparks as the metal was sawn through, until a crane lowered the last section of track onto a waiting truck. A few months later barely any traces remained at all. Now, years afterwards, only World Square station remains, protruding oddly from the side of the Rydges hotel building on Liverpool Street. It overhangs the pavement like a misplaced Lego block, interrupting the world above street level that was once the domain of the monorail.

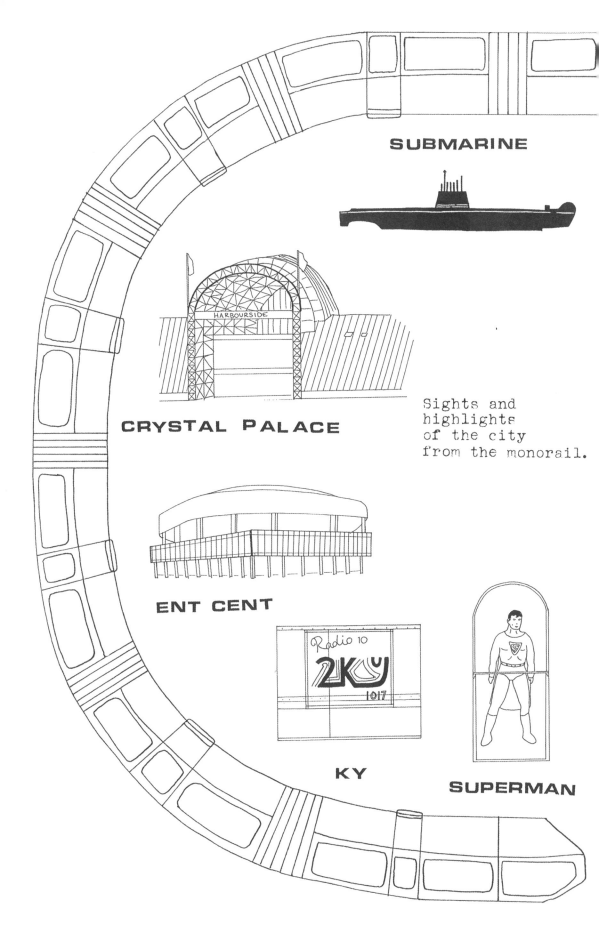

SUBMARINE

CRYSTAL PALACE

HARBOURSIDE

Sights and
highlights
of the city
from the monorail.

ENT CENT

Radio 10
2KY
1017

KY

SUPERMAN

PLANE TREES

10 VIEWS FROM THE MONORAIL

KNIGHT

DRUIDS' HOUSE

302   DRUIDS HOUSE   302

DRUIDS

KENT HOUSE

BRISTOL & CO PTY LTD REAL ESTATE

BRISTOL

KENT

Tourist guides to Sydney frequently detail the city's natural wonders: the harbour, beaches and bushland. They also describe the ever-growing city and its cosmopolitan appeal. In one of the city's first guides, the 1861 *Stranger's Guide to Sydney*, its 'immense stores and capacious buildings' were already being pronounced as equal in interest to its natural setting. Since then, a voluminous amount of tourist literature has been produced, all extolling these natural and civic virtues. One particularly verbose pamphlet from the mid-1960s, produced by the NSW Government Tourist Bureau, mixed things up by describing the 'forests of towering concrete' to be found in the city and the 'cobweb' of roads and highways that lead out into the suburbs.

The 1960s guide went on to describe Sydney's wild side, the madcap carnival evenings, 'noisy, hour-long "leg-shows"' and the visual effect of the floodlit harness-racing tracks at night. It also included a description of the city's restaurants and the welcome change that had occurred in quality and variety. No longer were they 'a gourmet's idea of "indigestion unlimited"', the pamphlet explained with relief. Sydney now had many world-class restaurants, from tiny backstreet cafés to banquet halls with in-house orchestras. Traditional steak-and-chips establishments were joined by restaurants with European and Asian cuisine, many of them established by postwar migrants who had invigorated the restaurant business.

There were taverns and wine bars, pancake cellars, theatre restaurants and supper clubs. These places offered experiences as much as they offered food, and many restaurants were carefully themed and decorated to enhance their atmosphere. Gleaming copper pots hung from the wooden beams in Mother's Cellar pancake restaurant in Kings Cross. The nearby Nagoya Sukiyaki House advertised its authentic Japanese food, decor and service. But none was more atmospheric than the Grotta Capri Italian restaurant in Kensington, which opened in 1955. The restaurant was designed to be an undersea fantasy land based on the cerulean ambience of the Blue Grotto on the island of Capri. The interior was fitted out as a series of grottoes with backlit fish tanks glowing from the walls, the ceiling decorated with fake seaweed and starfish, giant clams and shells. Diners ate their seafood pasta beneath stalactites strung with fairy lights as rivulets coursed underneath the transparent floor tiles.

The Grotta Capri might have had the most fantastical interior design but there was no shortage of restaurant gimmicks. The Cahills restaurant chain went for maximum variety, with themes as varied as The Tudor Room, The Hungarian Csarda and the South Sea Trader. By the 1970s there was The Summit revolving restaurant on the forty-seventh floor of Australia Square, 'where the view stretches practically forever'. There were theatre restaurants like the George F. Miller Music Hall in Neutral Bay, where diners watched performances of 'The Spring Heeled Terror of Stepney Green', or the more locally themed 'Lust for Power, or, Perils at Parramatta'. Then, despite the seemingly endless variety of restaurant experiences already available, a new kind of restaurant opened in Sydney, the only one of its kind in Australia. In 1970 the Captain Cook Floating Restaurant came to Rose Bay.

It was moored off Lyne Park, a harbourside reserve that already included a well-known Sydney restaurant, the Caprice. The Caprice was owned by entrepreneur James Bendrodt, surely the only person in the Australian Dictionary of Biography to be described as 'roller-skater and restaurateur'. In the 1930s Bendrodt had managed the Palais Royale and Trocadero dance halls, and was still an important figure in the entertainment scene when he opened the Caprice in the 1950s. The Caprice was built out over the water, and Bendrodt described its position as the 'dress circle' of the harbour. It offered sophisticated dining experiences in the form of long and elegant three-course meals. Quick service was disparaged in the preface to the menu, as it 'necessitates pre-cooking which is ruinous to food'. Diners had to be prepared to luxuriate in the experience.

The Captain Cook offered a similarly elegant dining experience in a multistorey, floating vessel. At its mooring the restaurant was a hard sight to miss for those travelling along New South Head Road towards Rose Bay. It was described as a unique 'galleon' but this was always an optimistic term for the three-level floating structure, made of fibreglass and steel, that more closely resembled a gigantic bath toy. The craft had been designed by the architectural firm Loder and Dunphy. They were better known for modernist church designs and a daring, never-built concept for the Peakhurst Bowling Club, in which domes hovered above bowling greens like enormous mushrooms.

Lyne Park has a history of unexpected structures, including Sydney's first international airport, the Flying Boat Base, which opened in 1938. Seaplanes made regular journeys to England, New Zealand, Lord Howe Island and Norfolk Island, carrying mail, cargo and passengers. For the few who could afford to travel to England by seaplane it was a luxurious but long journey. In 1938 the nine-day trip required thirty-one stops for refuelling – still much faster than the sea voyage. Passengers could stroll about the spacious cabin, play mini golf in the aisle, or watch the clouds from the windows of the promenade deck. This mode of travel was short-lived. The Second World War and advancements in aviation technology saw the flying boat service quickly superseded, although it continued operating in Rose Bay, flying to Norfolk Island until the 1970s.

By 1973 the Captain Cook had changed hands and was now known as Flanagan's Afloat, one of a number of Flanagan's fish restaurants owned by the entrepreneur Oliver Shaul. Shaul managed a portfolio of hotels and dining establishments that included the Summit Revolving Restaurant in Sydney Tower, which had opened in 1968. Shaul had strong ideas about what made a good dining experience, and the food was only part of it. Just as important was the atmosphere. His philosophy was that people wanted to enter a 'make-believe world' when they went to a restaurant. Flanagan's – the name Shaul chose for his chain of restaurants – evoked something of the cosy, hospitable environment he aimed to create.

The make-believe world of Flanagan's Afloat was different to the elegant dining experience the Captain Cook had previously provided. Shaul reinvented the restaurant to appeal to families and casual diners who were more interested in fun than sophistication. The signature side dish of shoestring potatoes, proudly made from exotic imported American potatoes, was served by waitresses wearing floor-length brown velvet skirts. Their outfits matched the gold-fringed brown velvet curtains, part of the nautically-themed decor which also included anchors and lanterns decorating the walls. The restaurant was promoted to families with various gimmicks that accentuated the restaurant's harbourside location, such as free fishing lines for children under twelve.

Throughout the 1970s Flanagan's Afloat hosted functions for groups of businessmen and served up lunches to hungry sailors who moored their boats at Rose Bay: Shaul's weekly newspaper advertisement column often mentioned that diners could 'cruise in and tie up alongside'. A moment of calamity came in 1975 when an attempted robbery resulted in the shooting murder of the night manager. But the 1970s were for the most part a good decade for the floating restaurant. Shaul continued to expand Flanagan's, opening 'Flanagan's Aloft' on the Pacific Highway at Chatswood on the top floor of the BMA office building. This newly built high-rise office tower had a curved facade and an external lift that rose up the centre like a pneumatic capsule, towards the schnitzels and spiced garlic prawns on offer in the restaurant.

Back down on the harbour Flanagan's Afloat continued to operate until 1988. Then it became Imperial Peking Afloat, its new menu featuring Peking duck, mermaid's tresses and prawn fans. For a time it was as popular as it had ever been but, eventually, the restaurant's appeal began to fade. After changing hands again and being renamed Rose Bay Afloat, it eventually shut down for good. It sat empty for years, gradually falling into disrepair and becoming the target of much unsympathetic attention. People seemed to enjoy coming up with unflattering descriptions for the craft. It had gone from a galleon to the 'floater', 'grub tub', and 'one of the harbour's worst eyesores'. A bid to convert it into a fine dining restaurant by advertising entrepreneur John Singleton was rejected, plans to make it into a flying boat museum never came to fruition, and in 2007 the restaurant was for sale for $150,000.

News reports of the time convey the desperation of what seems like everyone involved to have Rose Bay Afloat removed from Lyne Park. The agents selling it complained of the many calls from daydreamers interested in converting the craft into a houseboat. This, they stressed, was not a realistic proposition. Before the restaurant dropped out of the news there was a hopeful turn: property developer Ray Chan had put forward $95,000 for it. His offer was motivated by nostalgia. He remembered fondly his twenty-first birthday dinner at Flanagan's, only a few years after his arrival in Australia, and felt a sentimental attachment to the now run-down craft, which he had hopes of restoring.

In October 2007, the floating restaurant – now camouflaged under a coat of severe blue-grey paint – was towed across the harbour to Waverton, then relocated to Snails Bay in Balmain. Here it languished, paint flaking and chipped, with FOR SALE signs in its windows. Apart from marring the view from waterfront properties nearby, and greeting the occasional visit by curious sailors, it awaited its fate under little scrutiny.

One afternoon in 2013 I head out in search of the abandoned craft. I travel along Darling Street, which follows the shape of the Balmain peninsula, leading down to the harbour. The name 'Darling' is all over Sydney, a collection of localities that call to mind a sweetheart's affection, despite their being named in recognition of a strict and unpopular 1820s governor, Ralph Darling. At the Balmain post office building, an architectural tiramisu of colonnades and columns, I turn off Darling Street into a web of narrow side streets. I pass rows of terraces decorated with iron lace and tiny brick semi-detached houses. These were once the homes of the workers who spent their days at the Lever Brothers soap factory, or down beneath the harbour, mining coal. The two shafts where men descended into the 'living tomb' of the mine operated on the western side of the Balmain peninsula until 1931. The shafts are long since filled in and covered over, and it is difficult to imagine a coalmine among streets where the wealthy now live.

At the end of Grove Street I find a slip of a park between two harbourfront apartment buildings that leads to the water's edge at Snails Bay. Unlike the wider and more picturesque Birchgrove Park nearby, this is just a patch of grass with a few trees. It ends in a stone wall above the water from which juts a thin, sagging wooden jetty. Once this area was a hub of shipbuilders' yards and maritime industries, but that was all long ago and now the harbour is quiet.

I sit on the wall above the water and look out towards the moorings, where the floating restaurant is tethered to one of the concrete platforms only a few hundred metres away. It has been years since I'd seen it and I have never been up close – only glimpsed it from the bus going by on New South Head Road. Snails Bay is a purgatory of sorts, where ships for sale or between jobs are stored. The floating restaurant shared the company of a similarly forlorn salvage barge, a tugboat, and a houseboat with the look of a beach shack set adrift.

The craft that was once Flanagan's has the defeated appearance of an unloved, empty house, weather-stained, windows cracked and grimy. Despite its sad state, as I examine it from the shore I, too, get to daydreaming. I think about the girls in long brown skirts serving mud crabs with shoestring potatoes, about Flanagan's Afloat's grand return to Sydney Harbour as a kitsch icon, about the day when it will be my multistorey harbour headquarters. Then my dreams subside and I observe the run-down craft for what it is. On this overcast day the harbour is almost the same colour as the boat's dark paint. Birds roost on the roof. It sways gently with the movement of the steel-blue water on which it floats.

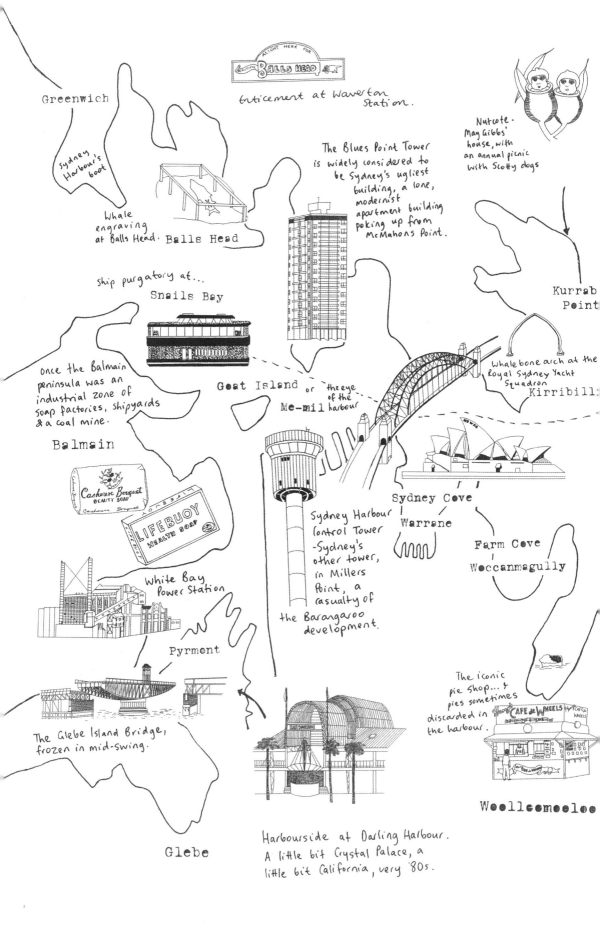

Greenwich

Sydney's Harbour's boot

ALIGHT HERE FOR BALLS HEAD

Enticement at Waverton Station.

Whale engraving at Balls Head. Balls Head

Nutcote. May Gibbs' house, with an annual picnic with Scotty dogs

The Blues Point Tower is widely considered to be Sydney's ugliest building, a lone, modernist apartment building poking up from McMahons Point.

Kurrab Point

ship purgatory at...
Snails Bay

once the Balmain peninsula was an industrial zone of soap factories, shipyards & a coal mine.

Goat Island or the eye of the Me-mil harbour

Whale bone arch at the Royal Sydney Yacht Squadron Kirribilli

Balmain

Cashmere Bouquet BEAUTY SOAP
LIFEBUOY HEALTH SOAP

White Bay Power Station

Sydney Harbour Control Tower -Sydney's other tower, in Millers Point, a casualty of the Barangaroo development.

Sydney Cove
Warrane

Farm Cove
Woccanmagully

Pyrmont

The Glebe Island Bridge, frozen in mid-swing.

The iconic pie shop... & pies sometimes discarded in the harbour.

CAFE DE WHEELS

Woolloomooloo

Glebe

Harbourside at Darling Harbour. A little bit Crystal Palace, a little bit California, very '80s.

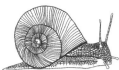

FROM ROSE TO SNAILS

The journey of the floating restaurant once known as Flanagan's Afloat.

◆◆◆◆◆◆◆◆◆◆◆◆◆◆◆◆◆◆◆◆◆◆◆◆◆◆◆

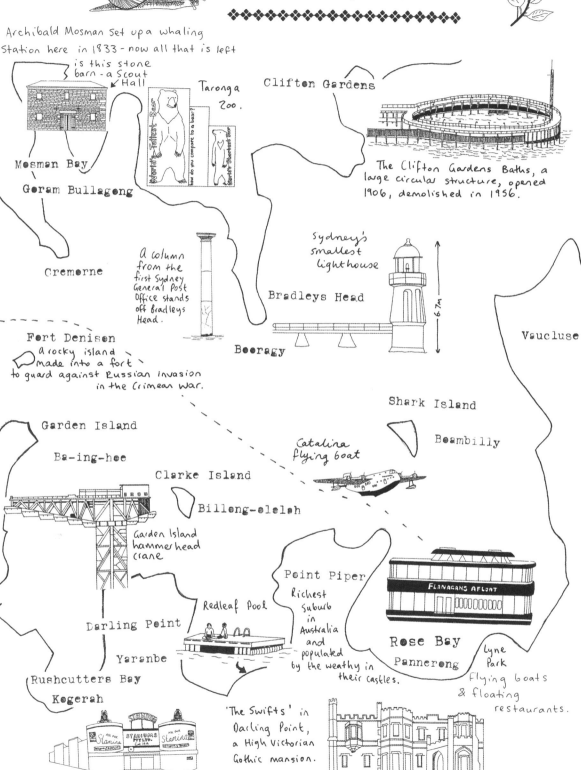

Archibald Mosman set up a whaling station here in 1833 - now all that is left is this stone barn - a Scout Hall

Mosman Bay

Goram Bullagong

Taronga Zoo.

World's Tallest Bear
how do you compare to a bear?
Shortest Shortest Bear

Clifton Gardens

The Clifton Gardens Baths, a large circular structure, opened 1906, demolished in 1956.

Cremorne

A column from the first Sydney General Post Office stands off Bradleys Head.

Sydney's smallest lighthouse

Bradleys Head

Booragy

6.7m

Vaucluse

Fort Denison
A rocky island made into a fort to guard against Russian invasion in the Crimean War.

Shark Island

Beambilly

Garden Island

Ba-ing-hee

Catalina flying boat

Clarke Island

Billong-elelah

Garden Island hammerhead crane

Point Piper
Richest suburb in Australia and populated by the wealthy in their castles.

Redleaf Pool

Darling Point

Yaranbe

Rushcutters Bay

Kegerah

FLANAGANS AFLOAT

Rose Bay

Pannerong

Lyne Park
Flying boats & floating restaurants.

STADIUM
STADIUMS PTY LTD CR 1911
Ask for Stamina
Ask for Stamina

'The Swifts' in Darling Point, a High Victorian Gothic mansion.

Sydney stadium at Rushcutters Bay: boxing matches, Beatles concerts, ads for 'Stamina self-supporting trousers'.

MILLERS POINT, BEFORE AND AFTER

Writing of Millers Point in her 1970 *Companion Guide to Sydney*, Ruth Park described its mood as 'drowsy and nostalgic'. Park notes the details of this peaceful place at the edge of the city, its terrace houses and narrow laneways. Cats sleep in the sun, streets follow the contours of the hills, steps lead down steeply to the wharves below.

In 2012, Millers Point is little different. If anything it is more drowsy, with activity on the wharves long ceased, their industries shifted south to Port Botany. The wharf area, once a hub of commercial shipping, is blank concrete, awaiting redevelopment into the parkland and high-rise towers of Barangaroo. Millers Point is land which has undergone many cycles of change and modification. Its English name preserves a moment from its early colonial history, when three windmills for grinding flour were built on the point. Its Gadigal name is Coodye, this high, rocky ridge with outcrops of sandstone looming above the harbour below.

Until the Argyle Cut was tunneled through the headland in the 1840s, the only way to get to Millers Point from Sydney Cove was over the ridge of rocks. It had been an isolated place, cut off from the rest of the settlement in the early days of the city. Despite its proximity to The Rocks, Millers Point developed a character distinct from its neighbouring suburb. The Rocks had a strong connection to the port and its industries but the people who lived there were a mixture of different trades and origins. Millers Point, by contrast, became the home to a tight-knit community of waterside workers.

In the 1900s the cliffs above the harbour at Millers Point were cut back to create one high wall along Hickson Road. Many houses were demolished and the rebuilding created the suburb as it exists today. These resumption and redevelopment works were a government response to an outbreak of bubonic plague in 1900. Plague sufferers were sent into isolation at the quarantine station at North Head and infected houses marked with yellow flags. While the living conditions in Millers Point and The Rocks were often poor, many believed the resumptions had more to do with clearing the area for future infrastructure projects, such as the Harbour Bridge, and the government's desire to bring the wharves under its control.

I approach Millers Point following the Hickson Road wall. During the Great Depression of the 1930s this stretch of road became known as The Hungry Mile, as men would go from wharf to wharf daily in the hope of obtaining one of the few jobs available. The austere cliff, half concrete, half sandstone, was the backdrop to their daily journey. The sandstone is gouged and striated and the concrete meets it in a line of jagged rectangles that look like a child's drawing of a city skyline. Moss and weeds grow in the cracks, and in parts previous structures have been consumed by the concrete. There's a flight of steps entombed in the middle of the wall, leading nowhere, and a boarded-up bunker.

At the end of the wall a zigzag stairway leads to Millers Point above. The stairs are steep, and as I climb the city's roar of traffic and the sounds of construction fade to a hum. At the top is a tiny patch of park with a bench facing out towards the harbour. Here a group of hospitality workers sit, smoking and discussing their boss. After a moment they grind their cigarettes out and creep back towards Kent Street. I sit in their smoky wake, looking out towards High Street, which follows the top of the cliff. The terrace houses here stand above the sharp drop down to Hickson Road, and were built around 1910 when the cliffs were cut back. Like much of the housing in Millers Point, they were once owned by the Maritime Services Board and were homes for the waterside workers and their families. In the 1980s the Department of Housing took over, and since then the residents, many of whom have lived here for generations, have feared losing their homes. Millers Point has become desirable real estate now that the wharf industries have ceased operations.

Afternoon sunlight streams over the houses. The white wooden balconies turn golden, the iron roofs gleam and people come out to sit on their porches. Stories of Millers Point often describe the community spirit and the strong sense of camaraderie that exists among neighbours. As I sit in the sun on the bench, High Street is animated by people going from one house to another or leaning over their front gates to talk.

Each house has some kind of distinguishing decoration. On the porch of one is a bird cage with two rainbow lorikeets inside and a bird feeder weighed down with pigeons, which scatter when I approach. On another windowsill is a row of quartz crystals shaped into points. One house near the corner is draped in Canterbury Bulldogs paraphernalia: blue-and-white scarves, flags and posters. This shrine has at its centre a real live bulldog, wearing a blue harness to match the rest of the display. The dog lies snoozing in the afternoon sun, half opening its eyes when I walk past. A piece of cardboard is tied to the fence, a warning written in blue texta:

BEWARE OF THE DOG. ENTER AT YOUR OWN RISK.
WOOF WOOF WOOF.

At the centre of this row of houses is a preschool where children are playing under tall plane trees. I turn up along the alleyway beside it and then along the lane behind High Street. It's so perfectly cool and still here that it feels like I've slipped into the backstage area of the city, a subconscious, clandestine place. On one side is the rear of the High Street houses with their back gates and downpipes, on the other a wall stained with slow channels of water seeping through the porous sandstone. Maidenhair ferns and shoots of asthma weed grow from cracks in the rock. The faint sound of a television buzzes from inside one of the houses, but otherwise this laneway is one of those places that could exist at almost any time in the city's history.

At the end of High Street there's another sliver of park shaded by two big fig trees. It's called Munn Street Reserve, after the road that once led down to the wharf below. There are many ghost streets in this part of Sydney, swallowed up by past redevelopments. Further east whole streets were demolished for the construction of the approach to the Harbour Bridge, which now feeds so seamlessly into the city it's hard to imagine what it would look like without it.

Although it is late August, this sunny afternoon feels like the first day of spring. A man and his daughter excitedly plot their afternoon, tearing the wrappers from their iceblocks as they cross over through the park and past the Palisade Hotel. A tall but narrow brick building at the crest of the hill above the cliff, the Palisade has the look of a pub at the edge of the world.

Behind the Palisade is Merriman Street, a dead end that runs to the tip of the headland. From here the city buildings are invisible. They are blocked by the houses in the foreground, as if Millers Point has broken away and formed its own island. At the end of the street is the Harbour Control Tower. It rises from the cliff, a utilitarian monument to surveillance. Atop the concrete stem is a round observation platform which towers over the houses below, which look delicate with their wooden shutters and iron-lace balconies.

The tower was constructed in 1973 on a site chosen for its proximity to the harbour's narrowest point, where its view was unlikely to be obscured by development. From the viewing platform in the cylindrical cabin at the top of the tower all harbour shipping movements were once controlled. The entrance to the tower is a white hatch crawling with ivy, locked behind a high wire fence. A concrete slab with tarnished metal letters announces the tower as the Port Operations and Communication Centre, property of the Maritime Services Board of NSW. Its 1970s aesthetic leads me to imagine the scene high up above me inside the control room. Here, men with sideburns and skivvies sip instant coffee from Maritime Services Board mugs as they peer through telescopes and talk on clunky olive-green phones with curly cords. In this world the houses across the street are inhabited by the grandchildren of wharfies, who have inherited tales of strikes and accidents, and whose dreams are full of ships.

For all my imaginings, I know the control tower is empty. Ship movements are now controlled by a radar system based at

Port Botany and the tower, like the headland below, has become the property of the government, managed by the Barangaroo Delivery Authority. Like the foreshore below it is under a spell of silence and stillness.

At the base of the tower is a small park. Half submerged in the rubber matting that carpets the playground is the prow of a wooden ship designed for kids to climb on. I sit up on it for a moment and look around. The surrounding streets are so quiet that I am surprised that there are other people in the park. A man wearing an apron patterned with flowers is cooking kebabs on a barbecue, while beside him a woman stares out towards the harbour.

Beyond the picnic area and the playground are steps that lead down to the streets below. I walk a little way along Rodens Lane, a thin street at the base of a sandstone wall which seems to exist in permanent shadow. Ruth Park mentions it in *The Companion Guide to Sydney* as a place where a blacksmith operated from a cave in the wall, hand-forging ironware and brackets as his family had done for generations. It seems possible that he might still be there, for the only details giving away the era I inhabit are a pair of behemoth televisions dumped on the skinny footpath. In what might have once been the blacksmith's cave is now a garden of moss, ferns and succulents. A broken ceramic gnome lies lopsided in the damp soil.

I follow the laneway until I arrive back outside the Palisade Hotel, sealed up as if it holds all the suburb's secrets. From here I look out over the High Street houses, under a warm spell from the afternoon light. Behind them the view of the city has reappeared, a crowd of towers and cranes, an encroaching future.

In 2015, three years later, the mood of drowsy stillness on High Street has gone, replaced by one of protest. Banners are hung over balconies, spray-painted onto sheets in stencil letters: *Millers Point Not 4 Sale*; *Say No to the Total Sell Off of Public Assets*. The street feels stripped, with many of the houses already empty.

In 2014 the sell-off of the houses and the relocation of the residents began. The Department of Housing declared the old workers' terraces too expensive to maintain, and determined the profits from their sale could be reinvested into public housing elsewhere. The sell-off was a shock to residents, but not without precedent. Since 1900 the adjacent neighbourhoods of The Rocks and Millers Point had been owned by the state government, and as the working harbour went into decline the land became an increasingly valuable asset. In the 1970s The Rocks was threatened by a redevelopment plan in which office towers would have entirely replaced terrace houses, warehouses and laneways. The area was saved by the actions of residents and the NSW Builders Labourers Federation. As the union for building workers, the BLF imposed a 'green ban', a strike that stopped work on sites slated for demolition and redevelopment. The ban was put in place to preserve the area's built history and also to ensure a community of working-class residents would remain in The Rocks.

As a result of the green ban the Sirius apartment building was constructed in The Rocks, designed specifically as housing for local low-income residents. It's a striking building, rising up alongside the Harbour Bridge like a staircase of glass-fronted concrete blocks stacked on top of each other. The architect, Tao Gofers, had previously designed a smaller-scale version of the Sirius as social housing at Sans Souci, a southern suburb on Botany Bay. To create the model for the design he had used Revlon eye-shadow cases, which had the correct dimensions for his square, glass-fronted apartment modules.

The Sirius was a controversial building when it opened in 1979, with its modular, brutalist aesthetic and roof gardens growing around purple air vents that resemble the funnels of an eccentric ocean liner. Now, as it faces threats of demolition, it has come to be recognised as one of The Rocks' most iconic buildings. Its prominent position beside the bridge meant that for almost four decades, anyone travelling past could not help but notice it as they looked towards the harbour. Like many regular bridge travellers, I developed the habit of looking over into the windows of the Sirius from the train, my eye catching on the 'One Way Jesus' sign reliably displayed in one of the windows. But now the sign is gone and most of the apartments are empty. The majority of residents have been relocated and the building's future is uncertain.

Millers Point escaped the threats of the 1970s but this time, despite community anger, relocations and auctions continue. The Port Operations Tower has been approved for demolition and, on High Street, houses are marked with yellow ribbons, suggesting the yellow plague flags that were hung in front of condemned houses in the last purge of Millers Point in the 1900s. 'No one wanted to be here when I came over 30 years ago, so now should I have to go?' reads a sign on the house closest to the zigzag steps.

The foreshore below is now the Barangaroo construction site, busy with trucks and machinery. Churning and crashing sounds float up from there, a mechanical, digestive clamour. A park is being constructed, the shoreline altered from the straight lines of the wharves, modified to conform to a shape from the past based on an 1836 map. Blocks of sandstone, each labelled with a barcode for correct placement in the overall design, have been assembled at the water's edge.

Earlier in its construction I went on an open-day tour of the Barangaroo development. I trekked around the foundations of the towers and then the headland park. I took in the development and its barcoded sandstone, bought tea from the food truck and patted a crocodile at the reptile petting zoo, but these were all distractions. My attention kept drifting to the streets above and the banners hung over the railings. The park where I would be able to touch the harbour water for 'the first time in more than a century' (as the promotional material promised) heralded the Millers Point houses' future as exclusive residences and offices, an enclave of wealth and privilege.

Millers Point was for decades a place out of step with the city surrounding it. Eventually the forces of profit, property and wealth caught up with it, despite the community activism which, unlike in the green-bans era, no longer has the political influence to intercede in development plans. Their fight continues, but many of the High Street houses lie vacant as construction continues on the foreshore below. The golden afternoon sun shines down on them and through the dusty windows, sending bars of light across the walls of their empty rooms.

Millers Point

Enduring, changing, disappearing.

Sydney's Other Tower

watched all that happened on Sydney Harbour

Port Operations and Communication Centre.

est. 1973 on Merriman St.

Demolished by concrete-eating robots in 2016.

Hotel Palisade

reopened after many years empty.

Once the pub of waterside workers, who called it the 'big house'

wool ship →

Dalgety's, one of the last remaining wool store buildings that once dominated the headland.

DALGETY'S NEW BOND and FREE STORES

container ship →

In 2012

based on pre-1836 shore line In 2017

Former container wharves

Barangaroo Headland Park

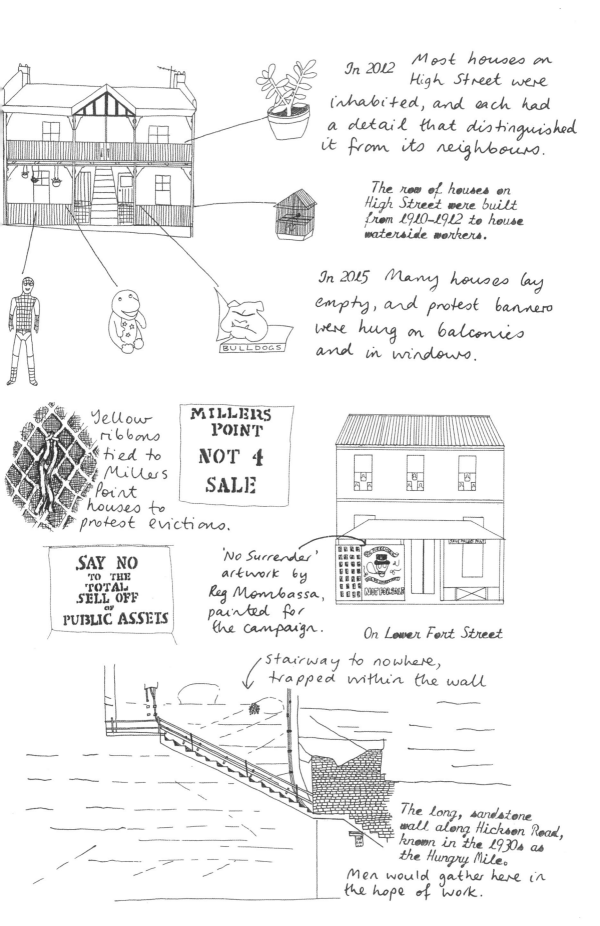

In 2012 Most houses on High Street were inhabited, and each had a detail that distinguished it from its neighbours.

The row of houses on High Street were built from 1910–1912 to house waterside workers.

In 2015 Many houses lay empty, and protest banners were hung on balconies and in windows.

Yellow ribbons tied to Millers Point houses to protest evictions.

MILLERS POINT NOT 4 SALE

SAY NO TO THE TOTAL SELL OFF OF PUBLIC ASSETS

'No Surrender' artwork by Reg Mombassa, painted for the campaign.

NOT FOR SALE

SAVE MILLERS POINT

On Lower Fort Street

stairway to nowhere, trapped within the wall

The long, sandstone wall along Hickson Road, known in the 1930s as the Hungry Mile. Men would gather here in the hope of work.

Down past the entrance to the Hungry Jacks a giant set of Olympic rings, tall and wide as a house, leans up against a concrete wall. When the Olympics were held in Sydney in 2000, these rings garlanded Martin Place. Now they mark the entrance to a salvage yard, backgrounded by a wall of shipping containers piled up like Lego bricks. Traffic provides a soundtrack to their existence, truck brakes gasping and sighing, planes roaring low overhead, coming in to land.

This is a typical St Peters scene: unlovely, surreal, resistant to investigation. St Peters is an in-between place at the edge of Sydney city. The suburb is divided in half by the Princes Highway, a north–south thoroughfare of trucks and traffic. Narrow streets of low brick houses trace one side of the highway. The shipping container yard and a stretch of wasteland are on the other, extending down towards the Alexandra Canal and the outskirts of the airport.

For thousands of years, like much of what is now known as Sydney, this area was forest. Colossal turpentine and ironbark trees made up the canopy, and the forest sloped down to marshland and a winding saltwater creek. Gadigal people walked the track that ran across the top of the ridge, and hunted kangaroo in the forest. When the land was invaded, the British stripped its trees and turned the earth inside out. The rich clay soil that once nourished the forest was found to be good material for brickmaking. From the 1830s brickworks multiplied, hollowing out the land with deep excavations.

As the city climbed upwards and radiated outwards, its buildings took shape from bricks made of St Peters earth.

The brickworks have long since closed, as have the rubbish dumps they went on to become, leaving a gouged, interrupted landscape. Peer through a gap in the corrugated iron hoarding along the Princes Highway and the ground drops sharply away into a bald, scraped pit, empty but for pampas grass and stray scraps of metal. There's little to see in this state of temporary abandonment, but much to sense: the violence exerted over this scarred land, the forces of industry and waste that have shaped its recent history.

I follow Campbell Road, which runs between Sydney Park and the boundary of the former rubbish dump. It is narrow and the rows of houses on either side line it precariously. Most of them are obviously empty. Wires hang down from the roofs where the electricity has been disconnected. They are recently vacated, their gardens still neat, rooms settling into darkness and stillness. From one, the bleat of an expiring smoke alarm sounds out in a forlorn Morse code. The same flyer sags out of each letterbox, displaying the acid blue of the WestConnex motorway development logo, advising the now-absent residents of the commencement of surveying, drilling and other geotechnical investigations. Within six months these houses will be demolished.

WestConnex is a monster awakening across the suburbs of inner Sydney. The road construction project, described as the largest in the southern hemisphere, has been stamped over St Peters. The project plans to convert much of the eastern half of the suburb into a motorway interchange, a coil of overpasses and feeder roads. In the promotional animated fly-through the wastelands are gone, replaced by a five-pointed star of looping roads that twist above patches of green parkland. Maps tell a different story, the thick blue lines carving through suburban streets.

The state government is blunt about the need for the new roads, and about the sacrifices required to fix Sydney's traffic problems. It is not the first of such proposals. In the 1970s the North Western Expressway plan had promised a similar solution, involving mass demolitions across inner city suburbs from Pyrmont to

Leichhardt. As a child I knew of it through the dotted lines slicing across familiar roads in the street directory. These lines exerted a fascination upon me. I'd open the directory to follow the lines of the ominous ghost road, etched across the city by a powerful pen. By then these dotted lines were all that was left of the plans, which had been abandoned due to widespread protests and a green ban. Forty years on, with such past successes in mind, residents have been fighting anew.

In speaking out against WestConnex, the writer Nadia Wheatley revealed Campbell Road as the archetypal neighbourhood for the setting of her 1988 book *My Place*, which follows the same area of land back in time in ten-year intervals. It is at first sight an unlikely place for literary inspiration, with its former rubbish tip, truck traffic and clinging rows of terrace houses. But writers are often drawn to such anti-monumental places, the sites of stories less often told. These houses on the edge of a hostile landscape have a striking presence, making you consider who might live here and how it might be to have this place as home. The houses wear their stories in details, in window decorations, bikes chained to fences and jade plants growing in pots on cramped balconies. Now at the end of the row there is a painted banner, a parting gift from the last residents: 'Our Homes are Being Stolen by Baird and his WestConnex Thugs. Will yours be next?' A caricature of the erstwhile premier looms at the edge, houses in his pincer-like fingers.

Live with a place for long enough and your personal mythology becomes woven into it, and it was so for me and these Campbell Road houses. Twenty years ago in the lot beside the entrance to the tip stood a lone wooden house. Two storeys, peeling white paint, half-hidden behind trees. It was separated from the terraces further up the street by a yard of stacked-up metal barrels, their bright colours faded with rust and grime.

The memory has been layered over with so many retellings I'm no longer certain which parts are true. One night I'm walking along with one of my housemates past Crystal Real Estate – a real estate agency we favour for its incongruous name and bottom-of-the-market rentals – and notice the house advertised for lease in the window. 'You know the one,' I say, 'on Campbell Road, the tip house.' We are fired up by the potential of moving our household to the edge of the world. Back at home we talk about it all weekend, so much so that this becomes our destiny. We will fly a pirate flag from the roof and make as much noise as we want. But when we call up to enquire it is off the market, already let.

After this episode the tip house was charged with additional meaning. An alternative version of my life was going on in there. If I looked hard enough I might catch sight of myself through the window, playing the drums or sewing a quilt or doing something else beyond the scope of my usual identity. This went on for years; I'd detour down Campbell Road just to check in with my alternative self. Then one day I went by and the house was gone. I stopped to stare at the patch of churned earth, as if by looking hard enough it might reappear.

The Campbell Road houses have stickers on their front windows announcing 24-hour monitoring, although there is no other sign of surveillance. This is an introverted stretch of road, deserted of people, only a willy wagtail dancing on a fence post, tail fanned out, movements hyperkinetic. Past the meat pie factory and the mega truck wash I turn into Burrows Road, which runs alongside the gloomy waters of the Alexandra Canal, Sydney's most polluted waterway. The canal was constructed in the 1890s along the path of Sheas Creek, a tributary of the Cooks River. The intention was to create a shipping channel linking Botany Bay with Sydney Harbour, but the canal was never completed. It ends suddenly in Alexandria, behind Sloy's Tipper Hire and the Swarovski head office, and trickles off as a stormwater channel.

In 1896, when the creek was being widened into a canal, workers discovered fragments of stone tools and the skeleton of a dugong with cuts to its bones among the sediment. A photo exists of the team from the Australian Museum overseeing the excavations, Victorian gentlemen with bowler hats and pocket watches, a black umbrella spiked into the mud behind them. Thousands of years ago people were hunting dugong here in the warm seas. Their gestures, preserved by these bones, return in a moment of overlapping time.

The canal flows behind warehouses and factories and the Burrows Road Industrial Estate. It is Sunday and the estate – two adjacent 1970s office buildings – is deserted, the roller doors pulled down. A motley row of chairs is on the lawn beside the canal, where the people who work in smash repairs and technical support systems sit for their lunches and take smoke breaks. I go to the canal's edge and sit there watching the skin of the water ripple with the wind. The water is moving, alive with tiny fish which flip up out of it like silver exclamation marks. This surprises me: I'd regarded the canal as a dead waterway, a kind of moat between the inner west and the inner east, traversed by neither craft nor creature. But this isn't so. As the fish settle back under the surface a cormorant glides down the centre of the canal, seemingly untroubled by the waterway's toxic sediments and industrial pollutants.

Out on Burrows Road again, I pass a woman zipped into a puffy jacket walking a big, plodding brown dog. We cross paths alongside the former premises of Rebecca Taxi Base, where an earthmover is positioned askew across the grid of parking spaces. Scuffing towards each other through the tide of disposable coffee cups and pie wrappers on the footpath, we nod as we pass one another, sharing the camaraderie that comes from walking in an unlikely place.

I turn into congested Canal Road, where the air is thick with fumes so strong I can taste them. I pull my scarf up over my nose as the diesel exhaust puffs from the trucks accelerating out from the shipping container yard, loaded with cargo. Above me a plane shrieks from the airport, angling up and away. As I trudge through it I remind myself that this confusion of traffic, industry and noise is as much Sydney as any other place within the city's boundaries.

On the corner of the highway the building that once housed the Dynamo Auto Electrician is painted with signs which announce its relocation. A St Peters icon, the Dynamo building occupies the edge of Canal Road like an oversized gift box. An early service station built in art deco style, it is white and square with ornamental parapets rising up like crowns on each side. When the Markellos family took over in the 1960s, their logo, a red lightning bolt through the name 'Dynamo', was painted atop the facade, and this has given the building its identity ever since.

When the site was acquired by the government for WestConnex, Dynamo Auto Electrician had no choice but to move. Soon after they had packed up the racks of engine parts which lined the walls, and taken down the framed photographs of the business through the generations, the building was boarded up. It was painted all over in white, the lightning bolt obscured. Then a high fence of grey panels trapped it inside the WestConnex works zone like a fly in a web.

The Dynamo was a local landmark, a shorthand for St Peters and its semi-industrial, edgeland identity. In 1986 it appeared on the front cover of an album by John Kennedy's Love Gone Wrong, a band known best for two patriotic, 'urban and western' odes to inner-west suburbs. 'Miracle in Marrickville' describes life among the factories where romance and mystery survives alongside struggle. 'King Street' is a tribute to walking down the street that to Kennedy is home and 'hub of the universe' (a nod to The Hub across from Newtown station, once a vaudeville theatre, but at the time of the song an adult cinema). On the album cover John Kennedy, with his quiff, suit, and black sunglasses, poses with the Dynamo in the background, declaring that such everyday places are worthy of celebration.

When Kennedy was being photographed outside the Dynamo in 1986, the Princes Highway was a stretch of car dealerships, motor mechanics and run-down old warehouses, surrounded by an industrial scene of rubbish dumps and gas-storage facilities. It could be an eerie, dangerous place, and at no time more so than on April Fools' night in 1990, when a fire at the Boral gas storage plant on Burrows Road produced an immense explosion. A fireball rose five hundred metres in the air, lighting up the surrounding area so brightly that it seemed to be daytime. Houses shook, windows rattled, the force of the blast stopped the engines of cars travelling on nearby streets. Some residents fled, fearing a nuclear attack or a plane crash, describing it to *Sydney Morning Herald* reporters as 'like the end of the world'. Others looked on in wonder, lining the Princes Highway and the hills of Sydney Park to watch the fires burn.

Living in St Peters then was to be in close proximity to the industrial edge of the city, the factories that stretched east through Alexandria and Rosebery. Residential St Peters is a grid of a dozen streets that run off the highway, tightly pressed rows of small, functional homes that have housed generations of workers from the nearby industries. In the 1990s St Peters also became home to punks and artists who had been priced out of rapidly gentrifying Newtown. St Peters was a tough place to live and the rents were low. After the opening of the third runway of Sydney Airport there was aircraft noise so intense that in 1995 four blocks of houses directly under the flight path were demolished, to be replaced by a bald park known as Sydenham Green. Added to this was the traffic, the waste dump, and the ominous presence of the '2044 boys' graffiti sprayed on the empty buildings.

St Peters had space in abundance for the kinds of underground cultures nourished by discards and margins. Warehouses became rehearsal studio labyrinths, corridors of closed doors muffling the thumps and squeals from the practice rooms within. The Salvation Army op shop perched above Swamp Road, almost at the edge of the airport, fitted out many a St Peters house with brown velour couches and CorningWare coffee pots.

Sydney Park became a post-industrial playground for the musicians and artists who inhabited the city's edge. The four brick chimneys at the corner of the park marked both its industrial past and its new, subcultural identity. The brickworks had closed in 1970 and the factory and kilns were left empty. In 1982 the industrial noise band SPK performed in one of the abandoned buildings, advertising the show on a flyer with a quote from *Vox* magazine that described their sound as 'a barren wasteland of screeches, diseases, and most of all excruciating pain'. On the night of the show the audience entered a post-industrial space of decommissioned machinery. The masked band members swung hatchets and hammers, smashing out rhythms half-human, half-machine on iron bars and metal drums.

The plans to convert the former brickworks to Sydney Park had just been announced. It was barren at first. For almost thirty years the disused brickpits had been a municipal rubbish dump. Trees failed to grow, their roots burned by the methane in the soil.

As more resilient trees were planted the park slowly came into life. It became a place for picnics and dog walks, and continued as a location for clandestine gatherings and marginal performances. In the 1990s Sydney Park became important in the free party scene, with Vibe Tribe dance parties held between the four brickworks chimneys at the corner of the park and the green slopes of its artificial hills. The parties grew in size and popularity until 1995, when the 'Freequency' party was shut down by riot police for being an illegal event.

Smaller events are still held at the park, like the monthly Sunday Dub Club, or the annual Punx Picnic, which gathers mohawked, longneck-toting revellers around the former brick kilns. There are not so many differences between the punks' picnics of twenty years ago and those of today. In the courtyard below the chimneys, musicians and audience merge, people reeling up to the microphones to sing and become temporarily part of the band.

Sydney Park, with its curved expanses of grass and pockets of trees, is a verdant moonscape, a constructed topography of rises and falls. From the top of the highest hill the park seems caught between the city skyline to the north, and Botany Bay to the south, where at night the airport glows with a sulphurous aura. It is a place to look out from as much as somewhere to consider what is underfoot. In the 1970s the park was a rubbish tip, and the polystyrene cups, milk bottles and broken toys that filled the city's trash bags are compacted down underneath the surface.

Rumour has it that buried somewhere among all this is the skeleton of a circus elephant, although the story has never been confirmed. There was a skeleton found in the park, but one much more ancient than a circus elephant. In 1910, a complete labyrinthodont skeleton was unearthed in one of the pits of the Austral Brickworks and sent to the Natural History Museum in London, where it is still on display. The creature, which resembled a giant salamander, lived in the lagoons here in the Triassic period, 180 million years ago. Excavations often uncovered the fossils of fish and plants from these long-ago lakes, delicate discoveries amid the harsh work of brickmaking.

On the eastern side of the park is a football oval and a sports pavilion. As I walk towards it the banners hung across the pavilion come into view. *Save Our City, Save Sydney Park*. Inside the pavilion it is crowded, with all the seats taken and people standing shoulder to shoulder in the remaining spaces at the edges of the room. On the far wall a long map shows the blue stripes of the WestConnex motorways across the inner east and west. The meeting starts with Uncle Ken Canning acknowledging Gadigal country and calling upon us to 'respect every aspect of what is left'. WestConnex, he says, comes from the same colonial mentality that invaded this land 228 years ago. As the meeting progresses, speaker after speaker echoes his message. With images of the ruptured landscape created by the early stages of the motorway on the screen behind them, councillors, scientists and local residents speak of WestConnex as an invasion into the environment and the inner-west community.

After the rally I leave the pavilion, passing by a little girl spruiking lemons for sale by donation. Lemons have become a symbol for WestConnex protesters, a token of the scheme's ineffectiveness. 'Homegrown in the inner west,' she tells me as I hand over two dollars. The lemon is small and underripe. I hold it up like a crystal ball, thinking of the back-lane orchards of the inner west, the lemon trees that grow over fences for anyone to pick as they walk by.

I walk down to Euston Road, which in the WestConnex plan will become a six-lane highway, carrying fifty thousand more cars per day. To achieve this, the edge of the park will be sliced off and the paperbark trees that line the road removed. Each of these paperbarks, like all of the trees threatened by WestConnex, has been wrapped in a strip of blue cloth in protest. Across St Peters hundreds of trees wear these blue ribbons, marking their condemnation.

At the corner of the park, where Euston and Campbell Roads intersect, I stop. The lemon feels heavy in my hands and I set it down as a kind of offering. When it touches the soil I hear a sound like an echo. It opens up into more reverberation, an industrial noise band playing in an abandoned factory or the repetitive beat from a secret dance party. The park is different when I look up. The green hills are transparent. Behind them is another scene, of brickpit craters, and then another, of an old-growth forest, and another, a lagoon and ferns. Labyrinthodonts cruise the waters, a scene overlaid by tall turpentine trees and kangaroos. A circus elephant lumbers out from of one of the pits and away into the distance. Smoke trails up from the brickworks chimneys. It merges with the clouds that move over and across this complicated landscape, all that has taken place and is taking place here.

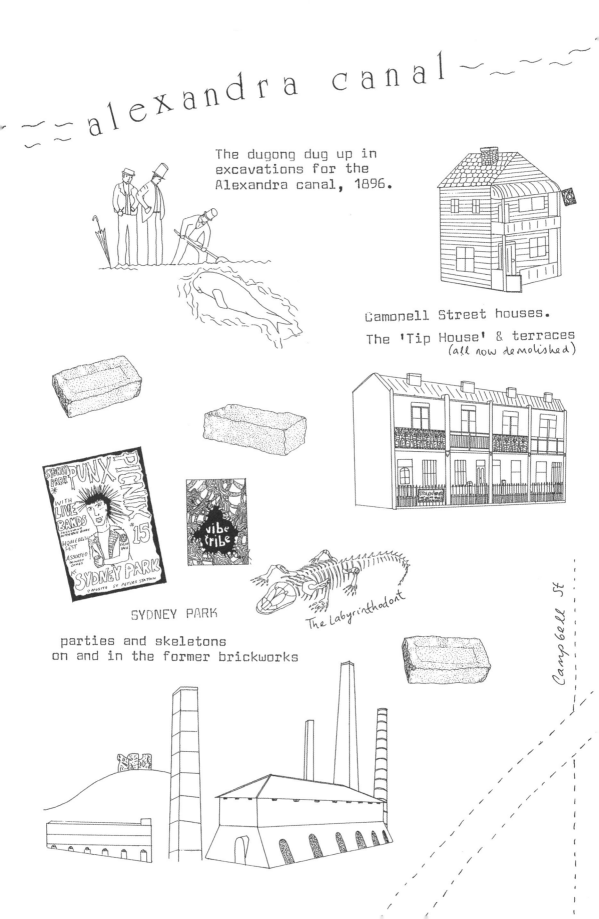

~~ alexandra canal ~~~

The dugong dug up in excavations for the Alexandra canal, 1896.

Camonell Street houses.

The 'Tip House' & terraces (all now demolished)

SYDNEY PARK PUNX PICNIK #15
WITH LIVE BANDS
HOMEBREW FEST
ASSORTED
SYDNEY PARK
OPPOSITE ST PETERS STATION

vibe tribe

The Labyrinthodont

SYDNEY PARK

parties and skeletons on and in the former brickworks

Campbell St

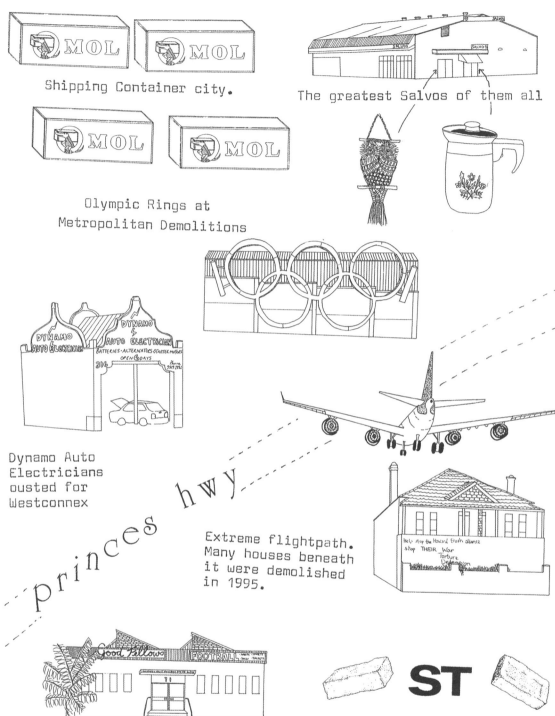

Shipping Container city.

The greatest Salvos of them all

Olympic Rings at
Metropolitan Demolitions

Dynamo Auto
Electricians
ousted for
Westconnex

princes hwy

Extreme flightpath.
Many houses beneath
it were demolished
in 1995.

Highway warehouses
(jerseys, ugg boots,
auto parts)

ST
PETERS

ANCIENT AND RECENT

on Gadigal land

MYSTERIES

Even after living in a city for a lifetime there are places that remain mysteries. Sometimes these are hidden from view, like Sydney's underground network of tunnels. Others are incongruous places, old or unusual, that exist despite everything else changing around them. They persist like islands, some mythologised, others ignored.

Of these mysterious places there is one that is literally an island – well, a road island at least – a triangle of land about six metres across at the intersection of Broadway and Wattle Street in Ultimo. Two wide fig trees grow there, their branches broad enough to keep the island in permanent shade. In the centre is a curved concrete structure with all entrances sealed seamlessly. Its yellow walls have a patchwork look from continual partial repaintings, covering the graffiti which it must be so tempting for taggers to inscribe upon its surface.

On one side of the island people gather, watching the relentless stream of turning cars for a safe break in which to cross the street. The new traffic lights, finally installed after decades of pedestrians taking their chances, have yet to break the habit of jaywalking across to the other side. Before the lights were installed it felt impossible to leave the edge of the island safely. It was only when the group of pedestrians reached critical mass and spilled across the road that there was a momentary rush of collective power.

Besides the people waiting at its edge to cross, few people linger on the island. There's little to linger for; aside from the concrete vault and the trees, there's only a garden bed of patchy ivy, a drinking fountain, and a square metal trapdoor set into a brick plinth, a hatch leading somewhere underground. The trunks of the fig trees are scarred and scratched at street level. Further up they are smooth and the branches spread out into a tangle which would be good to climb if you felt brave enough to get away with it. Posted on the side of the vault is a list of rules suggesting further illicit possibilities: there is no camping or staying overnight, no lighting fires, and no roller-skating allowed.

For as long as I can remember, the vault has been sealed. It is aesthetically unmistakable as once having been a public toilet block, but it's not its contents that are mysterious as much as why it has endured for decades in this enigmatic state. Its exterior is cared for, the graffiti painted over and the surrounding ivy garden kept clear of trash, but it serves no purpose other than adorning the island.

As is usually the case with incongruous places, there have been proposals to remove the island altogether. But for now it remains. Like the decorative 'ruined' towers of nineteenth-century follies, the vault is there for us to puzzle over, a monument to the inexplicable.

Most places that tend towards mystery do so by redundancy or eccentricity. These can be remains of infrastructure schemes that never came to be completed, like the 'road to nowhere' overpass underneath the Western Distributor flyover that cuts off in midair, or buildings abandoned for decades with signs so old they have five-digit phone numbers. These misfit places defy the neat, ordered vision of urban space presented as the aim of every proposal for change. They give a sense of the city as something organic, growing around its mistakes and false starts rather than erasing them.

At any given time I have a shifting roster of Sydney mysteries I keep an eye on. These are not grand mysteries but, like the island on Wattle Street, everyday places with some form of puzzling distinction that sets them apart from their surroundings. They are the weird structures, topiary monsters, sealed-up buildings and suburban castles that cause you to look again as you pass them by, leading you to wonder what they are and how they came to be that way.

MEMORIAL STORES

The pink-and-mauve facade of Marie-Louise Salon is a surprising sight among the shops on the main street of Enmore. Its curved windows are like two jewelled eyes; indeed, for a long time a large cardboard eye with spiky black eyelashes hung in each window. Then the eyes were gone and the windows redecorated with a collection of soft toys, pink and purple artificial flowers and Christmas baubles. Among the flowers was a framed photograph of a man in a police uniform, standing guard over the display.

Marie-Louise ceased to operate as a hairdressing salon many years before this window display of toys and flowers, but it didn't have the derelict feeling of an empty shop. The display changed now and again and the mail was regularly cleared out from under the door. It attracted a lot of attention, people stopping to photograph its pink exterior and to peek through the windows, although their curiosity was thwarted by the curtains which prevented any glimpse of the interior.

The Marie-Louise Salon was run by two siblings, Nola and George Mezher. Both were hairdressers and became public figures when they won the first-division prize in Lotto in 1982. Their winning Lotto numbers, they explained, were derived from saints' birthdays. Most Lotto winners choose anonymity, but the Mezhers were happy to appear in the media as they used their prize money to set up a charity. They established the Our Lady of Snows soup kitchen on the corner of Pitt Street and Eddy Avenue, in one of the archways of the viaduct below Central Station. The unusual name, Our Lady of Snows, harks back to a church in Rome, itself named for a divine miracle of the fourth century when snow fell in the middle of summer.

I would sometimes see Nola in the Our Lady of Snows van, holding up traffic while reverse parking on Enmore Road. If the salon door was open I'd go into Marie-Louise for a trim. I'd sit in a vinyl chair with a towel pinned around my neck, eyes wandering over the photographs and decorations surrounding the mirrors. Photos of Nola and George, pictures cut out from magazines, artificial flowers, jumbo-size novelty combs. Trays of curlers and bottles of blue rinse, swatches of different hair tints: there was always more to observe from my position in front of the mirror. Behind me was a row of hair dryers on pedestals, their domed heads like giant snowdrops. As Nola worked on my hair a cockatoo hopped over the backs of the chairs, chattering. When it got too close to where she was working Nola would command, 'Go to bed,' and the bird would hop back on its perch and tuck its head under its wing.

After Nola died in 2009 the Marie-Louise, with its commemorative display of pink and mauve objects, became one of Sydney's memorial stores. Memorial stores are shops no longer open for business that act as unofficial museums, in memory of people and times that have gone. George continued to maintain and modify the window display, visiting Enmore Road often to check on the salon and visit the St Luke's op shop next door. St Luke's also has a window display of cheerfully miscellaneous objects in haphazard arrangement: a bottle of Avon aftershave shaped like an alarm clock beside a Venus de Milo candle and an embroidery kit and a souvenir plate from Crete – a shifting spectacle of goods in limbo.

Enmore has been slower to gentrify than neighbouring Newtown. The rows of shops along Enmore Road are a timeline of sorts, moving unevenly between past and present. A stern statue of Queen Victoria, sceptre in hand, presides over the road from above the Queens Hotel. Elements of the 1980s and 1990s alternative culture that centred around Newtown and Enmore remain on Enmore Road, the Gallery Serpentine goth boutique selling corsets and gowns, the

Polymorph body piercing studio, the Alfalfa House food co-op with its share-house notices in the window. The road itself holds a deeper history, as an Aboriginal walking track, leading through the Gadigal and Wangal country that is the inner west West of Sydney.

At the same time that the Marie-Louise window display memorialised Nola, another memorial store existed on Liverpool Road in Ashfield. Like Marie-Louise it had two big, curved windows, this time painted yellow and red: Kodak colours. On one side was Koles Foto with a display of photographic paraphernalia, on the other Koles Universal, with an arrangement of 1970s linen tea towels in the window. The stores were run by a couple, Mrs Koles with the manchester store, Mr Koles the photographic store.

    The photo store opened irregularly. Once when I saw Mr Koles was inside I went in nervously to say hello. It wasn't that the thought of meeting him made me nervous; it was more that the store seemed an apparition. I looked in through the windows so often that it was strange to go inside, as if I was walking into a photograph. Inside, a tall, elderly man with black hair and big yellow-tinted glasses greeted me from behind the counter. I bought some film, explaining that I still liked to use it, and this was enough to start us talking. He told me he had wanted to be a photographer since he was ten years old. His first camera was made out of wood, he explained, stretching his hands out to indicate the size and shape of this invisible antique.

    I stood at the counter as he told me stories from his life. Many of them were about his wife, and as he spoke of her he looked towards the window of her store with its colourful tea towels. They had been married for fifty-nine years, he said and then told me, exactly to the day, how long it had been since she died. They were both Russians from Harbin, in cold, remote northeast China, and had emigrated to Australia after the Second World War. To make their surname easier for Australians to pronounce they had shortened it from four syllables to one. On the shops' signs the name Koles is equally as prominent as another fabricated name, Kodak, which was chosen by company founder George Eastman because he liked the assertive sound of the letter K.

I listened to stories from Mr Koles' life, about love and grief,
risk and change. He spoke with zest, as if by telling them he was
able to bring the times and the people back: playing in an orchestra
by the river one Shanghai summer, the intense cold of Harbin in
winter, coming to Australia with his wife. After her death Mr Koles
continued to arrange the window display in her store with floral
towels and patterned dishcloths neatly pegged to stands. Inside her
store the shelves were stacked with balls of wool, and from behind
the door a cardboard cut-out of a geisha holding a Minolta camera
smiled out into the street.

I'd hoped to visit Mr Koles again, but his store was closed every
subsequent time I passed by. I would always stop to peer in through
the glass at the cabinets of photographic equipment decorated by
Kodak promotional signs from different eras. The shop counter
was a still life, a mid-action scene of an open phone book, the page-
to-a-day calendar open on 17 January, a Yashica-branded ashtray
filled with odds and ends. Behind it the wall was hung with packets
of Polaroid film and Instamatic disposable cameras, and on a shelf
were drawers with packets of photographs indexed by surname, still
waiting for people to come and collect them. The very back of the
store was a studio set up for portraits, with a long green curtain and
spotlights. All this rested in a static arrangement, and I could stand
at the window and skim my eyes over it, noticing something different
each time. It was a museum to memory with its stacks of expired
films and outmoded cameras.

To look away from the Koles window was to re-enter the present-
day world. The Ashfield streets, busy as usual, with people queuing
outside the New Shanghai restaurant, the most popular of the
Liverpool Road Shanghai stretch that also includes Shanghai Night,
Shanghai Food House and Taste of Shanghai. As with the twin Koles
shops, many of Ashfield's stores come in multiples. Janny's Cakes and
Maria's Cakes side by side, both selling birthday cakes and red bean
buns. The two independent fruit and vegetable stores both advertised
their excellence: a choice between the paradise of Fruitopia, and
Ashfield Fruit Market, where people shopped underneath a banner
in cut-out wooden letters: *You've tried the rest / Now here is the best*.

Both went on to be demolished to make way for new developments. All along Liverpool Street, such pairings continue.

To visit the Sydney epicentre of anachronistic shops, I need only return to Parramatta Road. The Olympia Milk Bar, unchanged since the 1950s, is Sydney's best-known example, enduring for so long that it has come into notoriety. Now the dimly lit, cavernous milk bar has a Facebook fan club with thousands of members. Reports of fans' visits accumulate on the page, with descriptions of the milkshakes and cheese and tomato sandwiches consumed and accounts of conversations with the sometimes reticent owner, an elderly man whose background is the subject of much speculation. These reports often come to the same point of agreement: that the Olympia's consistent presence is a welcome counterbalance to the surge of change everywhere else.

There are a number of time-capsule stores along Parramatta Road. There is the never open but fully stocked Ligne Noire perfumerie, like a corner-store version of the Mary-Celeste, the ship discovered in the Atlantic Ocean abandoned with everything onboard intact. Nearby, Nelly's International Hair Salon is clad in particoloured brown tiles and has a red-and-silver sign with a silhouette of a woman with an afro and hoop earrings. Nelly cuts your hair while her Pomeranian runs in circles at your feet and the TV chatters in the corner.

These stores exist within their own bubble of time but they aren't memorials. Parramatta Road's most recent memorial store was Knispel Hardware, located among a run-down row of shops in Leichhardt. Like Ligne Noire, for a long time the shop was perpetually closed with all the stock remaining inside. The products were still on the shelves and the 1950s signs advertising Taubman's paints hung from the ceiling. The two front windows were arranged with a collection of hardware, artificial plants, tool catalogues and an oversized light bulb with the legend *KEYS CUT* painted on it. I'd had a key cut at Knispel years ago. With its origins in mind it became a lucky charm which I keep on my key ring, even though it is to a house I moved out of many years ago.

Then all the contents of Knispel Hardware were cleared out, the signs taken down from the ceiling and stacked against the walls, and the floorboards swept. The windows were emptied and only a few objects were left there, some artificial flowers and a red Eveready *CLOSED* sign leaning up against a wooden box. The windows became a memorial to Lois, the shop owner, who died in 2009. Taped to the inside of the glass were a series of photographs – Lois behind the counter, as a bride, with her family, heading out the door of the shop one day in her later years – and a piece of paper printed with the words *Lois Kyle (Peach), sadly missed*, and the details of her funeral service.

Most of the photographs were taken down soon after the funeral but the artificial flowers remained, and a dusty plastic Santa holding a bunch of balloons that would once have lit up when a power cord was connected. One black-and-white photograph was left, pinned to the back wall of the display window, of Lois in the store leaning against the counter. In it sun streams through the skylights and a wooden ladder is propped up against shelves that reach to the ceiling. Lois leans back on the counter with an air of self-assurance, at the centre of her domain, ready to dispense brooms and scissors and life advice to her customers.

When I was looking in through the door of Knispel the light from the skylight gave the room an eerie beauty, a sense of suspended animation. Shafts of sunlight illuminated the bare floorboards and the few items of furniture left inside. This was in contrast to the deteriorating exterior, the windows covered in graffiti scrawls and boarded up where they had been smashed, the doorway with piles of trash blown in from the street. All was coated with fine black diesel soot from the Parramatta Road traffic, a dust that quickly ages everything it covers.

These three memorial stores lasted for many years but eventually they changed. At Marie-Louise and Koles *FOR SALE* signs appeared, new and final window displays. Marie-Louise was the first. It was a shock to see that it was not exempt from change. There had been something eternal about Marie-Louise, as though it were a jewel

fixed so tightly into Enmore Road that it would always be there.
In Ashfield, a tarpaulin was hung up in the window of Koles'
photography store and, peeking in through the gaps, I saw that
the cabinets were empty of their cameras and expired film. Mrs
Koles' store also had bare shelves, apart from a sign wishing Merry
Christmas and a Happy New Year from a festive season long passed,
and a white cash register marooned in the centre of the counter.

Then boards went up to cover the windows of Knispel, soon to
be plastered in posters advertising beer and upcoming concerts.
In Ashfield, Koles too was boarded up, although in a more eccentric
fashion, with two domestic wooden doors with round metal
doorknobs in the centre of the hoarding. Then these disappeared
and new shops were revealed, two grey boxes. The *SOLD* signs came
down from Marie-Louise and were replaced by new ones, written
on pink cardboard. *Marie-Louise Memorabilia Sale. Grab Your Piece
of Inner West History. Sticky Beaks Welcome*.

A crowd of people gathered on the pavement outside Marie-
Louise on the morning of the sale. There were rockabilly girls with
their hair in pin curls, curious locals who had never seen inside, and
people who had once been salon regulars. One woman had lived in
Enmore since the 1970s and used to come past often and say hello
to Nola. The Marie-Louise always had a surprise, she said. Once
there were ducklings swimming around in a bathtub in the corner.
The windows of the store were constantly changing. Nola would
sometimes seat hair models in there, to read magazines and pose
as their hair was styled.

Eventually the pink door opened and the interior was for a
moment a tableau: the curtained mirrors and trays of rollers, the
pink and mauve capes and the bottles of blue rinse neatly arranged
on the shelves. The pink clocks on the wall ticked through the
minutes as the store was gradually dismantled, people buying things
here and there, the vinyl chairs and the vases, the pink towels
and bottles of Fanci-Full hair rinse. I picked out a giant novelty
souvenir comb from World Expo '88 and a bottle of blue rinse
as my own Marie-Louise souvenirs, and a pink business card for
'George and Nola Mezher, Leading Sydney Hairdressers'. A few

weeks later the building was gutted, with only the pink and purple facade remaining.

These memorial stores were, ultimately, expressions of love, and the shops extensions of their owners. The Marie-Louise was Nola and George, the Koles stores were a husband and a wife, and people came to Knispel as much for Lois as for paint or keys. All of the memorial stores faded slowly, remaining as objects of contemplation long after they had stopped trading. Even when their vestiges disappear entirely, there will be stories of blue rinses and ducklings, of expired film and linen tea towels. Keys cut at Knispel will still open doors.

MEMORIAL

MARIE LOUISE

The eyes were a constant of the ever-changing Marie-Louise window display, though over time they drooped into a tired expression.

No glimpses inside the Marie-Louise, every possible crack was sealed up with pink and purple curtains.

KOLES

Linen teatowels of flora and fauna, 70s cartoon girls, bunches of flowers.

The Kodak logo in every possible format and variation.

KNISPEL

Peer into the skylit interior.

The windows, once full of hardware and homewares, later became a memorial to Lois Kyle (Peach).

STORES

Everywhere a
potential perch
for the cockatoo.

Bottles of
Blue Rinse.

Trays and trays
of curlers.

Giant comb,
souvenir of
Expo 88.

Photo studio with
long aqua curtains
for portraits at the
back of the store.

The Minolta lady was
the guardian of
Koles Universal,
guarding the doorway.

Never-picked-up
photographs, memories
gone astray.

Almost everything
you could ever need.

The latest in
1960s house
paint, pastel
colours for your
cottage.

Giant keys to
advertise the
key-cutting service.

Beneath Sydney is a system
of tunnels and passageways mostly inaccessible to the world above.
Yet despite their clandestine existence, there are many places where
the above-ground and subterranean cities intersect. These clues
to the underworld are most often portals of some kind, manholes,
grates and hatches, although some of the clues are less obvious.
At Central Station the underground ghost platforms, numbers 26
and 27, are visible only for a few seconds if you know the right place
to look. Take the escalators leading down to the eastern suburbs
platforms at the far end of the station. Stand still and concentrate
on the horizontal stripes of the ceiling panels above you, specifically
the thin gaps between them. Halfway down you'll catch a glimpse
through to the ghost platforms, a fleeting sight gone in a blink as
the escalators continue to move you down to the trains below.

Thousands of people pass by the ghost platforms every day, the
majority without knowing of their existence. From the escalators it is
their lights that are most easily visible. Although the ghost platforms
are unused and rarely entered by railway staff, the lights are always
on, illuminating the grey scene. A small window in the door of the
lift used to provide a better view of them, identical to the platforms
below, although in raw concrete and without tracks running alongside
them. I would sometimes take friends for joyrides in the elevator
for a sighting, to the bemusement of others using the lift for more
conventional purposes. The spy-hole has been covered over but the lift
has buttons for the ghost platforms which I always press, just in case.

The ghost platforms are part of a city transport system that stalled part-way to completion. Similar spaces-in-waiting are found in the suburbs, in corridors of land set aside for never built expressways, or shops that remain forever for lease, as if cursed. These places are the architectural equivalents of the paths not taken in life, things begun but not pursued, a reminder of the flip side of decisions taken. I like to imagine that the trains that stop at the ghost platforms travel to all the potential Sydneys that could have ever been.

After years of these glimpses I visited the ghost platforms and found them as grey and clandestine as I had imagined. The tour was led by a retired railways engineer who wore a key on a string around his neck attached to a tag that said 'Ghost Platforms'. He told us his favourite things about the ghost platforms are their purity and sense of stillness. The scene was indeed still, though the air buzzed with a mechanical hum, as if the platforms were somehow alive.

The guide pointed out the holes in the centre of the platform, intended for escalator machinery but now filled with dusty debris. This reminded me to look out for the gaps in the panelling that gave the glimpse of the ghost platforms from the escalators. Now on the other side, I saw through to the lights of the bright, everyday station. The guide shone his torch up into the stubs of tunnels leading out from the platforms, illuminating rusty old scaffolding that looked like a gurney. 'You haven't asked about the rats,' he said, and I imagined fierce beasts with fangs and red eyes. 'Well, there aren't any. They prefer Town Hall, where there's lots of discarded McDonald's on the tracks.' We climbed down a ladder onto where the train tracks would have been laid and walked over the damp, clay-rich soil to the end of the longest tunnel, which ended abruptly in a concrete wall like the door to a gigantic vault.

The ghost platforms were constructed for an extended suburban network of railways stretching to Manly in the north, and east to Watsons Bay, Coogee and La Perouse. This plan was designed by John Bradfield, the engineer best known as the overseer of the Harbour Bridge's construction. His plans for a comprehensive rail system for eastern Sydney never came to fruition. Ideas for an eastern suburbs rail line had first taken shape in the late nineteenth century but it was only in 1979, after a long history of plans, proposals and revisions, that the eastern suburbs railway opened. It was much reduced from Bradfield's plan, of which bits and pieces had been built and abandoned, including Platforms 26 and 27 at Central, and tunnels extending out from the City Circle's underground stations.

Without Bradfield's full rail network Sydney's public transport system became frustratingly slow and piecemeal, involving long bus rides to the north and east. But the scheme's traces have given Sydney an underground world of intrigue far beyond that of a failed railway project. The longest of the abandoned city rail tunnels are those that extend out from the north and south of St James Station. This is a secret, chthonic world known to the few who can access it, legally or illegally, as a landscape with varied terrain and its own folklore. In the Second World War one of these tunnels was converted for use as an air raid shelter, with concrete blast doors at either end. In this tunnel now is a bell, a faceted metal structure that resembles an oversized gemstone. It was constructed by the artist Nigel Helyer who in 1992 broadcast on ABC radio the tolling of the bell every midnight for twenty-one days. The bell was left in the tunnel after the performances and now has an arcane presence there, like a remnant from a long-ago temple. When struck, the sound of the bell resonates between the walls of the chamber like a call to worship.

Other sections are rougher, resembling caves more than railway tunnels, with crumbling pathways and ladders against rock faces. Just east of Macquarie Street one of the tunnels has flooded into an ever-deepening lake. Lake St James, as it is known, was formed over decades by water seeping through the stone. The flooded tunnel is rumoured to have been the secret bunker of General Macarthur, the supreme commander of the South-West Pacific region during the Second World War. He and his staff were said to have accessed the bunker via doors in a rose garden above. Now its most well-known inhabitant is an albino eel, named Eric by some of the urban explorers who have slipped past railway security to brave the tunnels and set sail on the lake in inflatable dinghies.

Stories of the tunnels are a braid of rumours, history and

legends. Sydney is not the only city to have developed an underground mythology. While the archetypal modern city is one of high-rise buildings and towers, the subterranean elements of cities have a quieter and more curious presence – and are no less persistent – in the urban psyche. Subways, underground car parks and subterranean shopping malls are regarded as natural extensions of the urban scene above, but the hidden elements of the underground give us the potential to escape the city altogether. Stories like *Alice's Adventures in Wonderland* or *Journey to the Centre of the Earth* take their energy from the idea that secret underground worlds exist, in other dimensions, through magic portals.

The underground lies beneath the present moment of life on the surface, an alternative time-scale of pasts and dreams. The St James tunnels extend under the city but also into our imaginations. They are made of rock and concrete and earth, and also of fantasies and speculations. The spare greyness of the ghost platforms at Central make them seem like the city's bare bones, lying beneath the surface colour and detail. But they are one secret among many; to contemplate them is to wonder what else might be hidden, and what else there might be to know.

The disused railway tunnels are some of the best-known elements of the city's underground world, even if comparatively few people will ever enter them. The tunnels have been in and out of the news since their construction in the 1930s. First articles described the extensions to the railway network, then their repurposing as air raid shelters during the war. Later, from the 1950s, articles shifted away from the functional and towards the fantastical, with titles like 'Our Great Tunnel Mystery' and 'The City Underground', describing the descent into the 'eerie depths' and 'Sydney's catacombs'.

Other parts of the underground city have much less of a public profile, places where official visits are rare or non-existent. The urban explorers with knowledge of them are a surreptitious bunch. In the 1990s I sometimes came across copies of the zine for the Cave Clan, *Il Draino,* at the Black Rose anarchist bookstore in Newtown, and their mystique as a band of underground adventurers intrigued me. Here and there beside manholes and grates I'd notice the Cave Clan tag. The two Cs with a bolt between them had all the allure of a coded message. The members of the Cave Clan knew a different version of Sydney, an underground world of drains they infiltrated and named. I read about drains with names like Fortress and Eternity, and while I was too prone to claustrophobia to be a drain explorer myself I liked to imagine these underground realms, traversed by characters with equally curious names: Predator, Siologen, Trioxide, Ogre. They were urban superheroes, potentially underfoot at any moment as I walked the streets.

The more I thought about the Cave Clan the more I noticed the cracks and gaps that might lead somewhere else, details not intended to be noticed but surprisingly frequent in the urban landscape. For the Cave Clan, part of the excitement of drain exploration is the thrill of protest and subversion, of going into zones deemed private, dangerous, or inaccessible. The details of the underground environments are equally compelling in their silence and strangeness. Predator, a founding member of Sydney Cave Clan, described the compulsion for draining in 'A Sprawling Manifesto of the Art of Drain Exploring':

We like the dark, the wet, humid, earthy smell. We like the varying architecture. We like the solitude. We like the acoustics, the wildlife, the things we find, the places we come up, the comments on the walls, the maze-like quality; the sneaky, sly subversiveness of being under a heavily-guarded Naval Supply base or under the Justice and Police Museum.

Predator began the Sydney chapter of the Cave Clan in 1991. A well-known Sydney activist, he died from cancer in 2004, while still in his thirties. Inside the Maroubra 'mega-drain', which he discovered and named the Fortress, there is a tribute wall with candles and messages written by his friends and the urban explorers who have carried on his legacy.

Cave Clan members, with their attitude of subversion, are one form of Sydney underground aficionado. Others take a more traditional approach, such as Brian and Barbara Kennedy, the authors of *Subterranean Sydney: The Real Underworld of Sydney Town*.

Published in 1982, their book provides a historical account of underground Sydney through descriptions of its various tunnels. Of all of Sydney's tunnels, the Kennedy's pronounce the Tank Stream as 'the showpiece of subterranean Sydney'. I like to imagine the husband-and-wife team in search of it at Circular Quay, pausing to look through the hole in the cement where, they write, it is possible to see 'a small lake under the footpath', and seeking its outflow into the harbour.

The Tank Stream was for thousands of years a source of fresh water for the Gadigal people, flowing down to the harbour from the forest that became Hyde Park. It was also the decisive factor in determining the location of the city of Sydney, when the British saw its potential as a water source for their camp site. Immediately the stream came to indicate class division: officers on the eastern side, convicts on the west. Soon it became polluted and other water sources were found, but the Tank Stream's new identity was established, inextricably connected with the city's origins.

The Tank Stream has a mythical presence in Sydney. It lurks below the streets, running through pipes in the foundations of city buildings, its name appearing on bars and hotels and monuments. Tours of the Tank Stream are so popular that places must be allocated by ballot. On these tours, groups slosh through the drain underneath Hunter Street that now constitutes the stream. Kitted out in hard hats and safety harnesses, they wield torches to light the dark cavern as they follow the water's path back upstream.

One year I was lucky: I won a ticket in the ballot. Following the directions to meet the tour, I found myself stepping through an unassuming doorway at the edge of the Australia Square Plaza. If I'd ever noticed this entrance before, I'd not suspected it would lead into a small brick room with a sloping roof of exposed beams, like a subterranean lounge room. This room was built in the 1960s as a reception area for tour groups. Rows of gumboots were lined up at the ready and I sat on a bench at the edge of the room to pull a pair on. With hard hat and boots on I join the group to climb down into the chamber below.

The Tank Stream runs through a wide channel constructed

in slabs of sandstone. The space is not high enough to stand, and more than once my hard hat collides with the curve of bricks above. Crouched, we walk through the echoing passage, the thunking sound of cars passing over a manhole above punctuating the splash of our footsteps through a shallow stream of clear water. The tour guide describes her favourite details, the makers' marks that were inscribed into the bricks by convicts and how sometimes, with heavy rain, water fills the drain entirely. 'There's a noise like a train coming,' she explains, and then comes the rush. There's only a trickle today, a foot's width of water in the centre of the channel. The Tank Stream moves through this brick chamber and away to the harbour, escaping its enclosure.

Down here, with the water running over my boots, I have a sense of being at the city's source, a vital place where elements combine. Afterwards, back on the surface again, I find it hard to reconcile the dark, echoing world of the Tank Stream with Hunter Street above. The street is part of the business district, lined with sandwich bars and shops. In the centre of the strip is the entrance to the Hunter Connection shopping arcade, the ceiling mirrored like a 1980s nightclub, reflecting a mixed-up version of the street below in its angular shards. People head to and from Wynyard train station, caught up in the momentum of the city. Spending time underground has made me feel slow and reflective, out of step with the crowd. I stand back under the awning of what was once the Dymocks bookstore on the corner, looking for the blue line painted across the road that marks the path of the stream. Underground, beneath this faded blue line, the Tank Stream flows on.

Utility Tunnels

An under-city network that keeps the above-ground city functioning. Underfoot on Pitt Street, telecommunication workers traverse tunnels.

The Tank Stream

The "run of clear water" that convinced Arthur Phillip to choose Sydney Cove/Warrane for settlement in 1788. Then, it was a clear stream running through a ferny gully. Now, it is mostly enclosed in pipes that run through the basements of buildings like Australia Square.

Cave Clan zine, Il Draino - no longer in print...

Ghost Platforms

(C) CONCOURSE

(P.2) PLATFORM 26-27

(P.1) PLATFORM 24-25

At Central Station (26 & 27) built for the extensions of the railway network that never came to be. Visible in glimpses from the escalators. And there's a button for them in the lift.

THE CAVE CLAN NEWSLETTER
ILDRAINO
SEPT/OCT '94   SYDNEY   25th ISSUE
OPERA HOUSE DRAIN FOUND!

...but the Cave Clan are still exploring.

UNDERGROUND SYDNEY

Under the pavement, the pipes.

Graveyards

The city's first official graveyard was where the Town Hall now stands. Central Station was also formerly a graveyard.

In Memory of Eliz Steel died 1795 Aged

Excavations in 1974 revealed this fragment of a headstone under the Town Hall.

St James Tunnels
(and St James Lake)

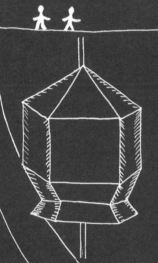

Around St James railway station and under Macquarie Street. In one is a large bell once used to create sound effects for radio broadcasts.

St James Lake inhabitant: Eric the albino eel.

Cave Clan

Drain explorers since the 1980s.

C/C

Experience a past version of the future on the **Domain Express Footway**

A network of subterranean moving footways never made it beyond planning stages but this one, which opened in 1961, is still rolling along under the Domain

At the crest of the hill at the top of Simmat Street in Condell Park there's a plain expanse of grass with a looming concrete water reservoir painted in grey and orange squares. The grass is strewn with wrappers, bottles and McDonald's trash, as well as weirder things like a bottle of nasal spray and a headless My Little Pony. It's the kind of place that teenagers drive to at night, at just enough a remove from the surrounding houses to be beyond surveillance.

On maps this park is known as Wattawa Reserve, Condell Park, but locals know it as Black Charlie's Hill. Charlie, an Aboriginal man whose full name was thought to be Charlie Luzon or Lopez, kept a vegetable garden here in the early 1900s. Every night at exactly 9 p.m. Charlie would fire one shot from his gun, a mysterious gesture without a recorded explanation. Now, Black Charlie's Hill is mostly covered by houses, apart from this patch of grass, with trees dotted around a small play area with a few swings.

From here there's a view down across the suburban streets of Bankstown and Punchbowl. It's a vista of tiles and treetops, the far-off high-rise buildings of Wolli Creek and Rockdale the only interruption to the pattern. From this aspect the usual bookends of Sydney city and the Blue Mountains are hidden from sight. The view is of an infinite suburbia, stretching to the horizon.

Despite its unremarkable appearance, the hill was once a location central to Australia's military operations. First the nearby Bankstown Aerodrome opened in 1940 as an air base and training ground for fighter squadrons. From above, the airport was camouflaged to look like a farm, and the hangars designed to resemble farmhouses in order to mask their true purpose. Artists including Max Dupain were employed by the military to devise methods of camouflage. The resulting constructions of netting, wire and fabric formed a false topography that concealed the existence of aircraft underneath.

The hill itself also acted as a kind of disguise, as beneath one segment of it the Bankstown Bunker was built. The bunker, a top-secret military operations centre three storeys deep, housed a maze of rooms, including one which displayed a gigantic map of Australia and the South Pacific area. In front of the map was a ladder for staff to climb when they needed to plot troop movements. There were chalkboards for noting the positions of enemy submarines and surface forces, and a large tabletop ocean map, with a hatch in the middle of North America for a person to stand in. From this hatch inside the map, the oceans of the world were within reach.

The Second World War transformed the environment of Bankstown above ground and below, just as it transformed the lives of local residents. Thousands of locals, many of them women, went to work at the Leightonfield Munitions Factory and the aircraft and weapons factory at Chullora. Bankstown became known as 'Yankstown' as American servicemen requisitioned the Capitol Theatre on Chapel Street for accommodation, and army huts and barracks were set up in the nearby Civic Centre.

After the war, some of the accommodation used for troops became provisional homes for migrants who arrived in Sydney, many of them from Central and Eastern Europe. The Villawood Migrant Hostel, built on the site of a former munitions factory, was a temporary home for many before they settled in surrounding suburbs. In the 1960s the Department of Immigration set up a Citizenship Advice Bureau in the new Bankstown Square shopping mall to encourage migrants to become Australian citizens. Photographs show the caravan set up beside the carousel clock in the shopping centre's central plaza, alongside a banner proclaiming the country 'A Land Worth Sharing'. Government attitudes have changed towards people seeking asylum; since 1976, the former Migrant Hostel has operated as the Villawood Immigrant Detention Centre.

If the war gave Bankstown a sense of centrality, the postwar period developed its suburban character. Before the war it had been a mixture of urban and rural land, but with the pressures of population growth – between 1940 and 1960 the population grew threefold – there was a boom in house construction and the suburban streets of Bankstown took shape. This was the heyday of the fibro cottage. Thousands of such houses were constructed on bald blocks of newly subdivided land. Fibro – thin sheeting made from fibrous asbestos and cement – was a cheap, versatile building material. A timber frame could be quickly clad in sheets of fibro, and a house swiftly assembled.

Walking along Edgar Street in search of the bunker I pass by some of these postwar houses. Their trees have grown tall, cacti and conifers now reaching the roof like pets grown into monsters. These fibro houses, like members of an expansive family, have gone on to different fates. Some are as neat as the day they were built, their pale walls bright in the sunlight, a perfect lawn in front. Others are surrounded by dismantled cars, their gardens unruly. In the 1960s these streets had a regular appearance, row after row of small white houses. Now this uniformity is gone. Cottages sit alongside the brick McMansions that are slowly replacing them.

This suburban scene is one of aspirations, new and old. The McMansions reflect a preoccupation with size and prestige, but the cottages they replaced were no less proudly thought of. In the 1950s and 1960s these cottages were the first home many people had owned. They symbolised a new, safe, suburban life, relief from run-down homes in the inner city or from wartime unrest. Their details have been for some the comforting, for others the alien, features of a new landscape.

Many current Sydney residents can trace their family story back to the postwar migrants of fifty and sixty years ago and this suburban scene. These are the kinds of houses that form the backgrounds for Instamatic snapshots, with children standing on the front lawn beside newly planted trees. In these photos the suburbs look stark, at the edges of the city as it grew outwards.

As Bankstown became residential its wartime identity quickly receded. The airport was converted for civil aviation with the majority of traffic being light planes. The bunker fell into disuse, sealed up and forgotten by most for decades. Then, in 1971, the editor of local newspaper the *Bankstown Torch* was given a tour by members of the RAAF, and a story with photographs was published. This revealed a place that people had known about through rumours but few had ever seen. Some years later the bunker was damaged by fire, and in 1975 a housing development was built on the land above it.

On the corner of Marion and Edgar Streets are the dark brick and wood villas of the housing development. Its internal streets are named after military aircraft: Mirage Court after the fighter plane, Jindivik Court after the target drone. Despite their combative addresses, the houses are an unobtrusive cluster. They are arranged around a central mound, a grassy hill with a few big blocks of sandstone placed randomly like discarded furniture. I walk up to the top, knowing the bunker is underfoot. Apart from the mound there are few clues to its existence. Like the summit of Black Charlie's Hill, this stretch of grass is deserted and my only company is provided by twists of food wrappers, a pale blue dinner plate, and a crushed packet of cigarettes displaying a gory photo of what might happen to your throat if you smoke them. Underneath the grass and trees and blocks of sandstone is the concrete shell of the bunker, five feet thick. Inside it are the burnt-out rooms where men once plotted how Australia would be defended from enemy attack, the walls streaked with soot and graffiti.

The entrances to the bunker are all sealed these days, although there are rumours that it can be accessed through an air vent in the backyard of one of the villas. A few notable visits have been recorded. Part of a1986 episode of the gardening and lifestyle TV show *Burke's Backyard* was filmed inside the bunker. In the 1990s it was visited on a number of occasions by members of the Cave Clan. During one of their expeditions a long-exposure photograph was taken inside the main bunker's control room. Shadowy figures appear like ghosts between the thick concrete pylons that hold up the roof, and a long snake of light zigzags across it from where a torch was thrown across the frame. The walls are blackened and stained with a few names written in paint on them: *Cave Clan, Predator, 29.1.95.*

All of this is beneath where I stand now, a wartime memory underneath the regular grid of houses and parks, roads and shops. I walk down out of the housing estate towards Marion Street and a corner store. It's a solid white building, a converted house, with sun-faded advertisements for newspapers painted on the awning. The advertisement in the centre, for the long-defunct *Daily Mirror*, has been painted over in white, but the name can still be seen faintly. The suburbs are full of such shadows, which persist until something comes along to cover them over.

The majority of houses built in post-war Bankstown were made of fibro. It was a cheap and versatile material and many people built their own homes. From a distance the rows of houses looked identical, but up close every one was slightly different to its neighbour.

Call your friends to invite them to a movie at the drive-in cinema at Bass Hill, a meeting of the orchid society at the Friendly Society Hall, or a game of bowls. Or maybe just an ice cream at the corner store.

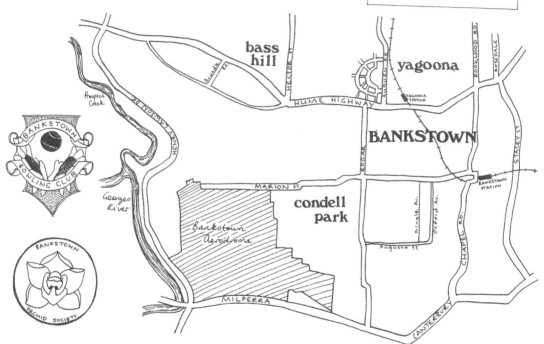

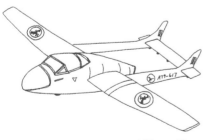

After the war the aerodrome was used by light aircraft and housed the de Havilland aircraft factory, where aircraft such as the de Havilland Vampire were built.

The map room of the Bankstown bunker, wartime underground operations centre that lay secret, forgotten under the streets of Bankstown until its rediscovery in the 70s.

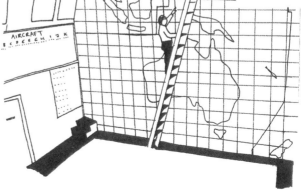

Guide to Bankstown

of the 50s and 60s

In post-war Bankstown the suburbs grew. Streets of fibro cottages, new houses, cars and appliances, leaving the old world behind.

Admiral televisions were one of the many products manufactured in Bankstown, and local residents worked in the Admiral factory, the Dunlop shoe factory, the Yardley cosmetics warehouse, among many others.

Take a drive up to the Bankstown Reservoir and gaze out over the newly built suburbia below.

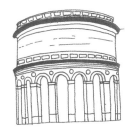

The offices of local newspaper The Torch were destroyed by fire in 1955. Torch owner Phil Engisch accused rival paper the Bankstown Observer of being responsible for the blaze.

100,000 people came to shop at Bankstown Square on its first day of opening, consuming 10,000 meat pies and 3 tonnes of donuts on the day.

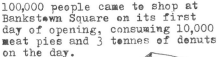

BANKSTOWN SQUARE

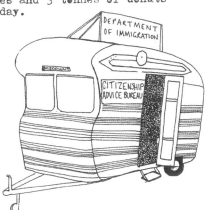

Bankstown Square and Roselands shopping centres opened in the mid 60s. A citizenship advice bureau was set up in Bankstown Square to encourage migrants to become citizens. Bankstown had a large migrant population, and the Villawood Migrant Hostel was the first Australian home to many.

Sydney's ugliest building is a contested topic. Some nominate the UTS Tower as the city's worst, a 1970s brutalist construction that resembles an elongated, rectangular pinecone. Others condemn the Blues Point Tower at McMahons Point. There, it is not so much the form itself that people object to as its conspicuous placement on the peninsula, the 25-storey apartment block disrupting the headland adjacent to the Harbour Bridge.

A more humble but equally unloved structure is the other contestant commonly nominated for Sydney's ugliest building: the Goulburn Street Car Park. This multi-level parking station was constructed over the entrance to the underground City Circle railway line in 1960. Perched precariously above the tracks, the concrete structure has a rather rickety appearance. From some vantage points it appears as if it is subsiding towards the railway line as it follows the incline of the surrounding streets. Trains travel back and forth from underneath it, as if the car park were consuming the trains and spitting them back out again.

Like the Domain Car Park and its futuristic moving walkway, The Goulburn Street Car Park was built at the height of Sydney's fervour for automotive convenience. As well as traffic pressures there were also aesthetic motivations for building it. The structure covered the entrances to the train tunnels, a string of dark archways that had previously been visible below Goulburn Street. Yet placing such a precarious-looking building on top of the railway lines only drew more attention to them. It also changed the experience of travelling to Central Station by train. Instead of a sharp emergence from the tunnel into the daylight there is now an intermediary zone, like a cave, where the street outside comes in glimpses through the concrete columns. Trains often travel slowly through here, and it is rumoured that they do this to avoid hitting the pylons and causing the car park to collapse.

After the slow journey out through the caverns, trains continue along the elevated track leading to Central. Looking over the Surry Hills rooftops from the train gives you a feeling of gliding above the streets. Through the branches of the plane trees that line Elizabeth Street is a view of multistorey brick warehouses, once housing tea merchants, garment factories and printing companies. The highlight of the strip used to be the animated neon sign for Sharpie's Golf House which, apart from the neon advertisement for Chateau Tanunda 'Brandy of Distinction' at the entrance to St James station, was the last remaining of the once-plentiful animated neon signs that decorated the city in the 1950s and 1960s. At night it lit up the rooftop with a red-and-green glow as a neon golfer hit a continual hole in one. The 'ball' was an arc of lights which travelled from one side of the sign to the other, from the golfer to a circle of green marked with a flag for the nineteenth hole.

The Sharpies sign is now also gone, tucked away in the archives of the Powerhouse Museum. All that is left where the sign used to be is a section of rusty scaffolding. I look down onto it from the rooftop level of the car park. This wasn't designed as a place to linger but there's a good view from up here, five levels above the street. It's like standing on an urban magic carpet, floating among the tops of the trees on an expanse of concrete.

I look across at Wentworth Avenue, a street well-supplied with vacant old warehouses in varying states of dereliction. The street was constructed after the Surry Hills slum clearances in the early 1900s, replacing the maze of lanes and houses that had stood there previously. Now the warehouses built in their stead have fallen into decline. The light shines through the top-storey rooms of Sheffield House, which has been empty since the 1990s. It stands out with its three levels of bay windows and huge but almost unreadably faded painted advertisement on its broad side wall.

Before neon signs were popular it was these kinds of painted advertisements that embellished city streets, enticing people to visit the City Boot Palace, or to buy Goldenia Tea from the Cash Grocer on the corner. Now the faded remains of advertisements of this kind are known as ghost signs. In cities across the world, ghost-sign hunters walk with eyes cast aloft, looking for faded hand-painted advertisements for long-gone products and services that act as clues to the everyday scenes of past eras.

I developed an obsession with the Sheffield House wall over years of trying to decode its ghost sign. Every time I passed by on the train I made another attempt to decipher it. Gradually, as the whitewash peeled away, the words became more visible, until one day I could suddenly read WINE in one script and PILLS in another. The ghost sign was two superimposed advertisements. The more recent one, I discovered, was for Penfolds Wine, the name written in the same cursive script that is still the company's logo today. Underneath it was an older advertisement for Dr Morse's Indian Root Pills, a patent medicine frequently featured on early-twentieth-century wall advertising. It purported to cure dozens of complaints including biliousness, rheumatism, neuralgia, grippe, palpitation and nervousness. I still look for it every time I pass, and mentally trace over its doubled message.

Further along the street is the Griffiths Tea building, a dark brick ruin with anarchist graffiti inscribed across the windows. Until recently these empty buildings were owned by the Wakils, a wealthy couple notorious for amassing multiple city properties they left empty and untouched for decades. Then, in 2014, they began to quickly sell them, and now Griffiths Tea is due to become apartments. Another warehouse, Key College House, will be converted into a hotel.

Looking out over the rooftops, my strongest thought is that everything I can see around me is going to change. It's changing already and constantly. Just a few blocks away the seemingly everlasting Oceanic Café, a place so old it had hat hooks on the walls and served lamb's fry as its signature dish, has finally closed down for good. Construction has begun on the Golf House Residences, where Sharpies used to be. Plans have been devised for the car park too. Although its proximity to the railway line makes it a difficult building to modify or remove, there have been attempts to improve its appearance. Covering the brick wall above the train line are panels patterned with seagulls. Plants have appeared on the exterior, trailing down over the concrete. There has been talk of a rooftop cinema or a conversion to an inner-city high school.

The rooftop of Sydney's ugliest building is a good place to contemplate change. Up here, I imagine the city as a network of forces, some benign, others destructive. There are cycles of transformation and stagnation, complex and overlapping. A persistent place like the Oceanic Café or the Marie-Louise will suddenly disappear. I'll stop at the edge of a building site, feeling both curiosity and horror at the deep excavations. Or I'll go into somewhere like the car park, for no other reason than to investigate it after having passed by it so often, knowing this is no guarantee it will remain. Ascending through the levels of water-stained concrete until I reach the top, my only company is the rows of waiting cars.

When devoting attention to such unlikely places, I think of the refrain from the Kenneth Slessor poem 'William Street': 'You find this ugly, I find it lovely.' Slessor was writing about Darlinghurst in 1935, with its neon signs for Tooheys Beer and Penfolds Wines, its pawnshops and cafés, its drinkers and sex workers. This was then the modern urban scene with its mixture of the garishly new and the traditional. This chaos, this mixture, is ever-present in Sydney; ugly and lovely are intertwined. Twenty-five years after Slessor's poem, architect Robin Boyd wrote *The Australian Ugliness*, a condemnation of what he termed 'featurism', the veneers, detailing and decorative kitsch that smothered the built environment of Australian cities and suburbs.

For Boyd, ugliness was the disunity brought about by featurism. It produced an inconsistent, cluttered urban environment, content with surfaces features at the expense of the deeper connection between human society and places. Whether or not these features

were as erosive as Boyd believed them to be, he was right about
the power of ugliness as a provocative quality, and of its ever-
changing nature. As Sydney changes, debates will continue as to
what constitutes the new form of Australian ugliness: whether it
be suburbs of McMansions, or the corridors of boxy apartment
buildings proliferating along suburban main roads.

However it is defined, there is something arresting about
ugliness that makes us pay attention. Ugly places disrupt the utopian
ideal of the ordered and beautiful city. The mystery of ugly places is
in their making us contemplate how they came into being, what kind
of ideals they represent, or what kind of processes might have caused
them to be the way they are. Sydney's ugliest buildings are enigmas,
around which dreams and desires for the city swirl.

SYDNEY MYSTERY STRUCTURES

Towers, offcuts & follies of the city & surrounds.

HARBOUR CONTROL

The harbour's all-seeing eye.

demolished 2016

NO SMOKING

The never-used chimney of the redundant-upon-completion power station in The Rocks.

ROAD TO NOWHERE

Abandoned Western Distributor on-ramp, a slice of road from nowhere to nowhere.

CIRCLE

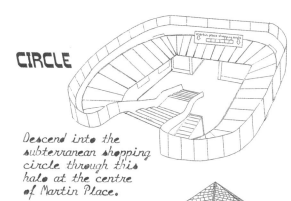

Descend into the subterranean shopping circle through this halo at the centre of Martin Place.

HANCOCK'S TOWER

demolished 1894

The city's first mystery structure, a watchtower where Robert Hancock was said to have imprisoned his wife.

BANDSTAND

Belmore Park bandstand, locked and caged.

MCKELL

What purpose serves these pebblecrete cylinders?

ISLAND

The Wattle Street Island, with enigmatic sealed centrepiece.

AQUEDUCT

Like a dinosaur skeleton, the Johnstons Creek Sewer Aqueduct extends across the valley.

ORNAMENT GRAVEYARD

Ruins of
the city past

by Kimio Tsuchiya.

PYRAMID

Pyramid Glasshouse,
Royal Botanic Gardens.

demolished 2015

GIFT TO
THE CITY

Thank John Frazer
for this monument
to thirst quenched
in the middle of
the street.

SCENT BOTTLE

Sewer vent disguised
as Cleopatra's Needle.

Named Thorton's Scent
Bottle after the
mayor in 1857.

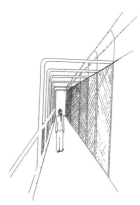

ELEVATED FOOTWAY

Cutler Footway, once a
tram line, now a precarious
ride on the 389 & a
skinny wooden footway.

UGLIEST
BUILDING

Goulburn Street Parking
Station, hovering above
the train tracks.

CENTENNIAL

Centennial Park yard
of mystery, elaborately
fenced, rarely traversed.

RESERVOIR

Petersham Water Tower,
proud as a temple at the
top of the hill.

TELSTRA

Bondi Junction
shrine to
telecommunications.

Turramurra is a suburb of gardens and tall trees, most often summarised as 'leafy' on the rare occasions it is mentioned in the media. It's a suburb I know well. As postwar migrants, my maternal grandparents made a choice between a block of land in Yagoona, in the city's south-west, or Turramurra, on the north shore. They chose Turramurra and lived there for the next fifty years, the rest of their lives. This choice saw me growing up with their home on Kissing Point Road as the nucleus of my life. It was a home of its time, a 1950s wooden cottage with a fibro extension my grandfather built himself in the 1970s. It had patterned carpet and flocked wallpaper and was filled with clocks. After he retired from his job in a university physics laboratory, my grandfather worked as watchmaker. At midday the clocks would strike out the hours in a chorus. I found this disruption comforting, imagining the house as a living thing, constantly ticking over.

Kissing Point Road runs south from the Pacific Highway, eventually ending in the bushland that surrounds the Lane Cove River. Its northern equivalent is Bobbin Head Road, which leads from the highway towards the Ku-ring-gai Chase National Park. It also had a feature from a romance novel, as it runs adjacent to the course of a waterway called Lover's Jump Creek. As far as I know there were no specific lovers and the creek was named, like many such Lover's Leaps, for its high rocks and waterfall. Despite this, as a child raised on Victorian-era novels about orphans and invalids,

I liked to imagine the lovers in their Sunday best, holding hands
a final time before they plunged into the waterhole below.

Bobbin Head Road also kindled my childhood imagination.
I knew the quaint word 'bobbin' from watching my mother at the
sewing machine and thought of the road like a thread unwinding
from a spool. The analogy fits: the road is long and winding, passing
by house after house. Then the houses stop and there's a golf course
and retirement villages, a rehabilitation hospital and a high school.
It ends in the bushland of Ku-ring-gai Chase National Park, which
forms the northern boundary of Sydney. The name Ku-ring-gai
is a version of Guringai, the name used for the language spoken
by the Aboriginal people whose country is north of the harbour.
The name Turramurra is a version of Terramerregal, the clan
whose country this is.

It has been a long time since I've travelled along Bobbin Head
Road but the scene is immediately familiar. Though the old cottages
are gradually being replaced by larger homes, change comes slowly
to Turramurra. It's the trees I notice most. In late winter the
camellias are in full bloom and the magnolia trees have flowered.
White cockatoos weigh the branches of liquidambar trees, nibbling
at the conkers before shrieking off to their next destination.

One of the final buildings on Bobbin Head Road is the dome-
shaped hall in the grounds of Ku-ring-gai High School, a pale grey
bubble that looks like a stranded UFO. During the 1970s a number
of these domes – named 'binishells' after their Italian designer, Dante
Bini – were built in NSW government schools. Their construction
became occasions for curiosity due to the unusual method used.
A thin layer of wet concrete was poured over a circular slab laid with
plastic and springs, and then quickly inflated while still wet to form
the dome. The structures attracted controversy when two binishells
built at Sydney high schools collapsed, one during construction in
Fairfield in 1975 and then another in Mona Vale in 1986, minutes
after students had left the hall. The rest of the state's binishells were
reinforced after these collapses, and the Ku-ring-gai binishell is still
here, emerging like a concrete blister among the pine trees.

There's an isolated mood to this part of North Turramurra.

It is completely surrounded by bushland, a strip of suburbia only a few streets deep before it becomes forest. Bobbin Head Road continues only a short way past the school before it stops at the gates to the national park, which are marked by stone pillars and a small tollbooth.

On entering the park there is an immediate shift as the atmosphere of the bush replaces that of the suburban landscape. Before the land that has now become the north-shore suburbs was cleared for colonial settlement, it would have looked much like this: eucalypts and woodlands, creeks and sandstone outcrops. There are walking tracks through the park and picnic areas here and there, but most of the land is forest. It's an overcast day and there is no one else in sight as I walk down the path to the right of the gates. I have only the birds and the wind in the trees for company. Here and there hot-pink ribbons tied to the tree branches mark out an orienteering trail through the bush, their artificial colour striking against the green.

A little way along the path the sphinx becomes visible, rising from a shelf of sandstone in the centre of an amphitheatre. The tremendous carved stone head has thick lips and deep-set eyes, giving it a serene but disquieting expression. Black paint or oil has run down its face and seeped into the stone, adding to this sense of unease. These dark trails, probably a work of vandalism, gives the sphinx a post-apocalyptic look.

Two small stone pyramids sit to either side of the sphinx, with a few plastic memorial wreaths resting against them. The sphinx is a war memorial and was carved in the 1920s by First World War veteran William Shirley. Shirley was a patient at the nearby Lady Davidson Hospital, which at the time housed ex-servicemen suffering from tuberculosis, and was bored by the usual convalescent occupations of leatherwork, basket-making or gardening. He had been a stonemason before becoming a soldier and missed practising his trade, which he was now too weak to resume. Hospital staff, on discovering a promising block of sandstone, suggested to Shirley that he might carve it into a model of the Great Sphinx of Giza as a memorial to his war comrades. Although Shirley had served on the Western Front, he was part of the 13th battalion that had been previously based in Egypt. Over two years he worked on the sculpture whenever his health allowed it. The sphinx slowly took shape and word of his tribute spread. When the *Sydney Herald* came to interview him in 1924 Shirley was humble about his project, saying, 'I have just been filling in my spare time…one has to do something'.

William Shirley's health remained poor, and he lived for only a few years after completing the sphinx. It is an enigmatic presence in the bushland, sitting alone in its stone lair as the creatures in the surrounding forest rustle the leaves. Occasionally the sphinx is the focus for memorial services attracting wreaths and bright-red artificial poppies. More often it presents its mysterious smile to people heading out into the walking tracks through the park, and then again on their return.

The amphitheatre, steps and pyramids form an unexpected geometry, a stage set in waiting. The sphinx faces the mainmast of a ship, the HMAS *Adelaide*, which has been erected in front of the amphitheatre as if the entire vessel might be buried underneath. Standing in front of the sphinx, I wait for it to test me with its riddle. No message transpires but a memory does, of a place not far away, about halfway back along Bobbin Head Road. When I was a child my parents would drive past it, knowing how the place fascinated me, but I've not seen it since. I farewell the sphinx, compelled to find it.

I turn off Bobbin Head Road, guided by my memory. After a few detours I am successful. It was the pyramids on either side of the sphinx that had made me think of this house, an anomaly amid an otherwise unremarkable residential street. Shaped like two adjoining pyramids, the house rises up from behind a grassy mound, a pair of steep-sided structures clad in dark roof tiles with a long, low annexe. It's a house utterly unlike its neighbours, or any other in the suburb – perhaps any other in the city. The pyramids are all tile, no windows, giving the whole place a furtive appearance. Nevertheless it has the trappings of a suburban home – a hatchback in the driveway and mail poking out of the letterbox.

Places like the pyramid house taught me early that mysterious details were everywhere, there for the noticing, even in the quietest suburbs. A network of unusual houses overlaid my mental map of Sydney so powerfully that I still look out for them now, thirty years later. Driving down towards the Spit Bridge, for instance, I watch for the moment the Spaceship House comes into view. The house perches on the steep hillside above Middle Harbour. One room bulges out, a concrete and glass bubble that brings to mind a James Bond villain's lair. I can only imagine that, inside it, people are wearing lurid flared pantsuits, drinking cocktails and plotting world domination. A less conspicuous but still unusual house is on Edgeware Road in Enmore. The Skinny House is a house-in-miniature tucked in-between two of regular size. It may or may not be the narrowest house in Sydney, but it is the most meticulously decorated of tiny houses, with steep tiled front steps and a little balcony trimmed with iron lace. I think of it as a dollhouse, full of miniature things.

People live their everyday lives in these houses as I do in mine, but these houses promise a different kind of everyday. They have an energy about them, a twist in time and space. As a child growing up in a suburban landscape they became my talismans, and I am still led by their sense of mystery into thoughts of other worlds, and all that the city shows and hides.

windsor

Sunday drives here to go swimming in the river & visit "Australiana Village".

When we lived here Sydney felt far far away, our house was an island

kenthurst

my room

I liked to climb up this.

"Ned Kelly", the cockatoo at Hargreaves Nursery.

Galston Gorge

"hairpin turns"

Powerline terror! I saw a report on A Current Affair & afterwards they terrified me. I'd shiver when we drove underneath them.

The shops at 'Round Corner' - ruffled dresses in the fancy dress hire.

dural

library. second favourite place to be besides my room.

Horse-riding, Soul-searching.

I'd ride a toothless horse called "Coffee". One day my dad forgot to pick me up afterwards & I started to walk home: I felt like a storybook orphan.

pennant hills

Pizza Hut, and Kentucky Fried Chicken (with rotating drum sign) here, and Waitara McDonalds (with train themed decor) - culinary highlights.

FOX VALLEY ROAD
Lucinda Avenue
COMENARRA PARKWAY
KISSING POINT ROAD

The first house I lived in red shag carpet the garden ended in a cliff.

view of the faraway city

blacktown

drive-in cinema Star Wars / E.T. double feature. Preview for Poltergeist terrifies me.

Frank the bear at Macquarie University. My grandfather took me to visit him.

Saw 'Return to Oz' in an old cinema which seemed like a castle.

parramatta

Mostly unknown lands lie south of the harbour - apart from visiting relatives at Chester Hill or Burwood, a visit to the children's hospital at Camperdown, an eisteddfod at Toongabbie and other, now forgotten excursions.

limit of maps

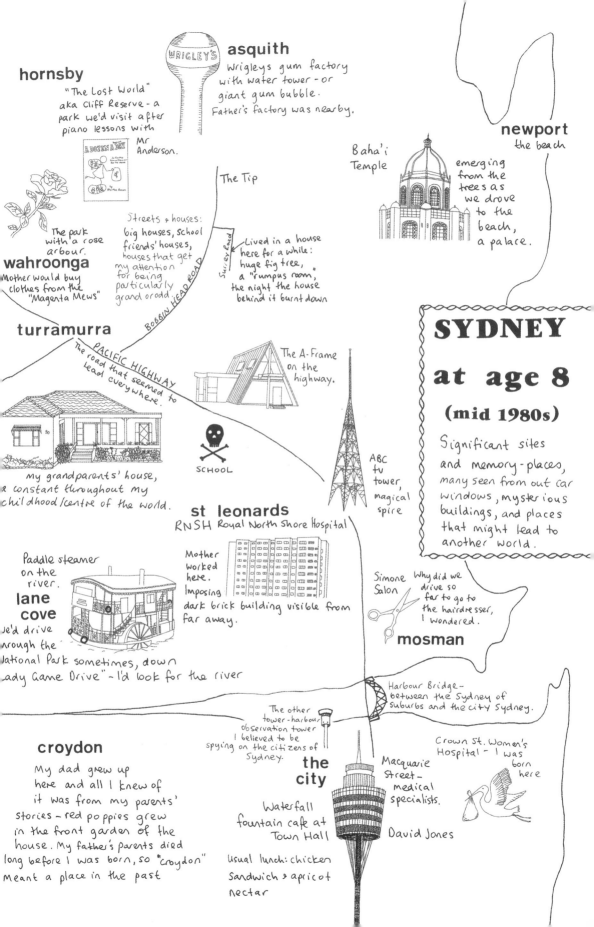

hornsby

"The Lost World" aka Cliff Reserve - a park we'd visit after piano lessons with Mr Anderson.

A DOZEN A DAY

asquith

Wrigleys gum factory with water tower - or giant gum bubble. Father's factory was nearby.

WRIGLEY'S

newport
the beach

emerging from the trees as we drove to the beach, a palace.

Baha'i Temple

The Tip

The park with a rose arbour.

wahroonga
Mother would buy clothes from the "Magenta Mews"

Streets & houses: big houses, school friends' houses, houses that get my attention for being particularly grand or odd

BOBBIN HEAD ROAD

Surrey Road

Lived in a house here for a while: huge fig tree, a "rumpus room", the night the house behind it burnt down

turramurra

PACIFIC HIGHWAY
The road that seemed to lead everywhere.

The A-Frame on the highway.

SCHOOL

ABC tv tower, magical spire

SYDNEY
at age 8
(mid 1980s)

Significant sites and memory-places, many seen from out car windows, mysterious buildings, and places that might lead to another world.

my grandparents' house, a constant throughout my childhood / centre of the world.

st leonards
RNSH Royal North Shore Hospital

Mother worked here. Imposing dark brick building visible from far away.

Paddle steamer on the river.

lane cove
We'd drive through the National Park sometimes, down "Lady Game Drive" - I'd look for the river

Simone Salon

Why did we drive so far to go to the hairdresser, I wondered.

mosman

Harbour Bridge - between the Sydney of suburbs and the city Sydney.

The other tower - harbour observation tower I believed to be spying on the citizens of Sydney.

croydon

My dad grew up here and all I knew of it was from my parents' stories - red poppies grew in the front garden of the house. My father's parents died long before I was born, so "croydon" meant a place in the past

the city

Waterfall fountain cafe at Town Hall

Usual lunch: chicken sandwich & apricot nectar

Macquarie Street - medical specialists.

David Jones

Crown St. Women's Hospital - I was born here

The landscape of Milperra Road as it passes through Revesby and Milperra is made up of warehouses, parched lawns and signs for Hungry Jacks and McDonald's speared into the roadside. It's an industrial zone that sells equipment and parts, things for making other things. It's also a place where objects are recirculated. At the edge of Bankstown Airport is Pickles Auctions, with warehouses and storage yards that contain objects in transition, the repossessed, the abandoned and the lost.

Above the customer car park at the back of Pickles, tiny Cessnas quiver their way towards the runway in the next field. They cross overhead and then over a graveyard of burnt-out and damaged vehicles. It's hard to imagine these blackened truck cabins and mangled sports cars being bought by anyone, but auction houses reveal how almost anything can be useful or desirable.

Today is the viewing for one of the irregularly held auctions of unclaimed lost property from the Sydney Trains network. Items that have languished in the Central Station lost property office for too long are on display: the mobile phones, earrings, skateboards, cameras and musical instruments that no one has come in search of. It's an auction with a mythology. Those who have been speak of the plenitude of laptops and mobile phones, and of the intimate things lost and then unsearched for, like false teeth and wedding rings.

A procession of auction viewers follows the path to a warehouse. Inside, tables and cabinets have been set up around the perimeter to display the lost objects, which are divided into lots: a pallet of prams shrink-wrapped into one lumpy block, skateboards neatly arranged into sets of five. One of these skateboards is decorated with thick plastic stickers peeled from train carriages: 'keep clear of moving doors' and 'please vacate this seat for elderly or less mobile passengers'. Karma, perhaps, for it to end up here, between a box of yoga mats and an arrangement of fishing rods.

'How could you leave something like *that* on a train?' people say, staring at the guitars and sets of golf clubs. There's a crowd around the mobile phone cabinet, where groups of five iPhones have been bundled together with rubber bands as if they were misaddressed mail. There are thousands of mobile phones, escapees from pockets and bags, now presented en masse in a glass display cabinet. People peer eagerly in at the rows of dead black screens. Some are hoping for a bargain, others are shocked by the abundance.

As long as there have been trains, things have been left behind on them. Now, the items most commonly left behind are phones, but in the 1940s it was gloves. Back then, five hundred pairs of women's gloves made their way to the Sydney lost property office of the tramways and railways every month. Despite such differences, a1909 description of lost items from the railways is much the same as the lots offered in contemporary auctions:

Apparel of all kinds, from hats to socks and boots may be seen there; watches and chains, and more or less valuable trinkets of every description; whole forests of walking-sticks, umbrellas and parasols innumerable...bags and purses, tools of trade and domestic utensils...

In these early reports of lost property there is a familiar disbelief at the number and range of objects left behind, and a pleasure in listing the more unlikely examples. In 1909 the *Evening News* reflected that 'no one would think that so bulky an article as a shovel could be conveniently mislaid by its owner'. In 2010, the *Sydney Morning Herald* reported a similar sense of bewilderment about a fibreglass boat in that year's lost property auction. The auction manager had no explanation, only commenting that it was 'more the sort of thing you would row out to' than leave on a train.

Although it was more likely left on railway property than on the
train itself, such sensible suggestions are left out of media reports.
It is much more satisfying to think of the boat squeezed into a train
carriage and then abandoned.

Like the odd objects recovered from creeks and parks on
the annual Clean Up Australia Day, things left behind on trains
are fragments of stories that will forever remain obscure. After
Clean Up Australia Day, similar lists of unusual lost items emerge,
whether a church cash box found at the bottom of a creek or a bridal
veil twisted up in the mud of a mangrove swamp. Like these stray
things, the phones, jewellery and musical instruments at auction
have dropped out of people's lives. Most of them, I assume, escaped
in moments of forgetfulness or absent-mindedness, but as I will
never know for sure it is easy to embroider a fictional backstory.
The silver ring in the shape of a rabbit was a love token discarded
in an argument; the melodeon was left behind by the singer of an
indie-pop band after her first ever gig, the excitement of getting
through it making her forgetful. On and on, each item can be
attached to some kind of story.

Next to the copious iPhones in the cabinet are two stacks of vinyl
records, one topped with Nana Mouskouri's *20 Solid Gold Hits*, the
other with the soundtrack to *On Golden Pond*. Closer inspection of
the LP spines reveals Tchaikovsky, Val Doonigan, Transvision Vamp
and the perennial op shop LP favourite, Phil Collins. The records,
perhaps due to their vintage status, are behind glass in the display
case. The more disposable media, CDs and DVDs, are stacked in
boxes. I look over the barrier into the box of DVDs and see that the
disc on top of the pile is a copy of *The Great Escape*, a fitting title to be
the ringleader of DVDs that have parted ways with their owners.

Seal-top bags full of earrings and watches fill another cabinet,
along with cameras a man inspects one by one. Some of those
viewing are serious buyers writing lot numbers in small, spiral-bound
notebooks. Others are merely curious to see what the forgetful have
mislaid. A gangly guy in a Teenage Mutant Ninja Turtles T-shirt
takes notes as he examines the prints and paintings, which fill six
tables. Bush landscapes and English villages, lacquered puzzles of

world landmarks, a framed poster from the 1980s warning against the perils of improper film classification: it is hard to imagine how anyone could leave such items behind, unless perhaps they were deliberately abandoning them.

On top of one of the pallets in the book section is a novel with a Bookcrossing sticker on it, indicating it was left behind intentionally, as part of the movement that releases books in public places for strangers to find. Its incarceration in the lost property office was probably not the intention of whoever set free the novel *Daughter of the Crocodile* by Duncan Sprott, with its outlandish stories of the pharaohs. Looking up its tracking number on the Bookcrossing website reveals that it had last been discovered on the Sea Princess cruise ship near New Zealand. Despite its lost property incarceration, it at least got to see something of the world first.

Some objects do nothing but inspire speculation as to how they came to be here. Not claiming a phone or a Nana Mouskouri record is a reasonable thing to do. Leaving a pair of skis behind forever seems more unlikely. Other objects are surprising in their multitude, like the many hundreds of bikes with rusty chains and deflated wheels. People walk from table to table, wondering and discussing. The number of musical instruments is perplexing to one man, whose demeanour of wonder suggests that this is his first lost property auction. His friend, obviously more experienced with the methods by which musical instruments might be disposed of, isn't surprised. 'Ditch the violin, don't need to go to lessons anymore,' he scoffs.

Most of the objects left behind are forlorn things of minuscule value, wisps of clothing, uncomfortable high heels, sagging handbags. Browsers file past, examining the contents of the boxes, quickly assessing their worth to be minimal. A young man with a wispy beard pauses by a box filled with all kinds of headwear and picks up a top hat. He holds it for a moment, a meditative expression on his face, before placing it back with the rest of its kind.

More than the objects up for sale themselves, it is the dream world they evoke in those who inspect them that makes the lost property auction compelling. Looking across the forest of umbrellas, each neatly tagged with a cardboard label stating the date and station where it was found, I think of them as a year's sum of rainy days. Rain is capricious in Sydney, often appearing in short, intense downpours, easy to forget after it has swept through, and to forget your umbrella with it. There are tartan umbrellas, umbrellas with duck-head handles, umbrellas with pink frills and polka dots, all bundled together in a cluster of nylon and metal. I wonder what buyer might find a use for these hundreds of mismatched umbrellas being sold as one lot.

As in every big city, a tide of objects circulates through Sydney, changing as technologies and fashions evolve. The city's auction houses hold objects paused on the borderline of insignificance. Here their worth is measured, and they will go on to redemption or oblivion. This could be a microcosm of the city as a whole, where places and memories are constantly falling in and out of notice and importance as cycles of stagnation and change continue.

Rows of white plastic lawn chairs have been arranged in preparation for tomorrow's auction. The next morning the room will fill with bidders, and by the end of the day buyers will have been found for the boxes of sunglasses and bags of silver jewellery. The skateboards will find riders, and the clarinets, flutes and ukuleles will sound out notes again. As these objects are returned to use, the storage rooms under the sandstone arches of Central Station will begin to gather new collections of lost things.

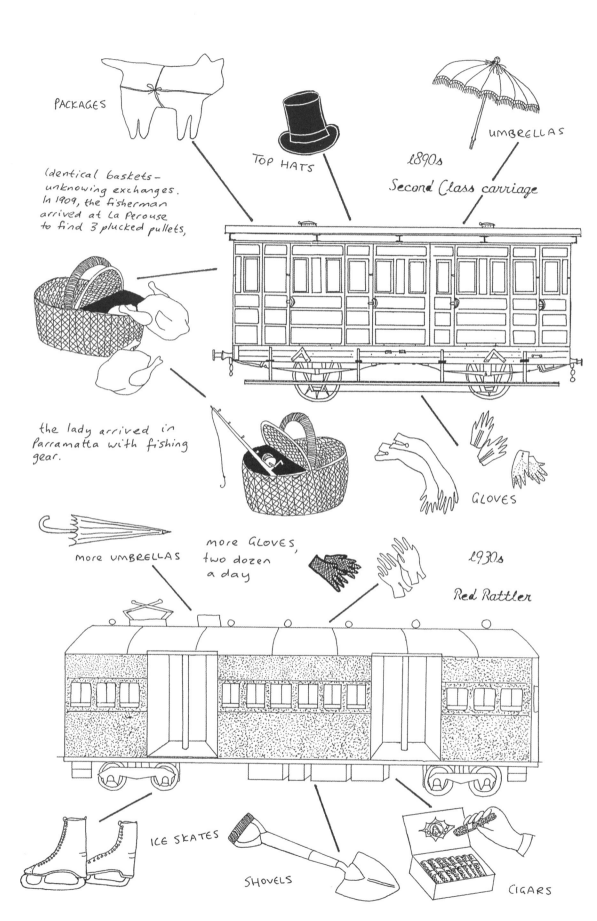

PACKAGES

TOP HATS

UMBRELLAS

1890s

Second Class carriage

Identical baskets—
unknowing exchanges.
In 1909, the fisherman
arrived at La Perouse
to find 3 plucked pullets,

the lady arrived in
Parramatta with fishing
gear.

GLOVES

more UMBRELLAS

more GLOVES,
two dozen
a day

1930s

Red Rattler

ICE SKATES

SHOVELS

CIGARS

LOST PROPERTY

on Sydney trains

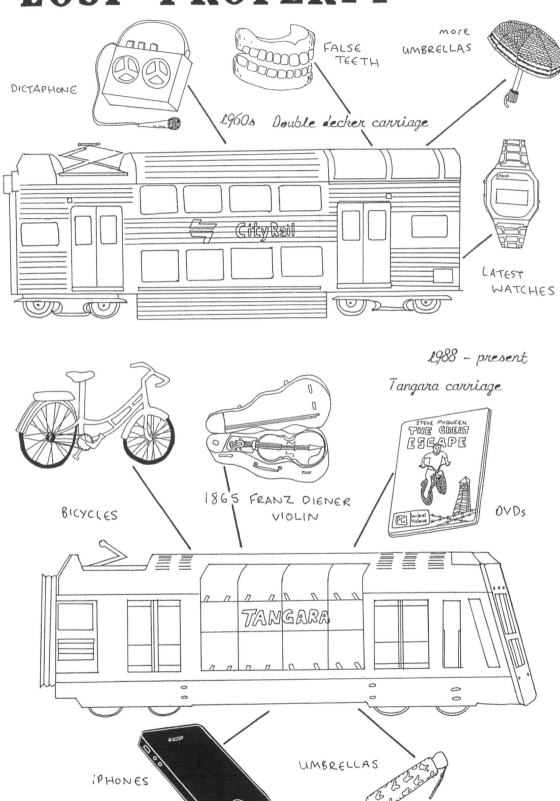

DICTAPHONE

FALSE TEETH

more UMBRELLAS

1960s Double decker carriage

CityRail

LATEST WATCHES

1988 – present

Tangara carriage

BICYCLES

1865 FRANZ DIENER VIOLIN

STEVE McQUEEN
THE GREAT ESCAPE

PG low level violence

DVDs

TANGARA

iPHONES

UMBRELLAS

COLLECTIONS AND NETWORKS

Think of everything that makes up a city like Sydney. The land underlying it, the hills and valleys and waterways, then the buildings and the infrastructure, the roads and the railways. Then the living beings which animate the urban scene, the people, the animals, the trees. Then think of the details in between, all the layers, all the particulars, intricate and ever-changing.

This is a practically impossible exercise. Cities are complex entities, made up of details in unlimited abundance. Some are strongly present and recognised as essential parts of the city's identity, while others are less distinct or noticeable. No matter their prominence, details are the key to the patterns and networks which overlay and underlie Sydney. Becoming attuned to these specifics brings the city into a different kind of life. House names, ghost signs, scribbly gum trees, water towers, vacant lots – look for them and they appear with surprising frequency. Tunnels, letterboxes, factories, substations, red-brick apartment blocks, all such details can form a collection, or become clues to some kind of network.

Some of the city's networks are irrevocably part of the landscape, so often used they are barely considered. The light switches we flick, the taps we turn and the water that we watch disappearing down the drain are actions connected to a city-wide order of pipes and wires. Other networks are more obscure or ephemeral, but no matter how minor the detail, there is the potential to connect it to some kind of system.

Past versions of the city are preserved in a network of traces.
I used to often walk past some old graffiti on a low brick wall in
Annandale, painted in an uneven hand:

18 trucks with 200 cops
Passed this spot at 12:00 midnight 1.2.77
Taking, sneaking uranium to white bay
What more can I say?

Reading over this graffiti I'd imagine the convoy sneaking down
Johnston Street, people in their beds asleep and unaware except for,
perhaps, the one who came out to paint this on the wall. The faded
words open out into other details: the green-bans murals in
Woolloomooloo; the faded *STOP* of anti-Vietnam War graffiti from
the 1970s, still just visible on the sandstone wall that leads to the
Opera House; or signs by the roadside declaring a particular council
areas to be a 'nuclear-free zone'. In such details a network of protest
and activism is visible across the city.

Every map chooses its details. One often-reproduced bird's-eye
map of Sydney from 1888 presents the city from above, looking down
from the north side of the harbour. It shows the struggle between the
rectilinear and the organic that shapes the network of streets. It shows
the gardens and the wharves, the headlands and the warehouses.
But most of all it shows the smoke. From each steamship funnel and
factory chimney a wisp of black smoke emerges, their trails leaning
westwards. The drifts of smoke are softer than the clearly defined
lines of shores and structures. It is a city of smokestacks, each one
neatly plotted with its escaping thread of vapour.

As with the smokestack map, specific versions of Sydney
are articulated through contemplation and a sense of distance.
Details lead to tangents, and it can be hard to follow them when
caught up in the rush of everyday life. But if there's anything
I have learnt from observing the Sydney suburbs, it is the radical
potential of taking notice. Noticing the details of places not
intended for scrutiny can transform and change our perception of
them: not only the place itself, but the idea of the city as a whole.

We see its undercurrents and hidden stories, and we see the forces that change the landscape around us.

Much of what makes up the city, and especially the suburbs, isn't intended for close examination. Highway landscapes slide by the car windows – warehouses, petrol stations and fast food restaurants on repeat. Yet there are always disruptions to order, details that hook, places that lodge in thought and imagination. Scrutinising these places and following their stories describes a Sydney of margins and edges, of criss-crossing identities, a city of atmospheres and ambiences.

SYDNEY BESTIARY

Sydney, like many cities, sustains an uneasy relationship with its animals. Many only come to our notice when they encroach upon the human realm. Every building has been at some time invaded by the big, glossy cockroaches which stir every summer, a shock to newcomers and residents alike. Many a quiet night has been disturbed by the sudden appearance of a huntsman spider from behind the curtains. Sometimes, however, the city's threatening beasts come in a more menacing form.

Feral Pigs Invade Sydney. A front-page news headline sounded the warning. The pigs were on the move, having already reached suburbs such as Hurstville, Pymble and even Hunters Hill, only nine kilometres from the central business district. They'd swum rivers and crossed roads, coming ever closer to the centre.

What could a pig want in the city? There must be something calling them forth, a magnetic pull towards their deity, the greatest Sydney pig of them all. This is the bronze boar Il Porcellino, reclining on a sandstone plinth on Macquarie Street. A hoary, tusked beast, perched on the edge of a wishing-well fountain, Il Porcellino is a copy of a sixteenth-century statue of a wild boar. The original sculpture, kept in the Uffizi Museum in Florence, has spawned many copies. Sydney's Il Porcellino is one in an urban porcine network, counting pigs in cities like Oslo, Dallas and Madrid among its many siblings.

Sydney's Porcellino has been in his position outside Sydney Hospital since 1968, when he was donated by the daughter of former hospital surgeon Thomas Fiaschi as a memorial and a symbol of friendship between Italy and Australia. His smooth brass snout glows like an oversized gold coin, kept shiny by the hands of those who rub it for luck as they pass by. To provide further good fortune, Il Porcellino guards a wishing well in the form of an oversized piggy bank set in the plinth below.

Further north along Macquarie Street there is another animal idol, a bronze cat perched on the sandstone window ledge outside the Mitchell Library. Its front paw is held aloft and eyes uplifted in an expression of feline attentiveness. Inside the library, on the other side of the windowpane, is a room containing hundreds of editions of *Don Quixote*. But it's to another character that this creature owes its fame. Nearby, a statue of Matthew Flinders looks sternly out towards Macquarie Street, grasping a sextant, his foot atop a coil of rope. As well as a navigator, Flinders was also a cat lover. He was so taken with his wily ship's cat that he wrote a book in his honour. *Trim: Being the True Story of a Brave Seafaring Cat* describes Trim's intelligence, bravery, sure-footedness at sea and his repertoire of tricks.

Like Il Porcellino, Trim has his wild suburban counterparts in ever-expanding suburban colonies of stray cats. They haunt the nocturnal city, their territory the car parks and alleys that people desert after sundown. Cutting through an Ashfield alleyway one evening I came across a tiny grey kitten eating a slice of pizza from a box, like an internet meme come to life. A motley assortment of other cats were assembled around, black and whites, a ginger, a tabby, errant pets now taken to the streets. They fixed their glares on me, a warning to come no closer. These are the strays that prowl the streets with eyes glowing, slinking through cracks in fences, slithering out of sight under cars.

Dogs too have a central-city icon. As Trim dwells in the shadow of Flinders' statue, so the terrier Islay resides with Queen Victoria, in the square outside the Queen Victoria Building. Pause at the edge of Islay's wishing well for a few moments and he will start to speak. To locals his voice is instantly recognisable as that of conservative talkback radio presenter John Laws. His abrupt 'Hello' has startled decades' worth of people who have chosen

Islay's fountain as their meeting place. The monument, a wishing well at the edge of a circular sandstone structure, was constructed to hide the air vent necessary for the car park below the Queen Victoria Building; an ornamental grille disguises it as a nineteenth-century folly.

Islay was Queen Victoria's favourite dog and his signature trick was to sit up on his hind legs and beg for treats. The Sydney Islay recreates this pose and, with Laws as his medium, requests we 'cast a coin' into the wishing well for the good of deaf and blind children. A moment passes, enough time to drop a coin into the fountain. 'Thank you,' says Islay, regardless of whether a coin is dropped in or not, then concludes with a few mechanical woofs.

Before the bronze Islay existed, a more unusual creature attracted Sydney's wishes, the coelacanth specimen on display in a tank in the ichthyology section of the Australian Museum. A coelacanth is a prehistoric fish thought to have been extinct until one was discovered off the coast of South Africa in the 1930s. The museum's coelacanth became the wishing fish when people started dropping coins into its tank through a gap in the case around it. Eventually the coins discoloured the water and the wishing had to cease, though the coelacanth is still on display, keeping to itself the secrets of the deepest oceans.

These city idols in their frozen postures are safely contained. Their real counterparts are less predictable. Creatures that attract notice are often those that highlight human intervention, whether by their presence or their absence. Introduced species are the most commonly encountered urban animals: the rats, myna birds, pigeons, rabbits and foxes that have infiltrated the suburbs. Others, like the ibis, are native creatures pushed out of their habitats. These birds have found in the city and its rubbish bins a replacement for the inland New South Wales wetlands that were once their breeding grounds. Resolutely unpopular, ibis stalk through Hyde Park stealing sandwiches, alarming picnickers, probing the overflowing bins with their long bills and being photographed by the tourists who haven't yet learned that it's not the done thing to admire the 'tip turkeys'.

Like stray cats, ibis occupy leftover scraps of land, in-between places that humans overlook. They map out intermediary zones, nesting in the corridors of trees beside railway lines or at the edges of vacant lots. One such place is a block of land on Parramatta Road in Auburn, beside a car park for a cinema complex and the concrete channel of Haslam's Creek. A crowd of ibis have taken over a low, wide bush and turned it into a nest. The ibis spend all day here, honking and shuffling their wings while the traffic surges past. Though the nest could seem temporary against the drab built environment surrounding it, perhaps it is the other way around. Sydney is now the province of the ibis, which will defy the hostility of the factories, highways and construction sites to find a place to nest.

Animal stories in Sydney are often tales of encroachment, of creatures in places where humans don't want them to be. A dead humpback whale washes up in the ocean pool at Newport beach. It slumps hugely against the concrete walls like a fallen dirigible, beautiful, horrible. Two water buffalo escape from the filming of a mobile phone advertisement in Sydney Park and charge up King Street before being corralled in a Camperdown front yard. Possums thunder over roofs with steps like clumsy burglars. Brush turkeys emerge from bushland, raking the ground with their claws, strutting assuredly across suburban streets on a mission to destroy careful garden landscaping. Other animals are more elusive, some to the point of myth. The Penrith Panther is one such beast, a black cat-like creature said to inhabit the western outskirts of Sydney. There are regular sightings but never any evidence conclusive enough to determine whether the panther is an oversized feral cat or a wildlife park escapee, or if it exists at all.

Despite attempts to control the more unruly creatures – spy cameras to track feral pigs, poisoned carrots to cull wild rabbits, golf buggies rigged up with speakers playing industrial noise to move colonies of flying foxes on – the city's animals are a constant presence. Even if the real creatures can be elusive or pushed towards the margins, their likenesses are everywhere.

Beasts gentle and fierce can be found in plentiful numbers in the Sydney suburbs, looking down from walls, guarding parklands.

Painted on the side of a furniture warehouse in Enfield, the art deco
former Savoy Theatre, is the face of a giant bear. It ogles the street
below with a cross-eyed look as if it has just been hit on the head
by a frying pan. In gardens across the city concrete lions guard the
gates to family homes. One Petersham household has taken this idea
further by installing life-size concrete figures of a lion and a tiger in
their otherwise stark front yard. From a terrain of woodchips these
creatures snarl at passers-by, guarding the house and their prey,
an unfortunate concrete wildebeest which lies slumped between
the tiger's paws.

Elephants are another of the often-encountered inhabitants
of Sydney's suburban zoo. In the Sir Joseph Banks Pleasure
Gardens in Botany a trio of them troops across the parkland,
life-size sculptures made of wire panels and aluminium tubing as
if they have sprung to life from fences and playground equipment.
A smaller playground elephant lives in the Franklyn Street park
in Glebe, its red paint chipped from years of clambering children,
its tail a dangling length of chain. They have also been found at
another kind of playground, one of discarded objects: for many
years an elephant silhouette gambolled across the awning above
Chatswood's legendary junk store, The White Elephant. This great
barn of a store was a treasure trove for op-shoppers in search of first
edition comics, Astrakhan coats and mystery objects people could
not even imagine until they came across them.

The city's stories of real elephants are, like many tales of these
large, complaisant creatures, bittersweet. They were used for
entertainment, like the elephants that carried countless children
on rides through Taronga Zoo until the 1970s. Elephants were
also used for publicity purposes. In 1932 Australia's premier circus
company, Wirth's, set up a stunt in which a group of elephants
crossed the newly opened Harbour Bridge. Riding on their backs
were men in striped military jackets who paid a special toll of two
pence per elephant, a discount from the sixpence toll for cars.
The Robur Tea Company also used a Wirth elephant for publicity
purposes. Draped in a branded rug, the elephant made a tour of
Robur Tea Rooms from Maroubra to the city. Here photos were

taken: the elephant, her trunk in a giant teacup, sharing a table with two nervous-looking gentlemen in suits and ties; the elephant lurching through the front door, past the tiny wooden elephants created in her likeness in the window display.

Even though the age of circus elephants has passed, they remain a presence in the city's mythology, like the persistent story of the elephant buried somewhere underneath Sydney Park. The elephant has become the park's good luck charm, like the shoes and cat skeletons that were once bricked into houses to ward off evil spirits. The fate of Wirth's most famous elephant, Princess Alice, is another abiding tale, as it is said she is buried in the grounds of Ocean View, the Wirth's mansion in Coogee.

Although animal encounters in Sydney often occur when creatures intervene in the human realm, there are a few places which are unmistakably their domain. Here and there, as with the ibis nests, the animals have chosen where they want to be. In Parramatta, behind the Cumberland Hospital and alongside the river, there is a colony of grey-headed flying foxes. They hang in the branches of the pine trees and eucalypts, chittering and clucking, looking down with black, beady eyes.

I walk down to the water's edge. The river is shallow here and a concrete weir spans it. The flying foxes provide unusual company. There are thousands of them above me in the trees, in constant rustle and chitter and restless movement. Every so often one takes flight, stretching its translucent, leathery wings. Although the hospital grounds are close by, this is a non-human place, where the order of the flying foxes prevails.

Flying foxes are a familiar sight in the skies on summer nights. Their black shapes look as if pieces of shadow have detached from the dark and are slowly drifting above the rooftops. Sometimes I pick out one of them and watch it until it disappears from view. Although it slips beyond my vision I know it continues to travel, above and across the houses and gardens, the apartment buildings and factories, the cars stopped at traffic lights and the people sitting on their back steps smoking, the stray cats out exploring and the possums in the trees – everything that makes up the city.

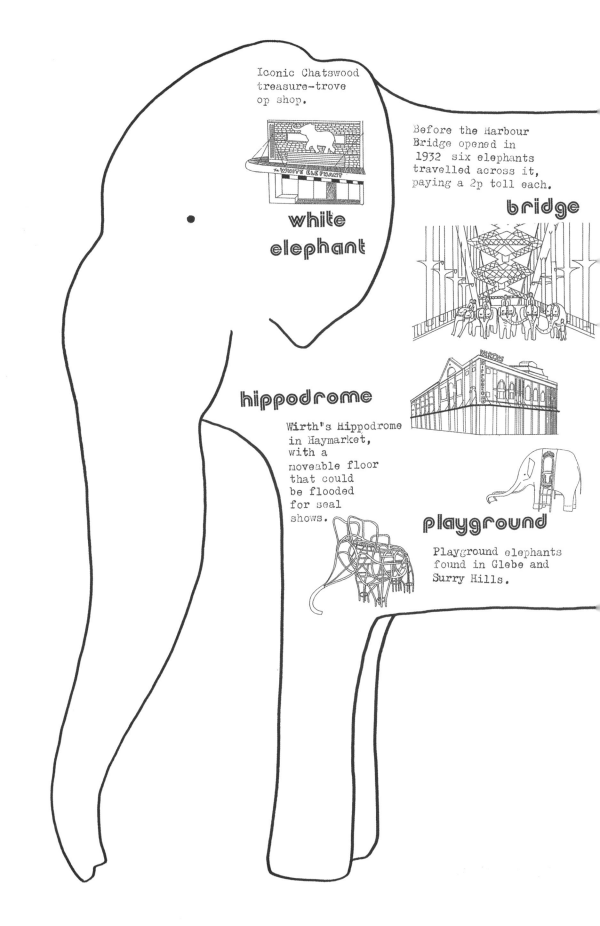

Iconic Chatswood treasure-trove op shop.

white elephant

Before the Harbour Bridge opened in 1932 six elephants travelled across it, paying a 2p toll each.

bridge

hippodrome

Wirth's Hippodrome in Haymarket, with a moveable floor that could be flooded for seal shows.

playground

Playground elephants found in Glebe and Surry Hills.

zoo

The old elephant temple – now they live in a cubist concrete mansion.

park

In Willoughby, Hallstrom Park adventure playground, based on Taronga Zoo, with stone elephant & 'musicosaurus'.

tea party

The Robur elephant on a tearoom tour in 1939. In the George Street tea room...

... and in Maroubra, at Bussell Bros. Grocers.

princess alice

Wirth's Circus' most famous elephant, star of Tamarama Wonderland

robur

skeleton

Buried in Sydney Park?

Life-size elephants at the Sir Joseph Banks Pleasure Gardens in Botany, site of Sydney's first zoo.

sydney elephants

pleasure gardens

SUBURBAN TIME

In 1983 the usually calm south Sydney suburb of Oatley was caught up in the fervour of anniversary celebrations. Through September and October, festivities grew in intensity: a family bush dance, a 'pageant of bridal gowns', a three-day bowling carnival and a regatta on the Georges River near the Pleasure Grounds. Then came the Clock Festival, the penultimate event in celebration of the 150 years of Oatley's identity as a suburb. Onlookers crowded the streets to watch a parade of floats representing the swimming club, the cub scouts and local businesses. Incongruous scenes paraded by, kids waving from inside a tent set up on top of a Land Rover, flanked by women in mob caps and frilled gowns riding pushbikes.

The nucleus of the celebration was the newly constructed brick tower in the middle of Frederick Street. Set inside the tower was a clock, a monument in commemoration of the suburb's namesake, watchmaker James Oatley. Oatley had in 1814 been found guilty of stealing two feather mattresses and sent to Australia. Like many convicts with specialist trades, his skills were useful and he soon became the colony's first Keeper of Clocks. It was a position of responsibility. Only the wealthy had watches of their own, and for most people it was public clocks that marked out the days.

Oatley is one of Sydney's middle-ring suburbs, built around three headlands on the Georges River. It is Biddegal country and a meeting place where the Georges and Woronora Rivers join. Two of the headlands are built up with housing, but the third is

a bushland park which retains some of the original vegetation:
the thick red trunks of angophoras, tall bloodwoods with rough grey
bark, old man banksias. Paths wind through the trees and rocky
outcrops. Near the baths on the eastern side of the headland is a
structure built as part of an unemployment relief scheme during
the Great Depression. Often these schemes were set up to construct
roads or pathways, but they sometimes included recreational
structures, like the series of concrete grottoes in Cooper Park in
Bellevue Hill that appear throughout the landscape like hollowed-
out ant hills. Here in Oatley a small sandstone castle was built as
a picnic shelter. Its roof is lined with battlements and it has high,
arched entrances leading to the picnic tables and barbeques inside,
a very suburban kind of fortress.

Since the festival in 1983 the clock has been the centrepiece and
symbol of Oatley. Driving into the suburb, past the disused bowling
greens and over the single-lane bridge that crosses the railway
tracks, I come across a sign pointing to the village centre. Its vinyl
letters are curled from decades of sunlight but the pun is legible.
Beside a cartoon image of the clock it reads 'Time to Visit', with an
arrow pointing to the turnoff.

In the town centre I note details that seem to have changed little
from the days of the clock festival: the amber glass lanterns on Oatley
Cellars, a 'gourmet shoppe' with photographs of Amsterdam canal
houses on the walls, a bakery with jam rolls and finger buns in the
window like a CWA cookbook come to life.

The clock is on its own island, in the middle of the road that
bisects the village green. Beside it a man is sharpening knives on a
wheel mounted on the back of his motorbike, the grating sound of
steel against stone rising from the machine. Then another sound
arises, a peal of electronic bells. It's the clock, chiming for 12:30.
It sounds for all the world like there is someone inside the brick
clocktower playing a tune on an electronic organ, and I imagine
a Sesame Street-style count in a cape seated behind a keyboard.

Despite its monumental aspirations, the Oatley clock looks to
have been assembled from fragments of the surrounding suburb.
The clock face is a modest white circle with Roman numerals for

the hours. The tower has a corrugated metal roof and iron lace panelling. At the back is a surprisingly ordinary door with a round aluminium doorknob, providing access for maintenance and daylight-saving switchovers. Protecting it is a screen door locked with a padlock, a later addition after vandals invaded the tower and destroyed the computers that controlled the mechanisms and chimes. A local welding business installed the door, taking it upon themselves to defend the clock against all future attacks. Thus fortified, the clock has kept good time ever since.

Sydney's suburban clocks are a unifying presence and a popular civic monument. No matter what other differences might divide people, time is a constant. A newspaper report in 1954 proclaimed Sydney as a city where 'you are rarely out of earshot or eyesight of a clock'. It described the largest – the clock on the Shell Building in Wynyard Square, almost six metres in diameter – and the most unusual. This, the article declared, was the Paddington Town Hall clock, which has letters instead of numbers to mark the hours. They spell out the message EDVARDUS THE VII, in commemoration of King Edward's coronation in 1902.

Once I began to take notice I found clocks everywhere, on council buildings and post offices, in train stations and on old factories. Many of these are utilitarian, but others have distinct personalities. The Fairfield civic clock, high up on its spindly legs, looks as if it is about to scuttle away. The war memorial clock at Little Bay is housed in a square tower like a suburban Big Ben. In Hornsby the sloshing water clock churns and hoots like a steampunk monster.

In Gladesville there is a plentiful supply of civic clocks. One occupies its own concrete island at the centre of an intersection. Unlike the Oatley clock it is a humble structure which has never had a festival in its honour. This clock is encased in a short, brick tower like a spike for a giant game of quoits. Another clock resides a few hundred metres away, at the centre of a town square of jacaranda trees and picnic tables. The clock, a plain black-and-white disc, is set high up on top of a metal pole. At its base is a plaque for the time capsule that was interred underneath in 1986. The capsule is due to be opened in 2036, revealing, no doubt, the newspapers, floppy discs and paper currency that passed as everyday objects only fifty years earlier.

Time capsules are messages from a self-conscious past, a combination of humility and hubris. The objects inside them are collected together as a way of imagining the future as much as speaking to it. There are time capsules embedded all over Sydney, in public buildings, civic plazas, universities and especially in schools. No schoolkid escaped the 1980s without being tasked to write a message to the children of the future, and to imagine the world of food pills, telepathic communication and hovercraft into which their letters would be received.

The Gladesville time capsule clock awaits the future, while other clocks are stuck in the past. Among these the post office clocks of Burwood (9:30) and Newtown (3:45) are notoriously frozen in time. In contrast to the celebratory descriptions of civic clocks from the 1950s, stories of neglect are now more likely to appear in the news. Surf club clocks, post office clocks and church clocks are among the wound-down and stopped casualties.

Clocks are animate objects that require our care, and through this relationship they take on a sense of humanity. Sydney's stopped clocks are obstinate things. They are symbols of forgetting and of apathy, all the states in which time slips away. There is no contemporary equivalent of James Oatley, Keeper of Clocks, who has the keys to the tower trapdoors and can reanimate the stalled mechanisms.

One afternoon, waiting to cross the street in Redfern, I looked up at the post office clocktower. The tower is a local landmark, an ornate cream and red brick construction with a copper dome. Australia Post had long left the building for smaller and more utilitarian premises, and with no one maintaining it the clock had fallen into disrepair. Rather than having stopped, however, this clock had sped up and was out of control. The minute hand moved quickly around the dial so that an hour went by in the space of a minute. I watched it as it raced through one o'clock, then two, then three, and onwards like the clock in H.G. Wells' *The Time Machine* as the Time Traveller drives the machine towards the future.

Times are changing in Redfern. The shops on the main street are now cafés and bars. The corner store with faded packets of paper towels piled up to the ceiling is gone, and Botany Road has become an epicentre for mid-century modern furniture showrooms. These smaller changes occur in the shadow of much larger ones, with public housing and community land in Redfern and Waterloo threatened by redevelopment. The Block, the heart of the Aboriginal community in central Sydney, has been the site of protests against the proposed changes. A tent embassy, behind tall white letters spelling out 'Sovereignty Never Ceded', protested for more than a year until Aboriginal housing was included in the new development. Now the camp has been packed up and the land where it was is a bare lawn backed by a long wall painted with the red, yellow and black of the Aboriginal flag.

Around the corner from The Block, on the bridge across from Redfern station, is another mural, one of the city's most enduring. Artist Carol Ruff led a group of artists and community members to paint the mural in 1983, along the brick wall above the railway tracks. Behind it the city buildings in the distance seem to float, distant and disconnected, peripheral to the mural scenes of footprints, figures, and the curves of the rainbow snake. Two lines of text, lines from a song by Joe Geia of the band No Fixed Address, remind all who pass by of the identity of this land:

40,000 years is a long time. 40,000 years still on my mind.

TIME TO VISIT

OATLEY

Kameygal land
on the Georges (Tucoerah) River.

Clocks everywhere

The Clock
Butchery

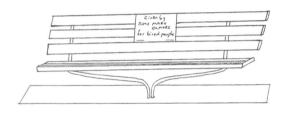

The commemorative
postmark.

At Oatley Park,
the seat donated
by Dame Mary
Gilmore "for
tired people".

star of the
$10 note.

The bowling
club badge

Hands set
at the time
of the first
bowling club
meeting,
10:15am.

Oatley Castle

Built as part of
a work relief scheme
in the Great
Depression.

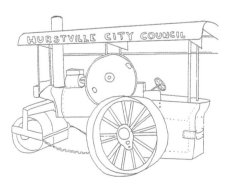

Owls,
swallows,
fairy-wrens,
plenty of
birds.

Playground steamroller.

Southern
Boobook Owl

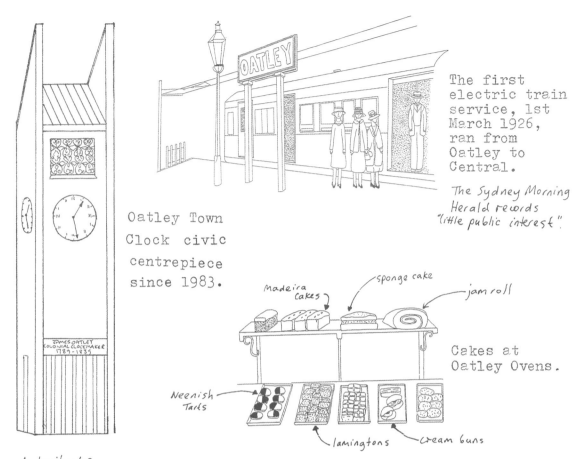

Oatley Town Clock civic centrepiece since 1983.

The first electric train service, 1st March 1926, ran from Oatley to Central.

The Sydney Morning Herald records "little public interest".

Madeira Cakes

sponge cake

jam roll

Cakes at Oatley Ovens.

Neenish Tarts

lamingtons

cream buns

A tribute to convict clockmaker and the suburb's namesake, James Oatley.

JAMES OATLEY
COLONIAL CLOCKMAKER
1789-1839

The Oatley Theatre, named after Radio City Music Hall. 1942-1962.

RADIO

Now the Oatley RSL Youth Club

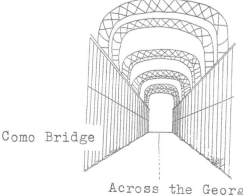

Como Bridge

Across the Georges River, to the Como Pleasure Grounds.

Woronora Dam pipeline.

Runs through Oatley on its journey between Woronora Dam and Penshurst.

WISHING TREE

When you enter the Royal
Botanic Garden the rush of the city recedes. This green world is
on the eastern edge of central Sydney, its pathways leading down
towards the curve of Farm Cove at the harbour's edge. Time is softer
here too. No one, apart from the lunchtime joggers, moves quickly.
Near the harbour wall two women sit on the grass writing postcards
and eating through a packet of raspberry tartlets. A man in a suit
lies under a tree, flat on his back with his palms facing up. A family
carrying a picnic basket pats the thick branches of the Queensland
bottle tree. Such scenes are repeated day after day. The gardens have
long been a place where people have come for respite from the city,
with their picnics, their books, their desires and wishes.

In the early years of the gardens, around 1816, a young Norfolk
Island pine tree was brought in by ship and its planting overseen
by Elizabeth Macquarie, the wife of the governor. As the tree grew
its legend grew also, so much so that by the twentieth century it
had reached a level of notoriety unmatched by any other tree in
Sydney. The origins of its identity as the Wishing Tree are unknown
but by the turn of the century it had become famous for its magical
properties, which were said to see one's wishes granted after the
performance of a simple ritual. The magic was activated by circling
around it three times forwards, then three times backwards, then
making a wish. The tree was especially popular with children and,
as one gardener noted in the 1920s, 'girls of the flapper age', with
their wishes for love and luck.

Throughout all this magical activity the tree was growing old and in the 1930s it was found to be dying. As sad at this was, it was generally agreed that Sydney couldn't be without a wishing tree, so a Wishing Tree Ball was held to raise funds for a replacement. In 1945 a new Norfolk pine was planted nearby, and on a day kept confidential to avoid protests, the original tree was removed. Its wood was turned into all manner of souvenirs – wooden egg cups, serviette rings, cigarette stands, vases – and sold by the Red Cross to fund aid for returned servicemen.

With the old tree gone it soon became clear that the replacement tree was failing to attract the number of people its forerunner had done. Smaller and less symmetrical, its crown having been damaged in a storm, it lacked both the grand proportions of its precursor and the status as one of the original trees of the Botanic Garden. The habit of wishing on the Norfolk Island pine soon became a memory.

The replacement Wishing Tree has also now been usurped by its distinguished neighbour, the Wollemi pine, one of the world's rarest plants. Once known only through fossils and thought to be extinct, in 1994 living specimens of these trees were discovered growing in remote bushland north-west of Sydney. Planted in the place of the original Wishing Tree, the Wollemi has its own magic, that of an ancient past. With it people can imagine a Jurassic scene of dinosaurs nibbling on its dark, shiny foliage.

As so few people remember the Wishing Tree these days, my suspicion is that its power is especially concentrated from lack of use. I start a slow walk around the garden bed that encircles it. No one nearby pays me much attention until I begin the backwards laps. It's hard to walk backwards and feeling self-conscious doesn't help my poise. I slowly complete three wavering circles. A man waits politely for me to lope out of the way so he can take a photo of a nearby tibouchina tree, which is flowering with bright purple blooms. I'm ready to explain my actions but no one enquires; instead, they stare from afar.

In the Wishing Tree's heyday it was so well known that anyone passing by would have known exactly what I was doing. Walking feats in general were once regarded as good entertainment.

In the 1840s one of Sydney's most well-known characters was William Francis King, the 'Flying Pieman'. A pie-seller and professional pedestrian, he was famous for embarking upon eccentric walking challenges. In his signature red breeches, blue jacket and top hat with coloured streamers trailing from it, he sold pies to the passengers at Circular Quay who were boarding the steamer to Parramatta. Then, in the trick that provided his name, he would race on foot to the wharf at Parramatta, arriving in time to sell the remainder of the pies to disembarking travellers. In another stunt he walked between Sydney and Parramatta twice a day for six consecutive days. Further feats included timed walking challenges carrying unusual cargo, such as a goat, a dog or a hundred-pound carriage pole. By placing bets upon himself, he made a living through his performances.

I finish my minor feat of reverse pedestrianism and stop to wish upon the tree. As I shut my eyes I think of all the other wishes that have been made here in the gardens, all the desires and hopes that have taken shape in people's thoughts. Love and success, peace and revenge, wishes earnest and fanciful. Some coming true, some not, but alive with possibility in the moment of wishing.

My wish made, I go to visit the casuarinas on the less-traversed eastern side of the gardens. They have sprung from the roots of casuarinas that grew here hundreds of years ago. Along with the four remaining red gums elsewhere in the gardens, they are a connection to the original trees of the cove. The wiry branches of the casuarinas have long, green-grey leaves thin as needles, and their furrowed bark covered in pale green lichen gives them a soft, ghostly appearance.

Trees connect to a different kind of past than that of the built environment. As the Wollemi pine links to a prehistoric world, the casuarinas connect to a memory of the land before colonisation. This place, later labelled Farm Cove, has the name Woccanmagully, and the flat area near the water was used an initiation ground for young Gadigal men. Here their passage to adulthood was marked by the ritual knocking out of a front tooth.

For the Aboriginal clans of the Sydney region, trees were

food and medicine, resources and totems. Nawi, the canoes used
to navigate the harbour, were made of long strips of bark from
stringybark trees, tied up at the ends and sealed with grass-tree
sap. Throughout the forests, trees wore scars where bark had
been removed to make these canoes, as well as shields and coolamon
vessels. The oval-shaped indentations in the tree trunks captured
impressions of these objects. Most of these trees were removed
when land was cleared for farming and housing, but some exist in
places where pockets of bushland remain, such as Ku-ring-gai Chase
National Park. Individual trees here and there wear these marks,
like the lone scar tree in Fairfield Park. An ironbark with an elliptical
hollow in the rough grey wood near the base of its trunk, it preserves
the shape of the bark section that was cut from it.

Upon claiming the Gadigal land by the harbour as their own,
the British immediately set about clearing it for settlement and
agriculture. Farm Cove was the site of their first, unsuccessful
attempts at farming. Their seeds failed to prosper, the wheat and
barley soon succumbing to disease. The colonists' relationship with
the land was one of struggle. On the map of 'hitherto explored
country' published in Watkin Tench's *A Complete Account of the
Settlement at Port Jackson*, areas of land in the Sydney region are
marked according to their perceived qualities: 'bad country',
'swampy and barren', 'nothing but rocks', 'wretched and brushy',
with the occasional 'patch of good land' here and there. Although
Tench was a curious and sympathetic observer of the Sydney
landscape, it is a map of disappointment.

Almost all these wetlands, scrublands and forests, the good
and bad country, were cleared to make the city and suburbs. Early
topographical paintings have the picturesque cast of a European eye
and by the time the first photographs of Sydney were taken there
are few trees to be seen. Sydney looks to be a stark place in the faded
sepia prints, defiantly man-made. After all the clearing of land the
new city would have wanted to celebrate its structures, rather than
the natural world that so much effort had been put into subduing.

In time, individual city trees became distinguished. A 1957 book,
the historical portrait *Sydney Looks Back* by Isadore Brodsky, includes

the story of a Moreton Bay fig in the square near the entrance to
Central Station. This tree was said to be the only one to remain
after the construction of the station fifty years before. Brodsky
writes of the tree as a constant presence, a witness to the coming of
the railway and the expansion of the city. The fig tree's persistence
was a way of measuring and marking eras. Trees are often used
as timekeepers. In the redwood forests of California, where trees can
live for thousands of years, sometimes the rings of a fallen tree will
be marked with historical events to show how centuries can pass in a
few centimetres of concentric circles.

Sydney's oldest trees provoke a similar sense of reflection and
witnessing. Great turpentine and ironbark forests once extended
across what are now the inner-western suburbs. Of this only a few
isolated trees are thought to remain, one of which is an ironbark
in the grounds of St Johns Church in Glebe. From this one tree
I imagine ironbarks covering the park on the corner, replacing the
roads and the buildings, the bakery with the mural of the blackbirds
and bats circling around a pie, the takeaway where my friends
and I would drive late at night to buy potato cakes, the pubs and
restaurants and yoga schools. So much of what I know and have
known here was once forest.

There are still pockets of bushland that trace out valleys, slivers of
green bracketing the suburbs. Many of Sydney's most celebrated trees
are, however, the introduced species planted to bring colour to the
streets. Their flowering bookends the seasons, the intense mauve of
the jacarandas in November marking the end of spring and the pink
ruffles of the crepe myrtles reaching their height in the late summer
days of February. Purple tibouchinas, white magnolias, and yellow
wattles create an alternative city calendar, one of warmth and colour.

Before these trees became established the suburbs were new,
with freshly built houses marooned on bare blocks of land. Then
residents started to plant their gardens. Trees commemorated the
birth of children and the death of pets, screened out neighbours,
provided shade. Over decades these trees have taken on a life
beyond the intentions of their planting, growing big or lopsided,
erratically or enthusiastically. Now some conifers are so tall they

conceal the houses behind them, palm trees make front gardens into miniature tropical islands, and frangipani trees litter the footpaths with sweetly scented flowers.

Back in the city, a few months after making my wish, I return to the Botanic Garden to see if it has come true. I hadn't wished for love or for luck. Instead I'd wished for the rekindling of an old tradition. I take my time getting to the wishing tree, first visiting the genteel environment of the shady fern house, then the creaking bamboo groves where the stalks carry the carved-in hearts and initials of hundreds of lovers, and the cactus garden which stretches a desert through my thoughts, dusty and vast.

After I pass back out by the spiky pincushion cacti at the gates, I snap back into the present. Ahead of me the Wishing Tree comes into view. Underneath it is a young woman in baggy travelling clothes, a tightly stuffed rucksack strapped to her back, walking around the base of the tree. As I watch she stops and reverses, moving backwards with slow and deliberate steps, her wish gathering force in her thoughts.

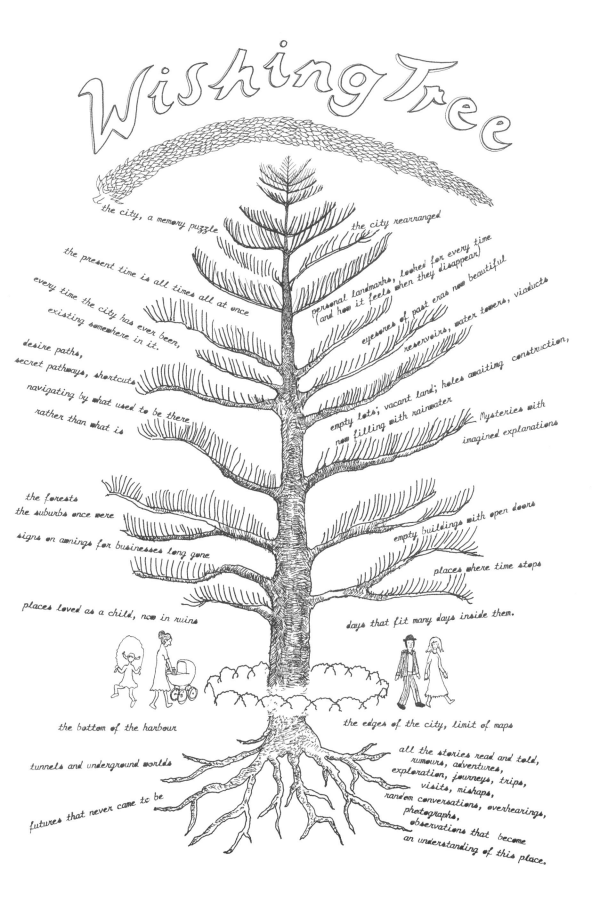

Wishing Tree

the city, a memory puzzle

the city rearranged

personal landmarks, looked for every time
(and how it feels when they disappear)

the present time is all times all at once

eyesores of past eras now beautiful

every time the city has ever been,
existing somewhere in it.

reservoirs, water towers, viaducts

desire paths,

secret pathways, shortcuts

empty lots, vacant land; holes awaiting construction,
now filling with rainwater

navigating by what used to be there
rather than what is

Mysteries with
imagined explanations

the forests
the suburbs once were

empty buildings with open doors

signs on awnings for businesses long gone

places where time stops

places loved as a child, now in ruins

days that fit many days inside them.

the bottom of the harbour

the edges of the city, limit of maps

tunnels and underground worlds

all the stories read and told,
rumours, adventures,
exploration, journeys, trips,
visits, mishaps,
random conversations, overhearings,
photographs,
observations that become
an understanding of this place.

futures that never came to be

Sydney Harbour Bridge, the city's central emblem, is not just one bridge. For as long as it has spanned the harbour it has been splintered into countless likenesses. These are dispersed across the city and the suburbs, appearing on café signs and plumbers' vans, skip bins and factory walls. No matter how far you go into the suburbs a harbour bridge will appear, reminding you of the city that encloses you.

The bridge was emblematic from its beginning. Built over the course of the 1920s, it was a jigsaw puzzle that slowly reached completion under the eyes of the city's residents. Upon its opening in 1932 souvenirs immediately went into circulation. Enthusiasm for the bridge was such that people wanted it small enough to be grasped as a medallion, pictured on a tea set or remade as a glass sweet-dish, with the bridge as a handle and the bowl as the harbour below. Some souvenirs have become artworks in their own right, such as the shellwork harbour bridges that Bidjigal women have made for generations. They were first made to sell to the tourists who came for day trips to La Perouse. Now elder Esme Timbery's harbour bridges, made out of shells glued to velvet-covered forms and sprinkled with glitter, are a well known icon of contemporary Aboriginal art.

Of all the multifarious bridges, there is one so large it can be considered the city's second, understudy harbour bridge. It is a surprise to anyone on an interstate bus coming into Sydney from the south. If the sleepy traveller jolts awake at the right moment in the

last hour of the journey this harbour bridge appears like a mirage by
the roadside. They might only be on the Hume Highway just past
Liverpool, but outside the window and long before schedule, there
is Sydney's famous bridge.

This harbour bridge is positioned over the entrance to the Peter
Warren automotive empire in Warwick Farm. At thirty metres long
it commands attention, although it is one of the few Australian
'big things' – along with the Leyland Brothers World replica Uluru
at Karuah – to actually be smaller than its original. Like the original
Harbour Bridge, the Warwick Farm version is topped with flags and
draped in lights for special occasions. Underneath it is a harbour of
asphalt which leads to the car dealerships beyond. The Peter Warren
compound occupies a lot across from the racecourse and sells
what seems to be every make of car imaginable. Here, newer and
shinier versions of the cars rushing along the Hume are displayed,
positioned on ramps, bonnets up and windscreens affixed with signs.

Warwick Farm, with its run-down motel, Masterton display home
village and horse-racing track, is at an expansive point in Sydney's
suburban sprawl, where there is plenty of space for warehouses and
car yards. Like many outer suburbs it's a place to be passed through,
bisected by a highway. By the Hume roadside, signs flash up offers
enticing drivers to stop:

GOLD MANSION PACKAGE $50 000!
ALL YOU CAN EAT ALL DAY
$1 WORLD

The signs are moored on a no-man's-land of lawn that separates
the road from the display-home village and steak barn that fulfil
these offers. On the other side of the highway is the racecourse,
its loop of sandy track quiet most days except for the twice-monthly
race meetings.

The idea to have a harbour bridge at the entrance to his car
dealership came to Peter Warren while he was watching the 1987
Manly vs. Canberra NRL grand final at the Sydney Cricket Ground.
The pre-match entertainment centred around the construction

of a replica harbour bridge in the centre of the field. Men in blue overalls carrying crossbeams raced to assemble them as young women wearing white bodysuits and Akubras swung their arms in choreographed unison. Each team in the league was represented on the field by a sign, a flag and a local representative, like the person dressed as a banana embodying Coffs Harbour. The spectacle included horses, kids in 'I helped make this state great' sweaters, and Julie Anthony singing the national anthem. Among all this commotion it was the bridge that caught Warren's attention and he wondered what was going to happen to it after the game.

Warren arranged for the bridge to be relocated to his car yard. It proved so popular and so good for business that it became a permanent fixture, and its image the dealership's logo. Cars bought there carry the sign of the bridge with the Peter Warren sticker on the back window, and at any time there are thousands of tiny harbour bridges out in the congested Sydney traffic.

Unlike the original, the Peter Warren harbour bridge is not so much grand as incongruous, a reminder of the city in a place that, almost thirty kilometres distant, feels far away from it. Cars rule in this zone of highways and automotive dealerships. There's not another soul out walking as I cross the neat lawn. On both sides of the bridge are brick pylons, faithful in detail to the originals, tapering at the top and decorated with archways. In one pylon is a trapdoor which I peer into through a crack, expecting some kind of treasure or troll inside instead of the empty chamber that greets my eyes. This pylon has a plaque commemorating the opening of the replica in February 1988, in celebration of the bicentenary year as well as the release of a new range of Ford Falcons. The other pylon has a plaque in memory of Peter Warren, 'who had the foresight to purchase this land in 1976', and who died in 2006.

The pylons of the original Sydney Harbour Bridge, although they appear to be an integral part of the structure, are in fact only there for appearance's sake. John Bradfield, city engineer and overseer of the bridge's construction, thought the arch of the bridge alone looked too stark and that the addition of the pylons would convince the public of its strength and stability. For further reassurance before the bridge's official opening, its strength was tested with a load of ninety-two steam locomotives which were lined up end to end along the railway and tram tracks. Newspaper articles contained guarantees of the bridge's resistance to gales and extremes of temperature, assuring readers that 'all the critical points' had been tested with 'microscopic thoroughness'.

The Harbour Bridge pylons became a tourist attraction. In the 1930s the south-east pylon was filled with as many amusements as would fit inside it. There was a camera obscura, funhouse mirrors, a miniature railway, a 'mother's nook' for women to write letters and a 'pashometer', a contraption that purported to measure sex appeal. All of this was topped by the 'five million acre view' of the rooftop lookout. After its closure during the Second World War the pylon reopened with added attractions: a tearoom, the largest existing map of New South Wales, a post office, and a family of white cats that guarded a wishing well at the lookout. The cats tiptoed along the edges of the pylon wall as if it were a garden fence, in defiance of those who peered vertiginously over the edge to the ground far below.

Today's pylon display is more museum than amusements gallery, exhibiting some of the ephemera and signs from its previous incarnations. One is a painted figure in a bow tie that once hung at the top of the stairs. Inside its outline are the words 'Look behind you for the way to the top of the world'. This curious kind of message, in which one looks backwards to look forwards, is typical of what must have been the rather surreal experience of visiting the pylon, with its cats, animated dioramas, and promises of unusual souvenirs.

The thought of being at the top of the world is enticing and there is a long tradition of bridge climbing, both official and unofficial. Of the unofficial attempts the most dramatic was French high-wire artist Philippe Petit's 1973 walk between the tops of the two northern pylons. To those watching below, Petit appeared to be hovering in the air as he crossed between the pylons on a taut wire. On the road below, police gathered, readying to apprehend him. But how to capture a man in midair? Police officers stared up at the slight, black-clad figure balancing above. Eventually a rescue team climbed up inside the pylon, waited until Petit had crossed the wire, and seized him. In the video recorded of his feat, the cheers of the crowd watching from the walkway opposite can be heard as he's bundled into a police car. He was taken into custody but let off with a minimal fine, the audacity and artistry of his feat outweighing its illegality.

By the 1980s there were so many illegal bridge climbers that a guestbook was left on the summit for messages. Anyone who wrote in the book became a member of the Sydney Harbour Social Climbers Association, a tongue-in-cheek club whose code of ethics included such items as 'I shall not unplug the beacon at the top of the arch,' as well as the instruction to refrain from vomiting on the traffic below. Some climbers were serious, but many others were out on drunken adventures. Once they reached the top they could look out across the glittering mantle of electric lights reflected in the night harbour, a view all the more beautiful for being illicit.

The first climbers were the thousands of workers who constructed the bridge in the 1920s. They spent their days high above the harbour, in their overalls and cloth caps, without harnesses or safety equipment to tether them to the structure. Their work was dangerous, heating rivets until they were white-hot, tossing them from man to man until they were hammered in place. Six million of these rivets hold together the steel arch of the bridge, a structure which now seems so complete it can be difficult to imagine it was constructed piece by piece.

The men in blue overalls at the 1987 NRL grand final were paying tribute to these workers, as the replica bridge itself is a homage to the greater structure which it imitates. Tributes and homages have celebrated the bridge as a work of civic art as much as a work of infrastructure. In 1931, before the Harbour Bridge itself had officially opened, Aboriginal ex-serviceman Douglas Grant completed a war memorial in its likeness at Callan Park in Rozelle. Grant, like William Shirley who carved the Turramurra sphinx, had been a part of the 13th Battalion and served on the Western Front. After the war he worked as a clerk at the Callan Park Mental Hospital and with the help of patients constructed his ornamental bridge on the flat ground by the river at the back of the hospital. The welded metal arch is bracketed by sandstone pillars and spans a wishing well. In Grant's day many of the residents who lived or passed through the hospital were ex-soldiers suffering from shell shock after their traumatic war experiences, and the memorial connected this experience with the city's new symbol of unity.

Many more personal bridge tributes have been constructed in the suburbs. Giuseppe Bianchi's 'Abruzzo Museum' in the garden of his home at Smithfield featured a wooden harbour bridge model he had made, along with Italian landmarks such as the Leaning Tower of Pisa. In Miranda, retired carpenter Norm Grundy made a version of the Harbour Bridge out of 75,000 matchsticks, the first of the series of iconic Sydney structures he has constructed from matches. Less dramatically, in homes and businesses across the city Harbour Bridges are made out of Lego, carved out of ice, stamped on business cards, and constructed in miniature as garden ornaments.

On any day in Sydney, as traffic surges over the Harbour Bridge, art gallery visitors pause in front of the 1930 Grace Cossington Smith painting *The Bridge in Curve*, in which the half-finished arch seems to vibrate with the energy of its making. In the Bridge Climb souvenir store, tourists stand before racks of merchandise, caps and shot glasses and drink bottles patterned with the arch. Out at Warwick Farm, the replica bridge decorates Peter Warren's car yard like a garland as people drive underneath it, joining the traffic in their new cars.

SYDNEY HARBOUR BRIDGE

EIFFEL TOWERS

artarmon

triangle

And

Triumvirate of
TV transmission
towers.

awa

Wireless House,
once the tallest
structure in
Sydney, with roof
top tower
modelled on the
Eiffel Tower.

bondi

The cheapest
houses in Bondi
can be found
beneath the
Telstra Tower.

canterbury

Once a radio
factory, a
smaller,
suburban relative
of the AWA.

lidcombe

The spire of
AR Plastics,
providores of
perspex and
weighbridge
guardians.

HARBOUR BRIDGES

and the teacups, souvenir spoons, napkin holders, matchstick models, jam dishes, snowglobes and coathangers.

SYDNEY IS AT YOUR FEET

sydney harbour bridge

The lookout in the south east pylon, once the home of a family of white cats.

World's largest (but not longest) steel arch bridge.

haberfield

Domestic tribute spans the drive-way of this Haberfield house.

callan park

War memorial by Douglas Grant in the grounds of Callan Park. Completed before the actual Sydney Harbour Bridge.

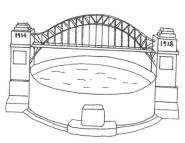

la perouse

Shellwork Harbour Bridges by Aboriginal women artists of La Perouse.

warwick farm

Liverpool's Harbour Bridge at the entrance to Peter Warren automotive empire, once, a Grand Final prop.

WARRAGAMBA

Warragamba is far to the west, at the furthest possible edge of what could be considered Sydney. Although inextricably linked to the city, it is a place known to most through reference rather than experience, its name synonymous with the dam that is the city's main source of water. Here the natural and the manufactured overlap: the concrete dam wall, all three million tonnes of it, holds back the waters of Lake Burragorang, a drowned valley with a volume four times greater than Sydney Harbour.

Though roads are often described as the city's circulatory system, it is the system of utility pipes that keeps the city alive. Warragamba is elsewhere but it is also everywhere, the origin of much of the water that flows from the city's taps. The dam's rising and falling levels are monitored like vital signs. In 2007, when the water level dropped below a third of its total capacity, Warragamba became associated with potential catastrophe. Its name haunted dusty cars and dry fountains. Rangers patrolled the suburbs on the lookout for breaches of watering bans, and it was a time of arguments and short tempers. At the drought's nadir, a man hosing his lawn in Sylvania died in a fight with a passer-by over his flouting of the restrictions. Eventually the weather patterns turned, and a year later the dam was filling again.

There's a weird sense of balance on either side of the dam wall, with the lake to one side and a steep concrete drop to the other. Despite hearing the percentages of the dam's levels in news reports throughout my life, it wasn't until I walked out on the road that extends across of the dam wall, I thought about how the dam came to be made. To the west, Lake Burragorang stretches out between the dense forests of the surrounding hills, its surface a dark, glassy green. This peaceful scene is a manufactured one, however. Lake Burragorang is in fact the Burragorang Valley, country of the Gundungurra nation. In their Dreaming story the valley was carved out by a battle between the tiger cat Mirragan and the reptile fish Gurangatch. Now the folds and the contours of the valley form the shape of the lake that submerged it.

In the 1950s the inhabitants of the Burragorang valley, which included a number of townships, farms and industries, were forced to move. The land had been acquired and the valley was to be flooded to form the catchment area. Trees were felled and the timber used for scaffolding on the dam and workers' houses in Warragamba. Some of the valley's buildings were dismantled; others were left and now lie beneath the waters of the lake. If the water level drops low enough parts of the town reappear, vehicles, bridges and buildings rising from the shallows.

The air smells of eucalyptus and the drone of cicadas is the loudest sound as I read the commemorative plaques that list the engineers and members of the Metropolitan Water Sewerage and Drainage Board. Beneath me, under the roadway on the top of the dam, is a five-kilometre-long network of tunnels and chambers. To work inside the dam structure is to be inside a quiet, immense beast. One of the elements of this creature is on display above ground, a three-tonne valve, as weird as a piece of space junk. It is a contraption of concentric rings, painted green like a steam engine. For almost fifty years it operated down inside the dam's machinery, but now it is stranded on the surface, a monument to the hidden workings of the structure.

Once, before security was tightened and tours ceased, visitors could go inside the wall, following a route through the networks of tunnels. They could also cross the suspension bridge, a remnant from the dam's construction, which traversed the valley. People could make the vertiginous walk across it to take photographs in front of the dam wall, posing as if in midair.

The supports for the suspension bridge, which burnt down in the bushfires of 2001, are still visible in the terrace garden. This is much changed from the neat flowerbeds, rockeries and ornamental conifers that in times past won prizes in gardening competitions. The gardens are dry and choked with leaves and bark, and only the hardiest of the plants remain. The sun is incessant and there is little shade to provide relief. Curls of bark snap underfoot. A man puffs his way up the terrace garden stairs, his giggling daughter sitting on his shoulders, but otherwise the only person in sight is a security guard snoozing on a chair underneath a sunshade.

The face of the dam is familiar to me from news broadcasts – a row of gates above a steep, concrete drop. At its base, far down below, there is only a small pool of greenish water. When the dam reaches capacity, water gushes down the wall in a powerful torrent toward the pool below. The overflowing water also provides an escape route for the migratory eels that live in the lake. During spills they can be seen sliding down the wall to begin the long journey north through the waterways to eventually reach the Coral Sea.

The long-finned eels that live in Lake Burragorang begin their lives far away, in the Pacific Ocean near Vanuatu. Tiny eels drift thousands of kilometres south on ocean currents, gradually ending up in the Nepean River system and finding their way to Warragamba. Undeterred by the hundred-metre-high wall, the eels move up around it through rivulets and drains, finally reaching the deep lake, where they stay until it overflows, continuing the cycle.

Today only a few wide, slow trickles course down the dam wall, which is patterned by grey-brown streaks. Over time the concrete has discoloured, giving it the appearance of bark or stone, something organic. Concrete is a fundamental material of urban construction but wide expanses of it can often seem more geological than manufactured.

Inside the nearby museum, collections of objects and ephemera remind visitors of the dam's history and construction. One cabinet contains specimens of eels and red-bellied black snakes in IXL jam jars. Another displays construction instruments, the intricate slide rules and planimeters used before computers came to guide civil engineering projects. A film of the dam under construction plays alongside the display. In the faded yellow tones of 1950s colour footage, engineers examine core samples of rock and men pour the interlocking concrete blocks that make up the dam wall. Their industrious movements repeat as the film plays on a loop, and the dam is built over and over.

During the twelve years it took for the dam to be constructed, many of the workers lived in the township of Warragamba, a village of fibro cottages and numbered streets a few kilometres away. In the centre of the town, for every shop that is in business there is another empty or boarded up. Since tourist access to the dam was restricted the shops have struggled. An old butchery with a pale-green tiled facade has its door sealed shut, thin beams nailed across it to prevent trespassers. Nearby, the Dam Lolly Shop, with its Wild West typography and 1980s brick facade, has a window display of For Lease signs.

It is late Sunday afternoon in summer and in Warragamba most shops are closed. The main street, which loops around a playground with picnic tables and gum trees, has a mood of deep stillness. Occasionally something happens to interrupt the quiet. A woman gets out of her car, struggling with a bunch of helium balloons inside a plastic bag, before disappearing into one of the stores. An old white bull terrier hobbles up the street and pauses outside the takeaway shop, as if waiting for an order. The takeaway is one of the few stores open. It's the kind of place that sells chips, burgers and random grocery items, the shelves stacked with toilet paper, canned fruit and packets of plastic toy soldiers.

The residential streets are quiet too. Most of the houses are the workers' cottages that housed the families of the dam builders. The cottage windows have striped awnings, there are caravans in the driveways, the gardens are planted with box trees and hydrangeas. There are few people on the street but on one front lawn a family group is assembled under a tree. They sit languidly on plastic lawn chairs, escaping the afternoon heat of their house, and follow my car with their eyes. I feel uncomfortably touristic, cruising the streets in my old pink sedan with a sticker of a flamingo on the back window.

Warragamba's tourist heyday extended from the 1960s to the 1980s, when the dam was an impressively new piece of civil engineering and the source of much pride. School groups on excursion and families on Sunday drives bought souvenirs of their visit: postcards of the dam and the town, rulers picturing dams of the Sydney region, giant pencils, souvenir teaspoons.

The dam was not the only local tourist attraction. In 1968 the nearby African Lion Safari opened, featuring lions and tigers which roamed free through the park as people drove through and observed them from the safety of their cars. Visitors entered the park through a double layer of fencing, passing by a series of warnings:

YOU ARE NOW IN LION COUNTRY.
TRESPASSERS WILL BE EATEN.

There were signs with reminders to keep the car windows wound up at all times and not to get out of the car, even in the case of breakdown. *SOUND HORN, DO NOT GET OUT!* At feeding time, jeeps painted in zebra stripes drove through the park and workers in khakis distributed hunks of beef to the lions from the safety of a caged trailer.

The African Lion Safari's television ads offered glimpses of the park's wild animals, helicopter flights over the dam and miniature train rides. For children it was an invitation to experience the exotic in the outer suburbs. They could come within metres of a strange mixture of animals from around the world, among them lions, tigers, bears, cheetahs and camels, even dolphins in this place more than seventy kilometres from the sea. Every time the advertisement came on I would imagine the thrilling scenario of a lion's vicious face appearing at the window of my family's Ford station wagon. To my disappointment, I was never to experience this for real, as the idea of driving through a reserve of lions didn't seem so appealing to my parents.

The block of land that was formerly the African Lion Safari is overgrown, its few remaining buildings in ruins and covered in layers of graffiti. The double row of fences is in many places damaged or fallen. Urban explorers overcome the fear that a gang of hyenas may remain inside, and go in to photograph the broken relics of the park. I'm content to cruise by, deterred by a less exotic threat as I remember the brown snakes in jam jars I'd just seen at the dam.

On the corner block across from the former African Lion Safari the barbed wire fence has been strung with 'No Trespassing' signs. Behind the wire and its warnings is a paddock with weird objects dotted among the trees. Concrete tepees, the remains of a miniature passenger train, a wishing well guarded by two wizards with pig-like faces. Among the creatures is a broken lion and a bear with one sagging arm. Like the animals frozen by the White Witch in *The Lion, the Witch and the Wardrobe* these concrete beasts appear as if they have been turned to stone on the spot. Further back inside the property are rusted cars and decaying fairground rides. The central scaffolding of a small ferris wheel stands by a grove of fire-blackened tree trunks and a playground rocket is beached on its side, its red and blue paint peeling. The grass and weeds grow long around these stranded objects, gradually obscuring them from view.

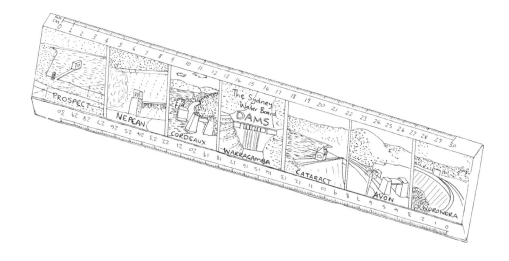

The Burragorang Valley
is a 'Special Area',
closed off to the public
... but not extraterrestrials.

Long-finned eels
slither their way up
alongside the dam to
reach the lake, the
final obstacle of their
4000km migration.

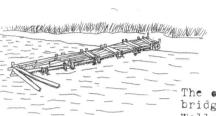

The old wooden
bridge across the
Wollendilly River.

burragorang
valley

The valley was drowned
to form the catchment
area for the dam.
Most buildings were
demolished, but some-
times remains emerge.

At the visitor
centre, snakes in
jars & huge machines.

the
dam

Red-bellied black snake,
venomous bushland
inhabitant.

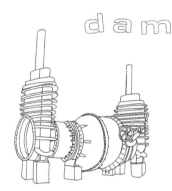

Larner-Johnson
needle valve, the
original outlet
valve for the dam,
now on display.

The gates of the
African Lion Safari,
closed 1991, but nothing
has yet taken its place.

lion
safari

Lions, tigers, &
for the faint-of-heart,
cockatoos on bicycles.

WARRAGAMBA

Beyond the edge of the city, everywhere within it.

Workers' cottages, neat & compact.

Butcheries and lolly shops.

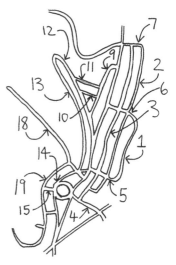

The numbered streets of Warragamba town with mystery omissions, 8, 16, 17.

The Spheroid Reservoir.

Curious collection of extinct playground rides & concrete creatures, behind a fence hung with 'No Trespassing' signs.

Locals call it the 'Devil's Playground'.

The creek first appears off Salisbury Road, behind a patch of unkempt grass. Ivy trails down into the concrete channel where a stream of milky stormwater flows north towards the harbour. The channel runs covertly between the back walls of the old jam and ginger beer factory buildings of Bridge Street, and the gardens of the cottages which line Cardigan Street.

Creeks cut through Sydney, tracing out irregular patterns. Water has determined the topography of the city, from the erratic outline of the bays and inlets of the harbour to the enduring paths of rivers and streams which now form suburban boundaries. Even when shaped and tamed, the creeks follow their original trajectories. Johnstons Creek still follows roughly the same path through Gadigal and Wangal country that it did before the land was cleared and the streets and houses constructed around it.

Two creeks enclose the suburb of Annandale: Whites Creek to the west and Johnstons Creek, the longer and more visible, to the east. It drains stormwater into the harbour, going underground and re-emerging, flowing behind back fences, or through strips of parkland, on the way to Rozelle Bay. I took solace in Johnstons Creek during the years I lived alongside it. It seemed so unlikely that a creek would exist amid the cluttered, concrete environs of Parramatta Road. It passes behind the 24-hour McDonald's, with its trash-strewn car park, then under the busy road, and then on past an eclectic, sprawling junkyard containing an ever-shifting configuration of discards.

Today I am determined to follow the creek from start to finish down to the bay, keeping as close as I can to its path. I watch the water flowing underneath the footbridge behind Cardigan Street. It's a hot day with screeching cicadas and searing sun and the heat seems to flatten everything. On the nearby street corner, men are smoothing newly poured pavement, carefully scoring the edges, trusting the sun to dry the concrete before anyone comes to scratch in their name.

At the end of Cardigan Street is the thunderous traffic of Parramatta Road. When this was a dusty thoroughfare in the 1840s there was a tollgate here at the creek, the lowest point of the surrounding land. Now motorists pass through mostly oblivious to the creek's presence. The only signs are a metal plaque on the footpath near the fence beside a cracked 'Municipality of Petersham' marker inlaid into the cement. On the other side of the road, the patchy remains of its name are painted onto a wall.

I cross Parramatta Road and head down the alleyway to the junkyard. It is as odd as ever. There are sections of shipping containers marked with messages, not graffiti so much as labels, *White Wolf*, *Blood Storm*, beside the rusted cabin of an old ute up on pallets. I walk up a path to the arch that overlooks the creek as it runs underneath the road. This space between two old commercial buildings has always been a little spooky. It is the kind of place you wouldn't want to run into if you were being chased. The path curves and stops at a dead end, tucked out of sight of both the road above it and the junkyard beside it.

The building on the Camperdown side is an antiques warehouse, its facade painted with harlequins. On the Annandale side was a row of eight Edwardian-era shops, which stood until they were demolished illegally by a property developer in 2011. Since then, as the case against the developer has progressed through the courts, the lot has languished. Weeds grow from piles of rubble, the remains of the foundations still marking out where shopfronts used to be. When I lived across from this building I could see into the backs of these shops and came to know the routines of the people who lived in the flats behind them. In the morning a man would stand shaving on the back steps of the rug store, looking in a mirror nailed to the back door. In one of the windows was a trophy, and I'd look over towards it from my balcony, speculating at what sport or achievement it was for. But this was long ago. Amid the weeds and rusted metal of the now vacant lot a scruffy black-and-white stray cat watches me. I turn towards the water running below the archway at the end of the pathway and the cool air rushes up to my face from the cavern of wet stone.

On the other side of the junkyard is a section of creek where the concrete is crowded with tags, a haunt of graffiti writers. The path alongside the creek ends as it flows between buildings. But I don't climb down in order to follow the creek – I go around through the industrial back streets and towards the foreboding, windowless concrete compound beside which the path resumes. The building used to be owned by a bank and in those days I imagined it full of gold, with a dragon curled up on top of the glittering hoard. Now it's a different kind of vault, a self-storage facility, full of objects that people can't quite fit into their lives. For a while I knew a man who, having nowhere else to live, tried staying in one of the self-storage units in here for a few months. He told me it confirmed something he had long suspected: he was not the only one to be doing it.

In the next section of the creek a group of plumbers and Sydney Water engineers are having a meeting about 'Stormwater Channel No. 55', as Johnstons Creek is officially known. They congregate around one of the pipes that feeds into the creek and then, business concluded, stand on either side of the channel and shake hands across it.

The creek is wider here as the water gathers in force, moving towards the harbour. On either side are tangles of asthma weed and drifts of ivy and wire fencing. It's the part of the creek most hidden from view but easiest to access, so the walls are painted with caricatures and faces, a fox holding a syringe of purple paint, a wizard with a bong. Every gap contains a scribble.

Here the creek was once a stream running over rocks at the bottom of a gully. When English economist Stanley Jevons lived in

Annandale in 1855, he found a path over Johnstons Creek was more
favourable than dusty Parramatta Road. He wrote how he would set
out walking: 'through close tall gum-trees and over picturesque rocks
for a full mile, when I come to a stream, an inlet of the harbour;
this is crossed by a bridge formed of a large gum-tree which has
been blown down and fallen across it, a long row of bullocks' skulls
being laid in the mud as stepping-stones on one side'. When I pass
along the creek I like to think of Stanley Jevons hopping from
bullock skull to bullock skull in the marshy ground. Now it is this
concrete drainage channel with spray-paint inscriptions on its sides.
It is no longer picturesque but has the covert atmosphere of a
secret pathway as it passes between streets, cuts underneath roads,
goes underground and reappears, weaving in and out of the built
environment that has been overlaid upon it.

Like Jevons, when I lived in Annandale I often walked along
Johnstons Creek. My favourite part of the familiar journey was
encountering the aqueduct. It stretches across the valley like the
spine of a gigantic dinosaur, bleached by the sun, each arch another
vertebra. It passes over the creek on tall concrete pylons before
disappearing into the higher ground on either side of the valley.
Later I found out it was built as part of the sewerage system in the
late nineteenth century, but until I knew this I saw it as something
decorative, a concrete adornment to the landscape.

When the aqueduct was built the land was bald, stripped of trees
with only a few houses placed haphazardly nearby. Photographs
of Annandale from that era could be of a Victorian suburb being
constructed on the moon. The grainy black and white prints give
the barren ground a lunar ambience. In one photograph the newly
built aqueduct extends across the frame, bisecting the land. Rows of
terraces in the distance stop abruptly mid-row. In the foreground
a horse and cart is being driven by a man in a suit and bowler hat,
a polite visitor to this fragmented terrain.

The creek passes underneath The Crescent, a curving road which
hems the eastern edge of the suburb. By now the channel is wider,
although the water in its centre forms only a trickle. The tags and
graffiti have disappeared and the only decorations on the concrete

are the trails of water which flow down from the stormwater pipes. On the north side, cranes and scaffolds attend the construction of the new development where the trotting track used to be. Behind this the Glebe tram sheds, once derelict and full of decommissioned carriages, are barricaded with fences, awaiting conversion to a food hall. The access road is presided over by a security guard sitting under a tree, who breaks up the monotony of her day by nodding to everyone who walks past.

There aren't many people out on this hot day. An elderly man swaddled in long sleeves, long trousers, a hat, gloves. Joggers with expressions of masochistic vigour. A dog walker with a pug, a terrier and a griffon bruxellois panting at the ends of their leads. Although he's not out today, this is the territory of Mark, Sydney's happiest dog-walker. He is regularly encountered here with a cadre of assorted dogs, telling everyone he passes something like 'You're beautiful! Sweet Jesus loves you!' He modifies his greeting depending on who it is he's accosting, and can be counted on for a unique compliment. As I walked past him with a male friend once, he yelled to me, 'The only person more handsome than your boyfriend is sweet Jesus!'

The brick arches of the elevated railway track cross the creek and extend through the park. The arches closest to the oval were once used to house the flock of sheep that kept the grass on the oval in check. At night, their lawnmowing duties over, they were herded back under the arches. Now the arches house a hockey club's headquarters, a Men's Shed, an offset printer and a memorial wall for dogs, with inscriptions for Sunny, Precious, Rastas and Kayne: King of the Park.

Behind the viaduct is an overgrown patch of land. The pathway that runs alongside it is known as the 'street with no name', and is said to be one of Sydney's most haunted places. There have been a number of murders here since the 1960s, the bodies found in the undergrowth. Somewhat more benignly, the ghost of a man who was hit by a train when trying to save an injured possum is said to stalk the nearby railway tracks.

On the other side of the viaduct the fences end and it is easy to step down over the low wall and into the concrete channel of the creek. I step over the mossy mud and towards the water. I've been following Johnstons Creek for an hour or more but this is the first time I've been close enough to touch it. But I don't dip my fingers into the water. The surface is cloudy, with bubbles of scum on the surface, run-off from last night's rain.

The bay water and sediment is contaminated by heavy metals after decades of industrial waste leaching into the creek. In the nineteenth century, Rozelle Bay was surrounded by noxious industries – the Glebe Island abattoir, tanneries and soapworks – and then in the twentieth century by the timber and shipyards that were the last vestiges of the working harbour. One of the shipping companies was A. E. Rawson, a tugboat company that specialised in rubbish disposal. In 1939 they had the task of disposing of the *Stalwart*, an obsolete naval ship; around the same time the company also needed to dispose of hundreds of tonnes of onions exported from Egypt that had rotted by the time they reached Sydney. The onions lay stinking on the wharves until the *Stalwart* came along. The ship was filled with the onions, towed out to twenty miles beyond the Heads, and detonated. This was the end of the *Stalwart*, but not its cargo. Two weeks later the onions began to return, washing up in great numbers on Maroubra Beach. Word got around and scavengers arrived to search among the onions for those that were still edible.

A miscellany of things wash up out of the harbour and appear at the shoreline. I walk along the edge of the creek until it merges with the bay, the water shifting from grey to green. There are the usual pieces of rubbish, plastic packets, a condom, a split and sodden orange. Once, in this spot, I looked down and saw a dead rat and a passionfruit floating in a surreal partnership, companionably bumping up against each other. Whenever I return here, I almost expect to see them again.

There are vestiges of mudflats here, some mangrove trees and a strip of muddy sand patterned with bird footprints like haphazard arrows. I look up across the bay, past the wading ibis at the end of the sandbar, to the cars travelling over the Anzac Bridge.

I'm not the only one at the water's edge. Along the wall, solitary people are sitting at a contemplative distance from one another. The distant roar of traffic, planes going overhead and the mad laugh of kookaburras from the fig trees form a soundtrack to their contemplation. They look out across the bay to the shipyards and the ruins of the White Bay power station, with its tall chimneys and hulking turbine hall. We all share the same view, but everyone looking out lays their own thoughts across it.

I reach the end of the path where there's a small beach and a dog wading into the water to retrieve a ball. The wheezy squeak of the ball in between the dog's teeth fades as I turn back past a vacant lot decorated with homemade Merry Christmas banners. The banners are painted on tarpaulins, detailed with hearts and peace signs. These have been made by Maurice, the window-washer who is out patrolling The Crescent in his Santa outfit, pacing up and down between the cars. When the lights change and the cars move off he returns to his base, a road island embellished by tinsel, feather boas and Santa hats.

Between the road and the beach there is a strip of vacant land. The lot at the end of the row was once a junkyard called the Thunderbird, operated by a man who had moved here from Oklahoma. His drawl could be heard weaving through the yard as you wandered among the wrecks of boats, statues, coils of rope and wire, and unidentifiable junk stacked up in rows. The last time I went in there I was drawn to a cardboard box among some rusty machinery. Inside there were half a dozen small brown puppies, and they turned their heads to blink up at me.

SYDNEY
at age 20
(late 1990s)

Inner west haunts, the home I chose rather than the home I was born into.

waverton
Visits to my mother and teenage bedroom.

glebe
Walking here along Pyrmont Bridge road, past the biscuit factory, abortion clinic and empty children's hospital. Then: cafes, books, Thai restaurants.

Jubilee Park

Giant fig trees I called 'broccoli', the old train tunnels. I would have my 21st birthday here with a cake shaped like a typewriter.

A screening of 'Picnic at Hanging Rock', my childhood self united with my present day one.

Glebe Point Road

Long blacks at Badde Manors.

Glebe Markets- buying paperbacks of Katherine Mansfield stories, clothes, greasy vegetarian Hokkien noodles.

Tyre swan in a garden in the back streets of Glebe.

"witch's cap" style of roof.

I'd come here to mope :-)

I moved out of home to Camperdown, a house with a high wall and an intercom.

camperdown
I lined up plastic dinosaurs along the balcony rail.

HANDY MART

"The Servo"- my friend Ryan worked here & I'd come to chat to him when I couldn't sleep.

Parramatta Road

The Witches' Houses on Johnson Street. Everyone dreams about one day living in one of them.

annandale

Johnson's Creek

junkyard near the creek, a tiny park with an old roundabout.

MAIL FRANKS CO.

Mystery terraces - no one ever entered or left, but they didn't seem empty.

Camperdown Park - not the one with the cemetery, the one with the rotunda.

Camperdown Velodrome - overgrown, a secret world. Soon to be demolished.

Annandale Vinnies. Also: Loyal Orange op shop.

ST VINCENT DE PAUL CENTRE SHOP

239 239

To Leichhardt and the rest of the world

The enigmatic Olympia Milk Bar.

Olympia MILK BAR | Ice cream

The archetypal anachronistic business.

World's Finest Chocolate

S. ALEXANDER CHOCOLATES

stanmore

All around, factories converted into apartments.

World's Finest Chocolate made the fundraiser chocolate bars sold by schoolchildren all over Sydney.

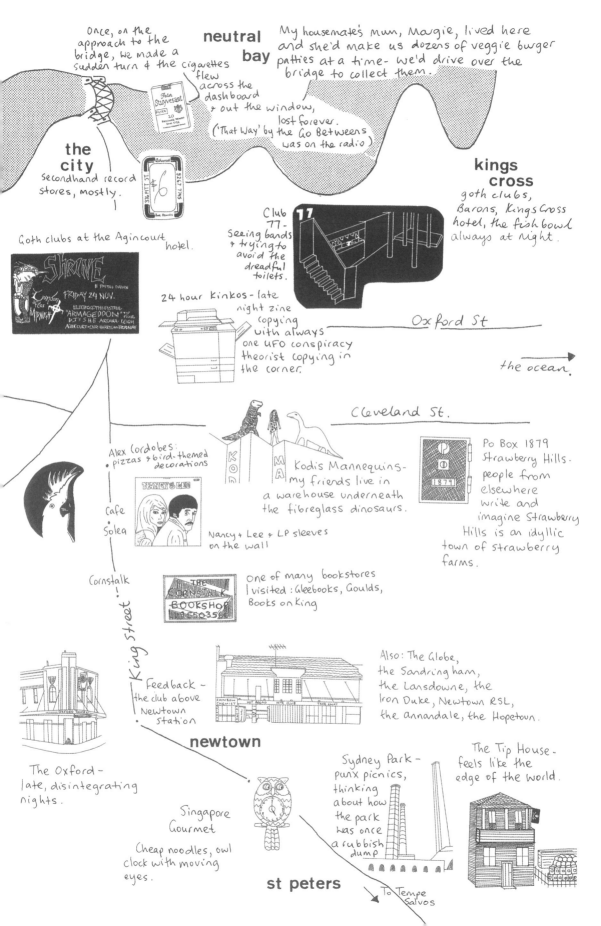

Once, on the approach to the bridge, we made a sudden turn & the cigarettes flew across the dashboard & out the window, lost forever.
('That Way' by the Go Betweens was on the radio)

neutral bay

My housemate's mum, Margie, lived here and she'd make us dozens of veggie burger patties at a time- we'd drive over the bridge to collect them.

Peter Stuyvesant FILTER 20

the city
secondhand record stores, mostly.

334 PITT ST. 9267 7145 $6

kings cross
goth clubs, Barons, Kings Cross hotel, the fish bowl always at night.

Goth clubs at the Agincourt hotel.

SHRINE
'TIL FAITH & DAWN
FRIDAY 24 NOV.
'ARMAGEDDON'
DJ's

Club 77- Seeing bands & trying to avoid the dreadful toilets.

24 hour Kinkos- late night zine copying with always one UFO conspiracy theorist copying in the corner.

Oxford St

the ocean

Cleveland St.

KOD
MA
Kodis Mannequins- my friends live in a warehouse underneath the fibreglass dinosaurs.

Alex Cordobes: pizzas & bird-themed decorations

NANCY & LEE

Cafe Solea

Nancy + Lee & LP sleeves on the wall

PO Box 1879 Strawberry Hills. people from elsewhere write and imagine Strawberry Hills is an idyllic town of strawberry farms.

1879

Cornstalk

THE CORNSTALK BOOKSHOP

One of many bookstores I visited: Gleebooks, Goulds, Books on King

King street

Feedback - the club above Newtown station

RAINBOW CHEMIST   HOT BREAD   NITE CLUB   TAKE AWAY

Also: The Globe, the Sandringham, the Lansdowne, the Iron Duke, Newtown RSL, the Annandale, the Hopetoun.

OXFORD TAVERN

newtown

The Oxford - late, disintegrating nights.

Singapore Gourmet

Cheap noodles, owl clock with moving eyes.

Sydney Park - punx picnics, thinking about how the park was once a rubbish dump

The Tip House - feels like the edge of the world.

st peters

To Tempe Salvos

Once, while waiting for a bus on Enmore Road, I noticed a handwritten notice affixed to the wall behind me. ROOM TO LET, its irregular capital letters spelled out in black marker, then STENMO and a phone number. I puzzled over what STENMO might mean. Was it an acronym? Or perhaps the name of the person to call about the room? I sounded out the word and all of a sudden it made sense. STENMO was Stanmore.

Although the sign has long since disappeared, every time I pass that patch of wall I remember Stenmo. It took root in my imagination as a rearranged version of Stanmore, with particular details of the suburb rising to prominence. The plentiful back lanes. The Stanmore Fish Shop, with its handpainted sign of a spiky blue wave, which sold paper packages of oil-sodden chips. The citrus trees overhanging fences and palm trees in the middle of roundabouts like tiny desert islands. Stenmo's mascot was the bassett hound that belonged to the group of old men who congregated in Weekley Park. It was a burly, grouchy dog that chomped at the grass around the benches where the men sat talking, and snapped at anyone who dared come close for a pat.

As far as DIY advertisements go, Stenmo is one of my all time favourites, and I'm ever on the lookout for similarly unusual street messages. I always stop to read community noticeboards and the flyers taped to telegraph poles or pinned to boards in shops, liking how this method of communication has endured despite the advancement of the digital age. Garage sales, lost pets, community meetings, objects for sale, the occasional rant or bizarre proclamation: these messages are all about proximity and immediacy, catching people's attention in the moment.

Community noticeboards develop their own microcosmic environments. Some are neat and orderly with notices written on identical cards. Others are less regulated, messy with layers of past notices and accumulations of tape and pins. These noticeboards display a full range of presentation methods: biro scrawl on lined notepaper, a photograph stuck on with tape, a streaky inkjet notice printed in Comic Sans and decorated with clip art.

Most noticeboards have a predictable selection of objects for sale: bed frames, wardrobes and dining tables. There is often a teenager looking for babysitting work. A room to let. Pets lost or for sale. VHS to DVD transfer. Each notice holds the trace of the person who made it, as a kind of public missive, reaching out to anyone who might walk by. Just by reading the notice I have travelled, at least in my imagination, to Paul's fully furnished room to rent in its bushland setting and experienced 'interaction with local wildlife', or met the person selling the 'car bra to suit Nissan Maxima' for $270.

Most community noticeboards have, on close perusal, one message that is a little unusual. Sometimes this can be due to the obscurity of the service offered or the item being sold, at others it is more about the style of the notice itself. Like Stenmo, another of my all time favourites employed a phonetic approach.

DOGS FREE
LABER DOOR AGE 8
SEPARD X AGE 8
RODY AGE 6
SI BA GIRL AGE 5
MALAMOTE
MOUNT DREWITT

The board where 'Dogs Free' was being offered was, as usual, covered in notices from this seller. Most of the time the board, in a walkway leading out from a shopping centre in Chester Hill, contained no other notices than theirs. The notices presented a bewildering array of toys, appliances, medical beds and hardware. They were written variously on notepaper, fluoro adhesive labels, photographs, and sometimes directly onto the surface of the noticeboard itself. This seller had such a cornucopia of items for sale that the notices sometimes spilled out onto the adjacent street furniture. On the metal shelf underneath the nearby public phone there were further messages written in the same familiar script: 'Stainless steel fridge age 3, $590', and 'Baby rocker with music auto stop, $150'.

Items would reappear on the Chester Hill noticeboard. For a time there was an explosion of notices offering rocking horses for sale. These included, in a puzzling twist, a photograph of a man wearing a T-shirt printed with the same advertisement for a rocking horse on it that was written on notices pinned elsewhere on the board. The man was facing away from the camera, towards an office wall-planner, and the text on the back of the shirt echoed other noticeboard messages: 'Rocking Horse, Suit small child 2–5, Padded All Round, $150, Urgent Sale.'

When notices get this strange I wonder if they fulfil some other purpose, besides actually selling the objects they advertise. It is tempting to imagine them instead as some kind of creative or personal project. The rocking-horse seller is still only a fledgling compared to Sydney's master of notices that exist beyond the noticeboard, known variously as 'Sign Man' or 'Bar Fridge Man'. Anyone who spent time in the inner suburbs of Sydney in the early 2000s would be familiar with Sign Man's particular style of advertising. He used objects – bags, chairs, paintings, shoes, eskies, belts, folders, a Dungeons & Dragons game board, anything, everything – as a canvas for his messages. They were written in white-out, always for beds or fridges or other domestic appliances. The stark white letters filled the surface of whatever object they were written on, be it a couch cushion or a landscape painting, listing the object, the price, and the phone number.

For years, a walk around Redfern and its surrounding suburbs inevitably involved an encounter with a domestic object branded with a notice for a queen bed or similar item. In his heyday the purpose and identity of Sign Man fuelled much speculation. Were the objects legitimately for sale? Was it art? Whatever their intention, they became art, or at least the collecting of them did. Their aesthetic qualities and their plenitude were compelling, and for a time no share-house mantelpiece was complete without a sign for a double bed or washing machine painted on some unlikely item. An exhibition of them was held at an artist-run gallery in 2004, and with this a link was suggested to Sydney's most famous signwriter, Arthur Stace, who chalked the word 'Eternity' on city streets hundreds of thousands of times between the 1930s and 1960s. 'Single Bed $100', it was suggested, could be the work of a contemporary, commercially minded version of Stace.

There was a simple way to find out who was behind the signs: calling the phone number. The usual outcome was that there was no answer, or the call went to a message saying the number wasn't available. I never got through to Sign Man but others persisted, although their reports only added to his enigma. Some said the person who answered laughed and hung up. Or a man answered and responded seriously to the enquiry, but said the single bed was sold. Or the caller made arrangements to meet Sign Man and even bought a bed from him. Some maintained that the person behind the signs was just a nice old guy, bemused by the attention he received. Others were sure it was a joke. Stories varied enough for a sense of unresolved mystery to accumulate.

I have my own Sign Man souvenir, scrawled over a print of winter trees in a blonde wood frame, 'Single Bed $100'. I removed it from its street-side location – a pile of trash outside the long-closed Castle Connell pub on Regent Street in Chippendale – but there were so many of these signs around the place that it didn't seem as if it would deprive the seller of customers. Other signs placed in more out-of-the-way positions persisted for longer. A black vinyl folder offering a fridge and dryer for $100 apiece hung high up over a pipe just off George Street in Redfern, becoming more discoloured and water-damaged until it finally disappeared after more than a year. It was readable to the end: white-out on vinyl is a durable medium.

Whatever their intention, these signs were a reward for people who looked closely at the otherwise ordinary pockets of space in which they were deposited. They were left in disused corners, hung on the fences of vacant lots or left in the corners of stairwells. They brought these unremarkable places into legibility and transformed the streets into one vast community noticeboard, on which messages could be found anywhere.

Notice Board

Free dogs & cheap appliances

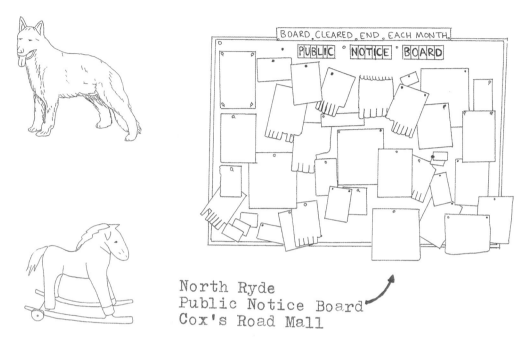

North Ryde
Public Notice Board
Cox's Road Mall

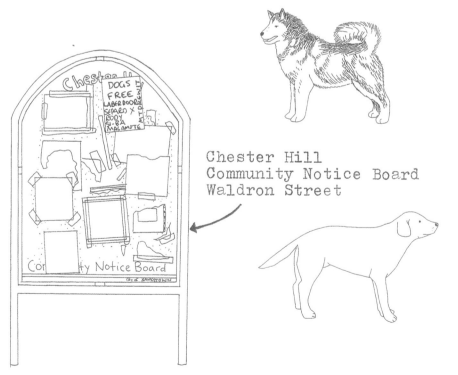

Chester Hill
Community Notice Board
Waldron Street

Castle Connell Hotel
Chippendale.

George Street,
Redfern

On the fenceposts
of Waterloo.

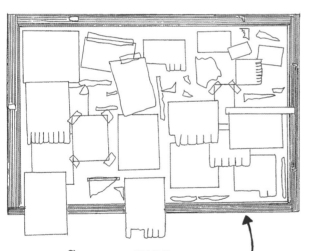

Summer Hill
Outside Romeos Supa IGA

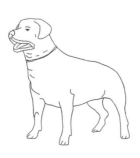

FIREWORKS

At the train station the indicator board is blank but we can see a train approaching, lighting up the dark distance. It creeps onward until it lurches into place at the platform. There aren't many passengers inside. It's approaching midnight, and by now most people have chosen their place to greet the new year. We stand at the doors, waiting for them to open and I imagine us as if looking from afar: a couple, both wearing red and black, going to a party perhaps, or to join the throng on the high ground of Sydney Park to watch the city fireworks in the distance. Other New Year's Eves we have done these things, but this time Simon and I have a bolder plan.

We step into a carriage and join the collection of stragglers inside. From the end of the carriage comes a loud phone conversation as a man tries to co-ordinate a meeting place at Circular Quay. Beside him, his girlfriend insists they drink all their alcohol first. 'Are they searching?' he asks his friend on the phone, before they stumble off the train at Central.

The carriage empties out as it travels through the city. By the time we're stopped at Wynyard we're almost the only people left on board. The train waits with the doors open. Echoing across the deserted station a woman's voice announces that the next stop will be Milsons Point. Then she begins the countdown. 'Three… two… one… Happy New Year!' Her words echo against their audience of tiles and stairs and the static faces of the models in the advertising billboards lining the tunnel. Then the doors close and the train moves off.

There's a minute or so of darkness as we travel through the tunnel, with only the regular wink of the fluorescent lights at the windows. Then the train gives a hoot and we are out on the Harbour Bridge. The smoke and sparks of the fireworks surround us. They explode and sizzle in clusters of colour as the train moves slowly along, as if the smoke which surrounds it has thickened the air.

On those New Year's Eves when I stay home and watch the fireworks on TV, I watch for the trains that creep along the bridge during the display. Amid the sparkling explosions a train always makes its way across in a slow-moving procession of lighted windows. Every time I see it I have wondered what it would be like to be on this fireworks train.

Watching from behind the doors is a tall, thin man who announces 'Happy New Year, everyone' to Simon and me, and to the two Irish travellers at the other end of the carriage who are ping-ponging between the doors on either side to see everything all at once. Down on the harbour headlands there are 1.5 million people, I later read in the news. From the train these crowds are indistinguishable, and it's only the boats massed in the harbour decorated with strings of lights that remind us of all the people who must be watching. The only figure we can see is the Luna Park face smirking at us from the other side of the bridge. And on the train it's just me, Simon, the backpackers and the tall man, a random party of five.

Travelling over the bridge we are inside the fireworks rather than watching them, and our delight at the spectacle is intensified by an edge of fear: the retorts boom, the smoke is thick, the sparks explode directly overhead. The smoke surrounding the carriage makes it seem almost like we are suspended in midair, flying through clouds. The carriage, despite the banality of its blue vinyl seats and the red smudges on the ceiling where graffiti has been removed, has the magic to float us across the harbour.

At Milsons Point we get off and catch another train back across the bridge. By now the display has intensified as it reaches its finale. Fireworks are raining down from the arch above and all around us.

Pink sparks fire out from the carousels positioned on the roadway along the easternmost lane of the bridge. Each explosion is as loud as a bomb and the carriage seems to shudder with every one. It's so thunderous and intense that our only response is to laugh.

Then the train enters the tunnel and we plunge under the city. The smoke and sparks and lights are all gone, as if the curtains had closed on the performance. Now we're just on a late-night train travelling west. Some miserable souls get on at Wynyard, couples who have had arguments and missed the fireworks and sit frostily side by side, unspeaking. After them comes a man holding a mechanical grabber, dragging on board the bag of soft drink cans he's collected. On the way home I stare at the shoe of the teenage boy stretched out asleep on the seat across from us. A chocolate freckle has been squashed into the tread of its sole, a perfect round of multicoloured sprinkles. The fireworks ride is already a secret, already past.

Only one other person gets out with us at Hurlstone Park, a man in his fifties wearing a polo shirt and slacks. We chat as we climb the stairs, telling him about our adventure on the train. 'Vanessa's good with timetables,' says Simon. 'She worked out the exact train that would travel over the bridge at midnight so we'd see the fireworks from the inside.' The man smiles politely at our enthusiasm. 'I saw the fireworks in 1978,' he says. 'I haven't needed to see them again.' At the top of the stairs he wishes us a Happy New Year and then takes off at a run, across Crinan Street and into the night.

NOTES

Aboriginal Names
Where mentioned in the text, Aboriginal place names and clan names are
from *Sydney's Aboriginal Past: Investigating the Archaeological and Historical
Records* by Val Attenbrow, Sydney: UNSW Press, 2010, pp. 9–13; 24–26.

Mirror Sydney
The Ruth Park quote describing the 'maelstrom of destruction and
construction' is from *The Companion Guide to Sydney*, Sydney: Collins, p. 60.

The Old Side: Hornsby
Artist Victor Cusack's description of the Hornsby Water Clock as 'a
cacophony of movement and flying water' is from the artist's statement
'Man, Time and the Environment: The Philosophy and Description',
published on the Hornsby Council website.

In a *7:30 Report* feature on the Hornsby Water Clock c. 1993, Victor Cusack
describes how chicken bones clog the mechanism of the clock and cause it to
malfunction.

Information on the Rock Around the Clock Festival and quotes from letters
protesting the clock are from the *Hornsby Advocate* published January–
June 1993. The 'pensioner ratepayers' were mentioned by B.J. Munro of
Hornsby, the 'Addams Family' suggestion was from Carlos A. Caruzzi of
Hornsby Heights, and the poem in which the clock 'weeps by the bucket'
was by P.A. Holmes, Wahroonga.

The Powerhouse Museum exhibition 'Paradise, Purgatory and Hellhole:
A History of Pyrmont and Ultimo', which ran from 19 March 2005 to
16 October 2006, presented the story of the Pyrmont and Ultimo quarries.

Fine Weather at South Head
The National Film and Sound Archive holds the newsreel footage of
'A 1906 Bird's-Eye View of George Street, Sydney, N.S.W.' (Full Title:

'A 1906 Bird's-Eye View of George Street, Sydney, N.S.W.: Cameraman
takes his life in his Hands in Perilous Trip. Whoopee!'). Title No: 106667.

The first recorded suicide at The Gap, of Anne Harrison in 1863, was noted
on the *Dictionary of Sydney*'s entry for 'The Gap', by Robin Derricourt. 2008.

The inquest into Anne Harrison's death was documented in the *Sunday
Times*, 7 November 1863, p. 3, under 'Coroner's Inquests'.

Upon his death in 2012, the work of Don Ritchie, the 'Angel of the Gap',
was celebrated in obituaries and articles including 'Death of the Angel of
The Gap: The Man Who Saved the Suicidal from Themselves' by Gwenda
Kwek, published in the *Sydney Morning Herald* on 14 March 2012.

Tony Abbott described the place that became Sydney as 'nothing but
bush' in a speech delivered at a breakfast for British prime minister
David Cameron on 14 November 2014.

Cora Gooseberry's description was quoted in *Eora: Mapping Aboriginal
Sydney 1770–1850*, State Library of NSW, 2006, p. 2.

Details of the wreck of the *Dunbar* in 1857 are recorded in 'The *Dunbar*:
A Melancholy Obsession' by Kieran Hosty, 2010, *AIMA Bulletin 34*,
pp. 57–66.

Sydney Beaches: A History by Caroline Ford describes the repeal of the
daylight bathing ban. Sydney: NewSouth, 2014, p. 50.

The 1907 Bathing Costume Protests on Bondi Beach have been
documented in *Sand in Our Souls* by Leone Huntsman. Carlton South:
Melbourne University Press, 2001, pp. 61–62.

Annette Kellerman's range of bathing suits were described in 'Annette
Kellerman: Mermaids and South Sea Islanders' by Angela Woollacott,
in *Race and the Modern Exotic: Three 'Australian' Women on Global Display*.
Melbourne: Monash University Publishing, 2011, p. 10.

Kurnell, Surrounded by a City

The story of the backyard-pool crocodile was recorded by the *Sydney Morning Herald* in 'Croc Found in Suburban Pool' by Kirsty Needham, 14 November 2003.

The reenactment of Cook's landing at Botany Bay is described by Katrina Schlunke in 'Entertaining Possession: Re-enacting Cook's Arrival for the Queen', in *Conciliation on Colonial Frontiers: Conflict, Performance, and Commemoration*, edited by Kate Darian-Smith and Penelope Edmonds. London: Routledge, 2015, pp. 227 243.

The image of Aboriginal people holding signs naming language groups and clans on the 1970 Day of Mourning at La Perouse is part of the 'At the Beach: Contact, Migration and Settlement in South East Sydney' photograph collection held by the Migration Heritage Centre, 2011.

The interruption by university students in a speedboat at the re-enactment of Cook's landing was described in 'Commemoration and Contestation at Kurnell' by Stephen Gapps. *Australian National Maritime Museum Blog*, 2015.

Stories of Kurnell, including a short history of the sandhills and a list of films shot there; and a description of the Tabbigai Cliff Dwellers homes, are available as part of *Kurnell: A Pictorial History*, by Daphne F. Salt, 2008. NSW Heritage Office.

The discovery of human bones at the desalination plant construction site in Kurnell was reported by ABC News in 'More Human Bones Found at Sydney Desal Site' on 15 October 2007.

The Wanda Beach Murders are used as examples of beaches as 'dark, empty places on the edge of suburbia' in Caroline Ford, *Sydney Beaches: A History*. Sydney: New South, 2014, p. 219.

The Cronulla Surf Museum includes photographs and descriptions of 'Voodoo' from the 1960s to the present day. Cronulla Surf Museum. 2016.

Bert Adamson's house on the cliffs was described in the *Sydney Morning Herald* in 'Bert and the Bureaucrats' by J.A.C. Dunn, on 16 August 1969. Images of his home appear in *Sydney Holiday* by Elizabeth Cavanough, with photography by Jutta Malnic. Melbourne: Lansdowne Press, 1967, pp. 48–49.

Penrith Arcades Project
The Rooty Hill RSL's name change from 'Vegas of the West' was reported in the *Sydney Morning Herald* in 'Vegas Goes West – Now Venue on the Menu' by Geesche Jacobsen on 10 March 2003.

The history of postwar shopping malls has been recorded in Dr Matthew Bailey's thesis, 'Bringing 'The City to the Suburbs': Regional Shopping Centre Development in Sydney, 1957–1994'. Macquarie University. 2011.

The changing history and uses of Penrith's High Street have been documented in *Once Upon a Road…: A History of Penrith's High Street 1901–1920*, compiled and edited by Colin R. Stevenson. Penrith, NSW: Penrith City Council, c. 1984; and *Penrith's High Street, 1814 to 2000: 186 Years of Progress* by Reginald Menz. Penrith, NSW: R. Menz, c. 1999.

Walter Benjamin's description of the arcades of Paris as a 'past become space' is from *The Arcades Project*, translated by Howard Eiland and Kevin McLaughlin. Cambridge, MA: Harvard University Press, 1999, p. 923.

Parramatta Road
Patrick White's story 'Five Twenty' was published in *The Cockatoos: Shorter Novels and Stories*. London: Jonathan Cape, 1974, pp. 169–196.

The *Dictionary of Sydney* entry 'The Road West' by Garry Wotherspoon, 2010, provides an overview of Parramatta Road's history and changing uses.

William Stanley Jevons' 1855 description of Parramatta Road is from *Letters and Journal of W. Stanley Jevons*. London: McMillan and Co., 2013, p. 51.

The Grand Midnight Star Social Centre era has been recorded in the entry on the 'Midnight Star Grand Ballroom and Social Centre' on the *Australian Museum of Squatting*, curated by Shane McGrath and Iain McIntyre.

Parramatta Road was described as 'a track through a morass' in the *Sunday Times* on 21 October 1900, p. 6, and described as 'an example of what a road should not be' in *Construction and Local Government Journal*, 30 October 1916, p. 15.

The 'gaily beflagged' reopening of the road was described in *The Cumberland Argus and Fruitgrowers Advocate*, 20 April 1921, p. 1.

The history of Fiona, the mannequin mascot of RA Motors, is recorded on the company's website, under 'About Fiona'.

Magic Kingdom
The Tamarama Wonderland was described in *Pictorial History Eastern Suburbs* edited by Alan Sharpe and Joan Lawrence. Sydney: Kingsclear Books, 1999, p. 111.

The opening of the Manly Water Chute was announced in the *Sydney Morning Herald* in a short article titled 'Manly Water Chute' on 15 December 1903, p. 9.

A history of Manly Wharf and Fun Pier can be found in *Seven Miles from Sydney* by Pauline Curby, Manly N.S.W.: Manly Council, 2001, p. 231.

Thank you to Ray Devitt for his stories of the Dizzyland amusement park.

The story of the staged kidnapping appeared in the *Sydney Morning Herald*, in 'Teen's Kidnap Story "Hid Tryst With Girl"' by Jano Gibson, 20 March 2007.

Documentation of the 1995 lion escape from the African Lion Safari appears in the NSW Parliament Legislative Council Questions and Answers No. 34, 5 May 1998.

Stan Leszewicz was quoted in the *Sydney Morning Herald* in 'Chainsaws Are Screaming As Suburbs Face Clean-up', 20 March 1990, p. 2.

Domain Express Footway
A ledger containing documentation of the Domain Parking Station and Moving Footway's opening ceremony and celebrations, on 9 June 1961, is held in the City of Sydney Archives.

The footway's 'taste for pedestrians' was described in 'The Year the Ground Shook Beneath Sydney' in the *Sydney Morning Herald*, 30 December 1961, p. 2. Further coverage of footway accidents appeared in the *Sydney Morning Herald* in 'When Your Pants Begin to Go' on 29 June 1961, p. 2; and 'Footway Strikes Again – Trousers Ripped Off' on 25 October 1961, p. 1; and in the *Daily Telegraph* in 'Girl, 2½, Hurt in Moving Footway' on 4 November 1961. These articles are in the City of Sydney Archives news clippings collection.

An illustrated history of the moving sidewalk can be found at Smithsonian.com, 'Moving Sidewalks Before the Jetsons' by Matt Novak, published 11 January 2012.

Charles Beauvais's sketches and designs are held at the Museum of Applied Arts and Sciences in the 'Charles Frederick Beauvais Automobile and Industrial Design Archive, 1920–1950'.

The articles describing the planned demolition of the Queen Victoria Building are 'Tear Down This City Horror' from the *Daily Mirror*, 26 September 1961, and 'Only a Bomb Will Shift It' from the *Daily Mirror*, 27 September 1961.

Plans for a network of underground moving walkways was discussed in the early 1970s, with the 'City of Sydney Pedestrian Network' of 1974 being one such plan. Further information can be found in the chapter 'Losing Ground: Post-Boom Planning' in *The Accidental City: Planning Sydney Since 1788* by Paul Ashton. Sydney: Hale and Iremonger, 1993. pp. 99–118.

'The Roads Must Roll' by Robert Heinlein was first published in *Astounding Science Fiction*, edited by John W. Campbell, June 1940, pp. 2–22, British edition.

The refurbishment of the footway in the 1990s was described in 'Domain's Footway Moves in the Right Direction' by Donna Reeves in the *Sydney Morning Herald*, 29 August 1994, p. 8.

The 'Traveldator' speed-dating event was held on the Domain Express Footway on the 9 June 2010.

Last Days of the Future
A collection of 'Sydney Citizens Against Proposed Monorail Pictorial Material and Realia, 1985–1987' is held in the State Library of NSW.

Frank Bongiorno gives an account of the legacy of the Bicentenary celebrations in *The Eighties: The Decade that Transformed Australia*. Collingwood, Vic: Black Inc., 2015, p. 241–247.

A collection of photographs by Rennie Ellis documenting the Aboriginal protests during the Bicentenary 'Parade of Sail' is held in the Rennie Ellis collection at the State Library of Victoria under the title 'Aboriginal Protest: Australia Day '88'.

'Welcome Back, Darling Harbour' was an advertisement printed in the *Daily Telegraph*, 14 January 1988, pp. 20–21.

The 'whisper quiet' attributes of the monorail were advertised in *The Sydney Monorail*, a brochure produced by TNT Harbour-Link in 1987.

The monorail was described as a ghost train in 'Holes in the Heart' by Valerie Lawson in the *Sydney Morning Herald*, 29 June 1991, p. 43.

Anthony Hordern & Sons department store's advertised claim that it sold 'everything from a hairpin to a harrow' has been documented among the

John Tipper collection of Anthony Hordern ephemera presented at his
Collecting Books and Magazines website.

A history of Anthony Hordern & Sons is recorded in *The History of Anthony
Hordern and Sons*, by T.J. Redmond. Sydney: Anthony Hordern, 1938.

A history of the Spanish Club on Kent Street was recorded in a radio
documentary, 'Adios to the Spanish Club', produced by Belinda Lopez and
Benjamin Ball and aired on Radio National on the Hindsight program on
24 November 2013.

Flanagan's Afloat
The 'immense stores and capacious buildings' were described in *The
Strangers Guide to Sydney*. North Sydney: Library of Australian History,
(1861) 1978, p. 3.

'Sydney Australia: Playground of the Pacific' was published by the
N.S.W. Government Tourist Bureau (undated, c. 1960s).

The description of the Summit restaurant's view as stretching 'practically
forever' is taken from *Summit* newspaper advertisements of the 1970s.

A collection of posters promoting shows at the George F. Miller Music Hall
in Neutral Bay, including 'Lust For Power, or, Perils at Parramatta' and
'The Spring-Heeled Terror of Stepney Green' is held in the collection of
the State Library of NSW.

The biography of James Bendrodt referring to him as 'roller-skater and
restaurateur' by Iain McCalman is published in the *Australian Dictionary of
Biography*. National Centre of Biography, Australian National University,
(1993) 2016.

Oliver Shaul's columns advertising his restaurants including the Flanagan's
chain were published in the *Sydney Morning Herald* from 1974–1976.
The floating restaurant was described as a 'galleon' by Oliver Shaul in
his 19 January 1975 column.

The Caprice menu describing the perils of pre-cooking is from a 1959 menu held in the collection of Woollahra Libraries.

A survey of the architecture of Loder and Dunphy appeared in 'Sacred Plans of Milo Dunphy' by Michael Bogle. *SL Magazine*, August 2013, Vol. 6, No.1, pp. 26–29.

'Rose Bay Airport' by Kim Hanna, on the *Dictionary of Sydney*, provides a history of the flying boats and airport at Lyne Park in Rose Bay. 2014.

A description of the brown-and-gold interior decor of Flanagan's Afloat is included in '$100,000 for Facelift on the Old Cook' restaurant review by Ted Moloney, *Sydney Morning Herald*, 8 April 1973, p. 102.

The attempted robbery and shooting of the Flanagan's Afloat night manager was reported in the *Sydney Morning Herald* in 'Fatal Shooting at Restaurant', 28 January 1975, p. 1.

Shaul's description of the 'make-believe world' is taken from the *Sydney Morning Herald*, 'Cook Climbs to the Summit', by Selwyn Parker, 13 February 1973, p.7.

Flanagan's Afloat was described as a 'grub tub' and 'one of the harbour's worst eyesores' in the *Sydney Morning Herald*, 'Floating Grub Tub on the Market for $150,000', 12 September 2007.

Ray Chan's plans for the floating restaurant were recorded in 'Hope Afloat: Restaurant Ship Enjoys 11th-Hour Reprieve' by Catharine Munro in the *Sydney Morning Herald*, 24 October 2007.

The description of the Balmain coalmine as a 'living tomb' is from a letter to the *Labour Daily* published in 1924.

Millers Point, Before and After

Ruth Park described Millers Point as 'drowsy and nostalgic' in
The Companion Guide to Sydney. Sydney: Collins, 1973, p. 66, The description
of the Rodens Lane blacksmith appears on p. 70.

A history of Millers Point can be found in *Millers Point: The Urban Village*
by Shirley Fitzgerald. Sydney: Halstead Press, 2009.

Demolitions in Millers Point and across inner Sydney in the early twentieth
century are described in 'Doomed Streets of Sydney 1900–1928: Images
from the City Council's Demolition Books' by Sue Doyle. *Scan Journal,*
Vol. 2, No. 3, December 2005.

The Hungry Mile era of Millers Point and the wharves is recorded in
'Home Life at the Hungry Mile: Sydney Wharf Labourers and Their
Families, 1900–1914' by Winifred Mitchell, in *Labour History,* No. 33
(November 1977), pp. 86–97.

The radio documentary 'Millers Point: Watching the Big Ships Come
In', produced by Nicole Steinke, includes oral histories from Millers
Point residents collected as part of a project commissioned by the
NSW Department of Housing. It was broadcast on *Radio National* on
the Hindsight program on 22 December 2013.

A visit to the Port Operations and Communications Centre is recorded
in 'Crows Nest on the Shore Controls Sydney Harbour' by Julie Kusko,
in *The Australian Women's Weekly,* 30 October 1974, pp. 18–19.

The documentary *Rocking the Foundations,* directed by Pat Fiske, covers the
history of the New South Wales Builders' Labourers Federation, including
the green bans. Sydney: Bower Bird Films, 1986.

The *Green Bans Art Walk and Exhibition* provided a contemporary visual
arts interpretation of green-ban sites around Sydney. It was a collaborative
project by the Big Fag Press in Woolloomooloo and The Cross Art Projects
in Kings Cross, 2014.

The eviction of tenants from, and uncertain fate of, the Sirius building in The Rocks is comprehensively documented by the 'Save Our Sirius' campaign. Information about the building has been provided by the archives of Tao Gofers.

Excavating St Peters
The history of brickmaking in St Peters is outlined in *The Brickmasters* by Ron Ringer, Dry Press Publishing, 2008.

My Place by Nadia Wheatley was published in 1988 by Walker Books.

A history of Alexandra Canal can be found in 'From Sheas Creek to Alexandra Canal' by Ron Ringer, *Dictionary of Sydney*, 2013.

The photograph of the excavation of the dugong, titled 'Excavation of dugong remains at Sheas Creek 1896' is held in the collection of the Australian Museum.

John Kennedy's Love Gone Wrong released the album *From Woe to Go* on Red Eye Records in 1986.

The description of the Boral gas tanks explosion on 1 April 1990 was reported by the *Sydney Morning Herald* in 'Inferno: Fuel Tanks Explode' on 2 April.

Details of the SPK show at the brickworks were documented on the website accompanying the book *Experimental Music: Audio Explorations in Australia* edited by Gail Priest and published in 2008.

Descriptions of the free party scene at Sydney Park are found in 'Sydney Park, free party playground' at ohmsnotbombs.net, by Peter Strong.

Memorial Stores
Nola and George Mezher's lottery win in 1982 and their use of the funds to set up the Our Lady of Snows soup kitchen, was recorded in the

article 'While Some Winners Stay Mum, Others Share Their Pot Luck' by Jonathan Pearlman in the *Sydney Morning Herald*, 2 August 2004.

The story of George Eastman devising the name Kodak can be found in *Kodak and the Lens of Nostalgia* by Nancy Martha West. Charlottesville: University Press of Virginia, 2000, p. 20.

The 'Olympia Milk Bar Fan Club' Facebook group was established in 2007 and as of June 2017 has 2274 members.

Thank you to Peter Doyle and Anne-Maree Prentice for their comments on the *Mirror Sydney* blog regarding their visits to Knispel and conversations with Lois.

The Sydney Underground
'The Bradfield Plan' for an expanded suburban railway network is described in *Sydney's Century* by Peter Spearritt. Sydney: UNSW Press, 2000, pp. 131–135.

Nigel Helyer's artwork 'An Unrequited Place' was a part of the Working in Public project, curated by John Barrett-Lennard and ArtSpace in 1992.

Newspaper articles on Sydney's tunnels are from the *Sydney Morning Herald*: 'Our Great Tunnel Mystery', 10 August 1958, p. 39; 'His World Was The City Underground', 2 July 1961, p. 66; the tunnels were described as 'Sydney's catacombs' in 'Tunnel Visions: Sydney's Underground Tours', 3 February 1995, p. 54; and the 'eerie depths' were described in 'Going Down Town', 5 February 1995, p. 18.

Predator's 'A Sprawling Manifesto of the Art of Drain Exploring' from 1999 is published on infiltration.org.

The Cave Clan and its members have numerous online resources, such as caveclan.org. An outsider's account of exploring with the Cave Clan can be found in *Strange Country: Travels in a Very Different Australia* by Mark Dapin in the chapter 'Drainspotting'. Sydney: Pan MacMillan, pp. 16–27.

Subterranean Sydney: The Real Underworld of Sydney Town, is by Barbara and Brian Kennedy. Sydney: Reed, 1982. The descriptions of the Tank Stream as the 'showpiece of subterranean Sydney', and the 'small lake under the footpath' are on p. 13.

The mythology of the Tank Stream as one of Sydney's 'thwarted waterways' is described in *Sydney* by Delia Falconer. Sydney: New South, 2010, pp. 33–34.

Bankstown Bunker

A history of the Bankstown area, including the story of Black Charlie's Hill, the Bankstown Airport and wartime Bankstown is documented in *Bankstown: A Sense of Identity* by Sue Rosen. Sydney: Hale & Iremonger, 1996. An image of the Bankstown Bunker is published on p. 123.

Max Dupain's war work devising military camouflage is described in *Camouflage Australia: Art, Nature, Science and War* by Ann Elias. Sydney: Sydney University Press, 2011, pp. 165–180.

Photographs of the Citizen Advice Bureau in Bankstown Square on 7 November 1966, taken by Curly Fraser, are in the collection of the State Library of NSW, under the title 'Dept. of Immigration photographs of migrants working at Bankstown Square and a Citizenship Advice Bureau set up with an exhibit on how to become "Citizens of Australia and British Subjects"'.

A history of the Villawood Detention Centre is available on the *Dictionary of Sydney*, 'Villawood Detention Centre' by Mark Dunn, 2010.

The editor of *The Bankstown-Canterbury Torch*, Phil Engisch, wrote in 1971 of the rediscovery of the Bankstown Bunker in 'The Torch Uncovers Secret RAAF War Base', 21 April 1971.

An article on the Cave Clan, 'Going Wonderground' by Lydia Roberts, also includes descriptions of the Bankstown Bunker as seen by Phil Engisch in 1971. *Good Weekend, Sydney Morning Herald*, 13 February 1993, pp. 6–10.

An article by Peter Treseder in *Australian Geographic* describes visiting the bunker in 1986. January–March 1994, pp. 17–18.

A recording of Don Burke visiting the Bankstown Bunker in 1994 is held in the collection of Bankstown Library, under the title 'WW2 Bunkers'.

Bankstown's postwar suburban architecture is described in *The Fibro Frontier* by Charles Pickett. Sydney: Powerhouse Publishing, 1997, p. 25.

A collection of newspaper articles on the Bankstown Bunker from *The Torch* and *Sunday Telegraph* is presented by the Australian Bunker and Military Museum website.

The photograph of the Bankstown Bunker during a Cave Clan visit was taken by Siologen and presented on his (now inactive) website at siologen.net.

The Ugliest Building
Discussions of Sydney's ugliest building are commonly encountered in the news media. An example is 'Two Thumbs Up For Sydney's Ugliest Building', by Jesse Adams Stein in the *Sydney Morning Herald*, 1 March 2013.

The City of Sydney archives holds a collection of photographs and administrative documentation relating to the Goulburn Street Car Park from the 1960s to the present day.

A history of the Sharpies Golf House neon sign is available in its listing in the Powerhouse Museum archives, under 'Sharpies Golf House Sign, 1958–1964'. 'Neons and Museums', a reflection on Sydney neon signs by Charles Pickett was published on the Powerhouse Museum's blog on 17 February 2014.

The Wakil property portfolio and sell-off was documented in 'Wakil Family Property Sell-Off: $200m Raised for Charitable Foundation' by Anne Davies in the *Sydney Morning Herald* on 13 December 2014.

The Kenneth Slessor poem 'William Street' was published in *One Hundred Poems 1919–1939*. Sydney: Angus & Robertson, 1944, p. 115.

The Australian Ugliness by Robin Boyd was first published in 1960 by Cheshire.

The Turramurra Sphinx

The history of the binishell in Sydney is documented in 'Binishells in NSW Schools' by Rebecca Hawcroft, *Architecture Bulletin*, Autumn 2015, p. 10.

Binishell construction and collapses are described in 'Dante Bini's "New Architectural Formulae": Construction, Collapse and Demolition of Binishells in Australia 1974–2015' by Alberto Pugnale. Published in *Proceedings of the Society of Architectural Historians, Australia and New Zealand 32: Architecture, Institutions and Change*, edited by Paul Hogben and Judith O'Callaghan. Sydney: SAHANZ, 2015, pp. 488–499.

The story of, and myths surrounding, William Shirley carving the sphinx memorial has been investigated in 'The Myth of the Sphinx' by Jenny Joyce in the Kuringai Historical Society Monthly Newsletter for April 2008, pp. 2–3.

William Shirley's quote is from the *Sydney Morning Herald*, 'A Modern Sphinx in Kuringai Chase', 6 June 1924, p. 8.

Sydney Lost and Found

The 500 pairs of gloves per month lost by women on Sydney Trains was recorded by the *Sydney Morning Herald* on 17 October 1941 in 'Lost Property: Forgetful Train Travellers', p. 6.

The quotes mentioning 'apparel of all kinds' and the lost shovel are from 'Absent Minded Travellers: Things Left on Tram and Train' in the *Evening News*, 17 February 1909, p. 3.

The boat as 'more the sort of thing you would row out to' is from the *Sydney Morning Herald*, 'Gadgets Up For Grabs in Giant RailCorp Lost Property Auction' by Ben Grubb, 9 September 2010.

Some of the unusual objects found on 'Clean Up Australia Day' were documented in 'Nationwide Clean Up Nets the Weird and the Wonderful' published in the *Sydney Morning Herald*, on 7 March 2005.

Collections and Networks
The 1888 'City of Sydney' map is by M.S. Hill and was published by Saml. Crump Label Co. A chromolithograph print is held in the collection of the National Library of Australia.

Sydney Bestiary
'Feral Pigs Invade Sydney' was published in the *Sydney Morning Herald* on 3 June 2014.

Trim: Being the True Story of a Brave Seafaring Cat, also published as *A Biographical Tribute to the Memory of Trim*, by Matthew Flinders, was first published in 1804.

The coelacanth's identity as the 'wishing fish' is mentioned in the Australian Museum's record of their 1939 specimen of a coelacanth, *Latimeria chalumnae*.

Sam Hood's photographs of the Robur tea publicity stunt, the 'Elephant's Tea Party', were taken in 1939 and are held in the collection of the State Library of NSW.

Suburban Time
Oatley's 150-year anniversary celebrations were described in *Oatley Writes...: A Souvenir Publication of Oatley's 150th Anniversary 1833–1983*, authored by the Oatley 150th Anniversary Committee and published in 1984.

'Sydney Is Clock Conscious', an article 'by A Special Correspondent', described the plentiful clocks of Sydney in a *Sydney Morning Herald* article from 9 February 1954.

Wishing Tree
The story of the Wishing Tree is outlined in *The Wishing Tree: A Guide to Memorial Trees, Statues, Fountains, etc. in the Royal Botanic Gardens, Domain, and Centennial Park, Sydney* by Edwin Wilson, Kangaroo Press, 1992.

The gardener's quote about 'girls of the flapper age' was recorded in 'The Wishing Tree: Age Tries its Charm' in *The Richmond River Express and Casino Kyogle Advertiser* on 8 September 1822.

A Complete Account of the Settlement at Port Jackson by Watkin Tench was first published in London by G. Nicol and J. Sewell in 1793.

Sydney Looks Back by Isadore Brodsky was published by Angus & Robertson in 1957.

Sydney Harbour Bridges
The amusements in the Sydney Harbour Bridge Pylon Lookout are recorded in catalogues and guides such as *Catalogue and Guide to Pylon Lookout, Sydney Harbour Bridge: All Australian Exhibition* from 1954, held in the collection of the State Library of NSW.

The story of two of the pylon lookout cats was recorded in 'Cats Live on the Bridge' in *The Sunday Herald*, 29 July 1951, p. 1.

Philippe Petit's high-wire walk between the two northern pylons of the Harbour Bridge is recorded in a documentary by his collaborators James Ricketson and Jesse Ricketson, *Philippe Petit Tightrope Walk on The Sydney Harbour Bridge 1973*.

The story of illegal bridge climbing culture was recorded in 'Illegal Bridge Games' by Jim Gleeson in the *Good Weekend*, 6 December 1986 pp. 54–58.

Warragamba

Surveyor Steve Rawlings described Warragamba Dam as a 'quiet beast' in the Water NSW video 'Caring for the Quiet Beast'.

The Path of the Creek

Stanley Jevons' description of crossing Johnston's Creek was written in a letter to Henrietta Jevons on 1st July 1855, and published in *Papers and Correspondence of William Stanley Jevons: Volume 2*, edited by R.D. Collison Black, and published in 1973 by Palgrave McMillan.

Reports of the Stalwart and its load of onions were plentiful in contemporary press, including: 'Ignominious End for Warship: Hulk to be Sunk with Rotten Onions' in the *Sydney Morning Herald,* 21 July 1939; 'Working with Tears in their Eyes: Men Load Old Warship' in *The Sun,* 21 July 1939; 'Beach Onions Defy Theory' in *The Sun,* 5 August 1939, p. 3.

Community Noticeboard

A collection of 'Sign Man' notices was exhibited at Slot Gallery in Alexandria in August 2004.

ACKNOWLEDGEMENTS

My gratitude to Ivor Indyk for his wisdom and ongoing support, to Nick Tapper for his astute editing, to Allison Colpoys for her beautiful work on the book's cover, to Harry Williamson, and to all at Giramondo for their assistance in bringing this book to publication. Many thanks also go to Peter Doyle and Kate Rossmanith for their guidance and enthusiasm in helping me shape *Mirror Sydney*.

Many people have helped me in the writing of *Mirror Sydney*, and I extend my heartfelt thanks to the many readers, friends, colleagues and mentors who contributed stories and thoughts about Sydney, and who were there for me during the writing of this book. Thank you to Keri Glastonbury, Stephanie Varga, Rachael Holt, Pat Grant, Sarina Noordhuis-Fairfax, Tim Wright, Ryan Scott, Chiara Grassia, Catherine Hoad, Kate Montague, Walter Mason, Lucas Ihlein, Lizzie Muller, Jessie Lymn, David Lever, Luc Sante, Ross Gibson, Sue Joseph, Jane Simon, Claire Reddleman, Willa McDonald, Ian Collinson, Matt Gear, Tim Sinclair, Michael Wayne, Ash Fry, Carol Ruff, Tom Carment, Joni Taylor and the New Landscapes Institute, Anwen Crawford, Emma Davidson, Tim Ungaro, Sam Cooney and The Lifted Brow, Naomi Doyle, Ray Devitt, Sam Wallman, Catriona Menzies-Pike, April Krause, Glenn Barkley, Darren Hanlon, Katy Plummer, Kuba Dorabialski, Jennifer Hamilton, Matte Rochford, Selina Springett, The Gentle Author, Tao Gofers, Rhonda Davis and Macquarie University Art Gallery, Emma Luketic and the Penrith Regional Art Gallery, Leigh Rigozzi, the NSW Writers' Centre, Daniel Mudie Cunningham, Miriam Kelly, as well as to the Olympia Milk Bar and the Ching Yip Coffee Lounge, where I often sat with tea and this manuscript. I would also like to express my appreciation to the many readers who have corresponded and commented on the *Mirror Sydney* blog.

Thank you to those closest to me: my mother Patricia, father John and sister Fiona for all your support and for fostering my interest in looking closely at the world around me. Love and gratitude to my friend Miss Helen, who passed away during my time working on this book. And the greatest of thanks to Simon Yates, whose curious mind and keen imagination transform any place we find ourselves in together.

Excerpts from *Mirror Sydney* have been previously published as follows: 'Guide to Bankstown of the 50s and 60s' was exhibited at the Museum of Sydney in 'Suburban Noir', 2013, curated by Peter Doyle. 'Magic Kingdom' and 'Sydney Theme Parks of the Past, Present and Future' were published in *The Lifted Brow* 20, 2013. The 'Penrith Arcades Project' map was exhibited at Penrith Regional Gallery in 'Mud Maps', 2014. A version of 'Parramatta Road' and the 'Parramatta Road Landmarks' map were published in *Sturgeon Magazine* 3, 2014. 'Underground Sydney' map was published in *Fluid Prejudice*, 2014. 'Sydney at Age 8' and 'Sydney at Age 20' maps were first published as an accompaniment to the zine *I Am a Camera* #17, 2014. 'Sydney Mystery Structures' map was exhibited at Gaffa Gallery in 'Groundwork', 2015, curated by the New Landscapes Institute. The 'Murals and Ghost Signs' map was exhibited at Verge Gallery in 'Second Circulation', 2015, curated by Dexter Fletcher. 'Sydney Elephants' was exhibited at Macquarie University Art Gallery in 'In the Loop: Feeding the Polyphonic Present', 2015, curated by Terry Pelarek, Selina Springett and Danielle Zorbas. A version of 'Johnston's Creek' was published as the artist book *Water's Edge*, with April Krause, 2015. 'Excavating St Peters' was first published as part of the 'Writing NSW' series on the *Sydney Review of Books*, 2016. A version of *Mirror Sydney* was produced as part of a doctorate through the Department of Music, Media, Communications and Cultural Studies at Macquarie University, 2016.

The Giramondo Publishing Company acknowledges the support of Western Sydney University in the implementation of its book publishing program.

This project has been assisted by the Commonwealth Government through the Australia Council, its arts funding and advisory body.

INDEX